Successful
Labor Relations

An Employer's Guide

NEW, REVISED EDITION

Successful
Labor Relations

An Employer's Guide

by Noel Arnold Levin

NEW, REVISED EDITION

With an Introduction by
David L. Cole

Fairchild Publications, Inc.

NEW YORK

For

Lonnie and Max

Contents

SECTION IV   Living with the Union

SECTION V   Renegotiating the Contract

SECTION VI
Union Weapons: How to Blunt Them

SECTION VII   Trouble Spots

SECTION VIII
Practical Handling of Key Problems

SECTION IX
Developments in Labor Relations

Topical Index

Topical references are to chapter. Where chapter title describes the topic, no index reference is made; therefore, the Table of Contents should also be consulted.

Introduction

A generation of exposure in the labor-management scene has not imbued me with over-optimism. Far too many participants in the field are driven by their emotions, giving the impression sometimes that they regard the absence of knowledge as a virtue of sorts.

Arnold Levin is realistic and rational, and his book reflects this. While he has good practical advice for management representatives, he does not neglect the philosophical and long range implications and objectives. Nor does he disregard the intermediate aspects. He projects the course and trend of decisions in labor law and by this means induces realistic understanding. He advises management how to conduct its labor affairs, yet his book is far more than a how-to-do-it handbook. It has missionary aspects because he is plainly sympathetic in the philosophical sense with collective bargaining and collective relationships in general.

This second edition of the book differs from the first in two ways. The writing is updated and made more current. But of equal significance, there is added a new Section—the last in the book— covering recent developments in labor relations. Here, the author departs from the technique in the first parts of the book of discussing primarily matters of direct concern to the employer. In this Section, are considerations of many of the basic problems, and analytical concern about the general theory and purpose of labor-management relations. He cites for instance, the long range sharing plan of Kaiser Steel and the Steelworkers Union as an example of the efforts of enlightened people to deal with the problems and fears of technology and automation. There have been too few such endeavors, but several have been engaged in and each has taught us something. There is no question but that thoughtful management and labor policy makers are eager for new approaches and want to know all they can about the few experiments that are under way.

In several parts of this new Section the author discusses the problem of finding a rational alternative to the strike weapon. While no one doubts the value of the strike, or its useful purposes historically and currently, nevertheless, there are indications that it has been relied upon too freely and often where it could readily have been avoided. Not every difference between an employer and his employees calls for resort to all-out economic war. The strike weapon is far too potent for this, and there is a variety of techniques available to resolve many of such differences which men of good will have found quite satisfactory.

The disastrous strike against the new *World Journal Tribune* in New York City which ran through the entire summer is an illustration of a needless use of the devastating force of the strike weapon. The issues involved, to my personal knowledge as special mediator, were not sufficiently basic or important to merit the rough treatment they were given.

The new chapters in the book cover equal employment rights, union administration, fringe benefit funds, the government's labor relations policies vis-a-vis its own employees, and the general development of collective bargaining. There are discussions of automation, the use of the strike, and the recruitment of union leaders, as well as consideration of labor's future demands. This adds a new dimension to Mr. Levin's book, raising it above the level of a trade or professional manual, or of a handbook on the strategies and law of collective bargaining. Its value is not confined by any means to employers. Observers and students of labor relations and the economic consequences such relations encompass can profit from the experience and thoughtfulness of this author.

DAVID L. COLE

Foreword

Labor-management relations is a major force shaping the American future. The dealings between companies and unions affect the productive capacity of the entire country. This, in turn, influences the social, political and economic development of our society. Consequently, labor-management relations are also a vital factor in the interplay between America and the rest of the world. Dependent on the attainment of harmony in labor relations is our ability to achieve and maintain a high standard of living for our citizens, to give aid to our allies and to support our defense effort. These are all essential elements in ensuring world peace, the survival of our nation and the well-being of its people.

It is the purpose of this book to explain the major aspects of the labor-management relationship. In order to do this meaningfully, this book explores many facets of the process. It is designed to treat in one readable volume the broad scope of collective bargaining dynamics and to cover practical details of day-to-day labor relations.

This book is written for management. It is not a philosophical treatise to extol the position of the employer, nor is it a diatribe against labor. Rather, it is published to enable management to protect and exercise its rights and to operate successfully in the framework of reality. It is written particularly for management's representatives, in all industries, who must work and deal with employees. The contents include what these supervisors should learn and what they must know. This volume is also for the attorney, teacher, student and all well-informed people who are interested in acquiring a comprehensive background in the labor-management field.

The information contained here may be subject to change as developments occur. Even between writing and printing, new decisions are being issued. In certain areas the law is unsettled. Different tribunals can and do render decisions which are inconsistent. As the personnel and philosophy of the National Labor Relations Board and the judiciary changes, so too do the rulings. Consequently, the author's statements regarding some aspects of the "law" are not merely a reporting of the latest case; they are a composite of his evaluation of the general trend of decisions, the most significant and articulate opinions, and the most realistic interpretations. Of necessity, in a volume seeking broad and general coverage some details must be omitted. Management in the construction and building trades and the garment industry will find special exceptions in the laws covering the scope of their permissible contractual relations with unions and other matters. Executives in transportation and broadcasting will find particular statutes which concern their industry. Before taking action, the reader must ascertain that his position is justified in light of the most recent, pertinent rulings. In order to be sure of its ground, management should consult counsel prior to taking a position. Some examples cited here are real; some are theoretical; still others are a combination of both. A discussion of further sources of information for the reader may be found in Chapter 33.

The author wishes to acknowledge with thanks the valuable secretarial assistance of Mrs. Alma Breen, Miss Jane Feingold and Mrs. Hazel Thompson.

Before the Company is Unionized

Why a Union Organizes

How a Union Organizes

The Employer's Evaluation

Recognizing the Union Without an Election

1

Why a Union
Organizes

The reply to the man who asks why a union organizes can range from the simple phrase: "To enroll the workers of an employer" to an involved dissertation on the history and goals of the American labor movement. Somewhere in between lies an answer which is an explanation of the working motivations and behavior of organized labor in the United States. It is essential for every businessman who deals with workers—from corporation president through production executives down to the ranks of plant, shop or facility supervisors and foremen—to know the answer to this question. To understand why a union organizes is to know what it is and how it works. Management of any enterprise in this country which employs workers must realize this, for all such management falls into one of two categories. Either the company has a union which it must cope with, or the company is not unionized and may sooner or later be confronted with a union seeking to organize its employees. Whether trying to live with or without a union, the employer's knowledge of unions and labor law will aid in the accomplishment of his goal. Top management must ensure that all levels of the company team dealing with personnel are armed with this background of understanding. Just as the salesman must know his customer, the engineer his machines and the comptroller his cost factors, so, too, those who direct people must understand the subordinate employees and the workers' union.

Ask a typical businessman why he is in business and his response will be: "To make money." If you put a similar question to a union official his answer will almost always be that the purpose of the union's existence is to improve the lot of the working man.

Unions' objectives include better wages, improved working conditions, shorter hours and more job security. Translated into action it means a fight for inclusion of clauses in collective bargaining contracts which will accomplish these aims in many ways. Transposed into results, these objectives involve an increased outlay of dollars by management for labor.

Improved status for the employee equals pay increases, minimums, maximums and progression raises, premium pay for overtime, ever decreasing work-week, seniority, job retraining to protect against displacement, grievance machinery, vacations, holidays, sick leave, pensions, severance pay, life insurance, plant safety and sanitation improvements, wash-up time, coffee time, portal-to-portal pay, and so on in an ever increasing list.

The implementation of the goals of unionization in any plant, store or facility always has two consequences—a greater expenditure of company funds and a reduction in absolute management prerogatives. But, as will be developed, wise management can minimize these tolls and under some circumstances win certain advantages for itself.

The objectives of labor which are keyed to improving the members' lot directly are the aims most frequently spoken of by representatives of the labor movement. However, parallel with these objectives there runs a second set of goals. These are based on preserving, strengthening and enriching the union itself. The local or international union has a continuous existence and is separate from its individual members, just as a corporation is separate from its stockholders and preserves a distinct legal existence throughout the transfer of shares from one stockholder to another. Thus, the union continues to operate though its members come and go.

The union's officials and employees are concerned about this aspect of trade-union growth when they organize. To this end, organizers stress those demands which are beneficial to the union as a whole, as distinct from demands which benefit the individual members. First there is the "check-off system." This provides for the employer's deduction of union initiation fees, dues and assessments from his employee's pay check and the remittance of these directly to the union, saving the union the difficulties and uncertainties of collecting from individual workers. Second is the "union shop" provision which requires that after a probationary period of thirty, sixty or ninety days, all future employees of the company must become members of the union. This, too, assures the payment of dues, if not the allegiance of all workers. In the opinion of union adherents it prevents the "free ride" by non-union members—keeps them from benefiting from a contract which the union has negotiated and for which union members have paid with their union dues. Third is the "maintenance of membership" clause which supplements the condition requiring that new employees join the union. This provides that all present employees must become union members after thirty days and must remain dues-paying members of the union during their period of employment. Other provisions designed to achieve these and similar purposes include the "closed shop," now illegal, which required that only union members be hired, and the "agency shop" which stipulates that non-member employees must pay a fee to the union, more or less like the union member's dues, to cover the union's expense in its representation of all employees, members and non-members alike. Incorporated in many contracts is a clause insuring "super-seniority" for the union's shop steward or chairman and, in larger plants, for members of the union's shop committee. This provides that in the event of a reduction in working force the union's delegate will be the last man in the company's employ to be laid off, insuring the union of consistent representation in the plant and putting a valued "plus" on union activity and a premium on the office of shop chairman."

Union representatives do not apologize for this aspect of their program. The union must be supported and invigorated, they argue, for the very purpose of enabling it to pursue and obtain its primary ends.

Those who are more critical of unions point out that for American unions today the means has become the end. Unions, like similar organizations, tend to burgeon. Able men like to build empires, and many unions are led by able men. Big unions cost money to support. Education, research, voter indoctrination, information, social and community service departments, the staff of organizers and recruiting campaigns are all costly.

There are those who indict union officials as greedy and ambitious, claiming that such men view increased membership as leading to increased dues and equating this with more money and power for the leadership. Unions today, like people, range from honest to dishonest, responsible to irresponsible, ethical to unprincipled. Within the same international union, individual locals may vary. It is essential that the employer know the union he is dealing with. The particular motivations behind the union's campaign will affect company strategy and can influence the outcome of the situation.

As the position of organized labor in the American power picture has shifted, its methods of organizing have changed. Historically, the combination of employees for the purpose of discussing wages and working conditions with an employer was a criminal conspiracy. The workers who engaged in these discussions underwent harassment, and their embryo unions were held by the courts to be liable for damages to the employer. Gradually the onus on concerted action was dropped. The combination of workers began along craft lines—carpenters, bricklayers, shoemakers, hatters, etc. But, as the rights of working men to organize emerged, there remained an equally strong principle of law that employers could resist their efforts. As late as 1917, the U. S. Supreme Court upheld the right of employers to discharge a worker who was active in organizing a union.

During the second quarter of our present century the pendulum started to swing. Federal legislation barred the employer's right to enjoin strikes. The climate of opinion towards organized labor improved. The depression, the New Deal Administration and the growing awareness of labor's voting power nurtured passage of the Wagner Act in 1935. This law, enacted by Congress and signed by Franklin D. Roosevelt, was hailed by labor as its Magna Carta. This, the National Labor Relations Act, guaranteed the right of labor to organize. Workers were given the opportunity to select their bargaining agents. Employers were compelled to recognize and deal with the duly designated collective bargaining representative of their employees. Basically this remains the law today. In the nineteen-thirties and the first few years of the nineteen-forties, labor organized. The American Federation of Labor, an affiliation of old, established international craft unions, found itself competing with a lusty new confederation of unions, the Congress of Industrial Organizations. Led by the miners' union, the CIO moved into the mass production industries—automobiles, rubber, steel, textiles, aircraft, electric appliances. By the end of the Second World War, many a citizen felt that labor, the "underdog" in the days of the Wagner Act, was no longer a weak and emaciated pup. It had grown to powerful strength. Vitality in the economic field was flanked on one side by financial security, large treasuries and assured income—on the other by political and social influence reaching from the grassroots to the White House and buttressed by political action committees.

Twelve years after the passage of this first significant enabling act, a Republican Congress voted in the Taft-Hartley Law which modified some of labor's rights granted by the Wagner Act. This second major law, called the Labor Management Relations Act, was not repealed by subsequent Democratic majorities in Congress and the unbiased observer can only conclude that the enactment of a law limiting certain powers of labor was in accordance with the will of Americans of both political persuasions.

In the first edition of this book, in 1963 was written: "In the past decade, three developments have major significance. First, Congress, concerned over labor's powers not curtailed by the Taft-Hartley Act and distressed by revelations of corruption in the labor movement, passed laws requiring disclosure of certain information relating to welfare and pension funds. And statutes were also enacted that were designed to ameliorate some existing problems and, moreover, to guarantee the rights of the individual union member from infringement by his union leadership. Second, the A F of L and CIO combined forces, bringing at least surface unity to the labor movement. By 1960, out of 17,500,000 union members in the U. S. over 14,000,000 were in the combined federation, and another 3,000,000 in various independent unions. Third, labor was on the defensive by the end of the decade. Unemployment was shearing membership rolls, automation raising an alarming spectre, and the Teamsters (expelled from the combined federation for unethical practices) was a healthy, if wayward, orphan with membership growing in contrast to the other labor organizations."

A review three years later shows little substantial change. No major legislation effecting the heart of labor-management relations has been passed. However, laws condemning discrimination because of race, color, national origin, religion or sex have been added. The AFL-CIO continues to hold together and there is scant talk of a split up. Unemployment has been stemmed. In fact at this writing it is at a low ebb. The fears of automation while remaining of long range concern are less discussed in the present context of high employment. The Teamsters continue as the largest union, but they are, nevertheless, beset with President James Hoffa's legal problems. In 1964 there were 16,841,000 union members representing about 22% of the total work force and 29% of non-agricultural labor in the U.S.

Today, nearly one out of every three workers in the non-agricultural labor force is organized in a union. The AFL-CIO has, within its ranks, 80 per cent of organized labor in this country. It is a federation of about 130 affiliated international unions. The supreme governing body is the biennial convention of delegates from all of these associated unions. The president, now George Meany, is assisted by an Executive Committee on which he sits with the secretary-treasurer of the Federation and six of its vice-presidents—themselves leaders of key international unions. These men plus an additional twenty-one vice-presidents form the Executive Council which runs the Federation between conventions. These two groups, with the General Board on which each affiliated union and department is represented, are the policy making arms of the AFL-CIO subject to convention rulings. Within the Federation are seven departments, binding together international unions which have certain jurisdictional areas or organizing problems in common. The major among these is the Industrial Union Department, headed by Walter Reuther, which includes most of the unions associated with the CIO before merger with the A F of L. The Federation has its own organizing department and staffs concerned with promotion of union label, education, civil rights, international affairs, investments, legislation, political education, publications, public relations, social security and research.

In fifty states there are councils of the AFL-CIO affiliates. In New York, for example, the state AFL-CIO represents some 2,000,000 members in the state and has its own branches for research, education and political action in Albany. There are also trade and labor councils of AFL-CIO locals in various cities which speak through their leadership for organized labor in the community.

International unions affiliated with the AFL-CIO and large independents such as the International Brotherhood of Teamsters, America's biggest union, have basically the same organization. The international—so called because it includes Canadian locals—is an association of local unions which usually assert jurisdiction in the same fields or trades. These locals, through their delegates convened at the general convention, elect the top union leadership. Most major internationals have staffs paralleling the function of the AFL-CIO specialists and are particularly active in the fields of information and public relations, research, education and lobbying. Between the local and the international, some subdivisions of organization may exist. Certain unions have regional organizations, others have directors for certain states or territories, and some have established special departments for particular functional subdivisions in their over-all jurisdictional fields. Many international unions charter joint boards in certain cities to exercise jurisdiction over all the affiliated locals in the community.

The local itself is the basic unit of the labor movement. Varying in size from under 100 members to tens of thousands, it may represent the workers in one company or it may be the bargaining agent for many separate firms' employees in a given geographical area. Locals are usually headed by an elected official—business manager or president—and staffed by one or more full-time professionals, called business agents, organizers, or delegates.

Beneath the facts and figures and behind the statistics and tables of organization lies a change in the spirit of many union organizers. The union movement in the nineteen-thirties was characterized as a crusade. Today, to call it a business would be more fitting. Labor unions are run like businesses—and big businesses to boot. In 1961 the United Mine Workers Welfare and Retirement Fund expended some $133,000,000 for pensions and medical care. Its assets at fiscal year end were nearly $105,000,000. The president of the Teamsters union was, in 1966, voted a salary of $100,000 per year and earlier had been granted permission by his union to appoint organizers with pay of up to $20,000 per year. The minimum dues for some 1,700,000 Teamster members is six dollars per month which means an income of nearly $125,000,000 annually. In Washington, the Bakers & Confectionary Workers International Union has a headquarters building costing $6,000,000 and other unions have spent another $25,000,000 building their offices in the Capitol. The six largest unions each have over seven hundred thousand members.

In 1967, unions are effective and powerful organizations—sometimes and in some places, on the defense—at other times in other areas, on the offense. The practical employer will respect the union for its strength and fortify management representatives with an awareness of organized labor's operations.

2

How a Union
Organizes

The union organizers approach the unorganized workers of an employer's work force in the same way that a salesman tries to convince a customer. The union organizers are salesmen, the workers are potential customers, and the product for sale is the union. It is important that management representatives know how labor organizers will operate and essential for management to follow labor's campaign. There are two reasons for this. First, awareness of labor's campaign will better allow management to reply. Second, the company may thus be alerted to any transgressions of the law by the organizing union and take steps to frustrate this. Knowledge of labor's campaign does not require espionage or interrogation, which is illegal. Campaigns are generally not secretive, and employers are often able to follow organizing drives by reading the pamphlets and throw-aways that are handed out.

The union drive starts away from the plant. It starts in a union's office. A worker in the plant comes to the union for assistance; or a disgruntled employer in contract with the union demands it organize a competitor who is presently benefiting from cheaper labor; or the union's organizing staff—through systematic or coincidental knowledge of the company—decides to organize it.

Sending in Trojan horses is frequently an effective technique for organizing workers. A union will often send its representatives into the personnel office and through regular recruiting procedures they will be hired. This device is particularly practical where there is large labor turnover, the community is not too small, and job re-

quirements are not too demanding. Where it is impossible to get
an organizer into a plant, the union representatives will have their
organizer meet with workers already employed with the purpose of
converting them.

After the organizers have made contact with some people in the
shop, they will endeavor to broaden this base of support. The first
steps in this direction include requests that the workers become
members of the union and sign applications, authorization forms,
or cards requesting an election. Organizers can and frequently do
hand out leaflets at the plant entrances and exits. Provided this is
done in an orderly manner it cannot be stopped. Usually efforts to
prohibit such propagandizing by invoking anti-littering laws, etc.,
will fail. Simultaneously, union organizers will visit workers at
their homes and fraternize with them at the lunchrooms or bars
they frequent. The worker can refuse to admit an organizer to his
home or cold-shoulder him in a cafe, but the employer can do
nothing.

At these early stages of a campaign it is quite common to find
employer representatives less worried by the possibility of union
success than they are curious about what the union organizers are
saying and promising. The temptation arises to call in an employee and question him about his relations with the union—who
has spoken to him and about what. The best advice an employer
can get at this point can be summed up in one word: "Don't."
Questioning a worker about his union activity is often deemed to
be coercive interrogation, which is unlawful, and may result in a
successful unfair labor practice charge against the employer.

After the initial passing out of leaflets, the union will usually
issue a call for a meeting. This will be held at the union hall, if
centrally located, or at an auditorium more conveniently situated.
As a general rule, the union has no right to demand that the employer grant it facilities on the company's premises for the purpose
of holding its meetings. In special cases, however, where the employer is particularly isolated and there are no other facilities for
a meeting place, it may gain this advantage.

From the first, and throughout subsequent meetings, the union
will endeavor to sell unionism in general and its own brand in
particular to the workers. The sales talk may stress two points:
first, how good the union is; second, how bad the employer has
been.

The affirmative side of the union's campaign propaganda starts with the obvious. The advent of the union, it is argued, will be accompanied by an increase in wages and by better working conditions. In effect, the general objectives of the labor movement as a whole are translated into specific promises applicable to the shop which the union seeks to organize. In almost every drive, certain planks appear in the over-all platform—an immediate wage boost, recognition of the union, institution of a seniority system, inauguration of grievance procedures, improvement in holiday and vacation time and an increase in welfare benefits. Supplemental to this, those benefits management has heretofore given on its own must henceforth be "guaranteed" to the workers. What was a privilege becomes a "right" to be incorporated into a contract binding on, and enforceable against, management. Those union requests which are keyed more to its own needs than to the needs of its prospective members (e.g.: the union shop and dues check-off), are usually soft-pedaled.

 Very frequently, inception of a union organizing drive corresponds with a specific incident which has irritated and aggravated the employees. Firing of a longtime employee, drastic cut-backs and lay-offs based on ability rather than seniority, failure to increase wages at a time when it is usually done, passing up Christmas bonuses, institution of automated machinery, an abusive and unpopular foreman, posting new plant rules—any of these can be the flint that sparks the drive. When there is such an episode, the union's organizers will frequently seek to make a *cause celebre* out of the problem and build their campaign around the specific incident, stressing the union's ability to solve the problem and to prevent its recurrence.

Management in an unorganized plant may well take a lesson from this. Actions of management should be carefully analyzed in advance for the reaction they will provoke from the work force. After careful analysis, a prudent company will move only where clearly necessary. Most significant, it will endeavor to neutralize its own moves in advance, either by thorough communication with workers and explanation of the necessity for the action or by endeavoring to balance the bad with some step favorable to the employees which will offset any bad feeling.

Specific local unions, in their drives, will stress their own particular advantages. Most unions try to convince the employees of their knowledge of the industry and its problems. Many claim a unique know-how in certain fields. This understanding of the plant, its product, equipment and operations provides a common ground between organizer and worker. And in this age of specialization, knowledge of particular operations by a union seems of value to the workers. The union will cite the benefits which it has obtained in competitive companies in the industry and, when appreciably better standards exist, will even show the contract. Several unions use the hallowed advertising technique of testimonial. Borrowing directly from Madison Avenue, they will cite the endorsement of their program by workers in other plants, important political figures, major national union leaders or others.

None of this "pro-union" approach is likely to disturb the employer as much as the other pincer in the tong—the "anti-company talk." In most cases, particularly where employer resistance develops, the union will spur its campaign with denunciation of the employer. The company's wages and working conditions are called sub-standard and unfair. The union asserts that workers are "captives," "slave labor," "behind an iron curtain," "victims of management and its stooges," "imprisoned," "under Gestapo control" and employed by a "vicious and treacherous employer." (All of the expressions quoted were used in one campaign alone.) The employer will suddenly find himself accused of many injustices.

As the time for decision nears, with either an election in the offing or the possibility of employer recognition, the union campaign intensifies. More organizers are at the doors to talk and hand out leaflets, more meetings are held, more promises are made. Certain refinements of techniques appear. One union, for example, will buy beer "all around" for prospective members. Another will back a bus up to the plant gate and take prospective members to its impressive newly-built headquarters where they can meet with top union officials and see satisfied members. This trip will include a guided tour of the welfare facilities the union offers—from dental chairs and examining rooms down to ping-pong tables in the basement.

Almost all unions assure the workers that if they do sign cards their names will be kept confidential. Some locals waive initiation fees for members who join during an organizing drive.

Perhaps the most persuasive and often-echoed argument presented to the workers is "What do you have to lose?" Conditions can only improve, the organizers argue, and the four or five dollars paid monthly in dues will be more than covered by a wage increase. This argument is a hard one to answer. It should not be evaded but can effectively be rebutted in only one way—management must actually tell the workers what they really can lose.

In addition to all of these techniques, the union may put an organizational picket line around the company and call its sympathizers out on strike. Such a picket line requires fast, decisive action by management as we shall see.

The union's campaign can be divided into two facets: what it says, and how it says it. The law has given wide scope to what a union may say in its organizing drives. Truth is not a criteria. For example: a union may, in its organizing drives, make erroneous statements about raises it has obtained elsewhere. If these statements are exaggerated, the employer's recourse is to rebut them. The Government will not generally step in to police the honesty or accuracy of campaign statements.

Recent opinions indicate that this wide latitude is being limited. The Board has held that a union's statements about wages in other plants that were highly inaccurate was grounds for setting aside an election where there was no way for the employer to know the true facts, nor time to proclaim them. The standard of free speech for unions and employers is different. An employer may not make promises contingent on defeat of the union. The union, however, may promise that it will get many things for the workers if it wins. There are union statements, however, which are proscribed. These include gross misrepresentations and words resulting in threats and coercion. While fraud and favors are permissible instruments of persuasion in this forum, force is not. The Government will direct the union to cease any violence or threats of violence or warnings of dire consequences generally. Such remarks are not protected activity.

The way a campaign is conducted is also important and is regulated by the laws. Just as the law guarantees workers the right of self-organization and the privilege of choosing their own bargaining agent, if any, it has also given organizers certain rights insofar as they influence people to make this choice. But this "right" to organize is not unqualified. It is tempered by the right of the employer to continue to run his business during a campaign. An employer must be alert to protect against abuses and to curb them.

3

The Employer's
Evaluation

Seldom does an employer receive advance notice that union representatives are about to descend on the company and commence an organizing drive. The information of the opening of such an effort comes in small bits and pieces, and usually by the time the employer is aware of what is happening the union is well on its way to developing a program. Rumors, a casual remark or a leaflet found are the usual heralds of such a campaign.

When the employer's representatives have actual knowledge that a campaign is underway, there are certain steps which they should take immediately. First, the company should select one person or a committee of workable size to coordinate all management action in regard to the union. If the company has personnel experienced in labor relations matters, such persons should, of course, be included in all deliberations concerning the union. Whether the company utilizes house counsel or an independent law firm, an attorney should be brought into the picture at the earliest possible moment. Again, it is important that such counsel be well versed in labor relations matters.

Second, the company's counsel must determine whether the employer (and, consequently, the entire labor relations situation which is developing) is under the jurisdiction of the Federal law or not. U. S. laws governing labor relations—including the Wagner Act, Taft-Hartly Law, Welfare and Pension Disclosure Act, Landrum-Griffin, Wage and Hour legislation, etc.—are based upon the premise that to a greater or lesser extent the activities of the employer affect interstate commerce. Those companies which are engaged in activities taking place solely within the borders of one state and not deemed to affect commerce are not covered by the acts of the U. S. Congress in this regard. In the case of these "intra-state" businesses, either the written statutes of the state or, if there are no such laws, the state's common law will govern the relationship between labor and management.

It is extremely important to determine at the very outset which authority will prevail. Differences between state and Federal laws are not simply procedural and often will substantially affect the outcome of an organizing drive. For example, under present Federal rulings a union seeking to have a representation election in a plant must present a "showing of interest" to the National Labor Relations Board, establishing that at least 30 per cent of the employees desire to have an election. Under rulings of New York State, however, a smaller percentage of workers showing interest is held sufficient to warrant an election by the State Labor Relations Board. Thus when an attorney in New York is called into an organizing situation by management, it is significant that he determine from the beginning whether state or Federal law prevails. This is just one example of important differences between the U. S. laws and parallel state provisions. For many years there existed blurred borderlines of authority between national power and state boards and courts. This "no man's land" is being gradually eliminated.

There are now certain objective standards which may be applied to determine if Federal jurisdiction obtains. The Labor Board has prescribed differing criteria for various industries. These standards determine whether or not the Board will assert jurisdiction. In most cases it is relatively simple to ascertain this. For example, in non-retail businesses if the inflow or outflow of goods shipped or services furnished outside the state exceeds $50,000 per year the Board will assert jurisdiction. In defining inflow and outflow, allowances are made for both direct and indirect transactions. Retail concerns, as another example, must have a gross volume of business in excess of $500,000 for Federal authority to be concerned. Public utilities and transit systems (except taxis) grossing over $250,000 a year will be covered by Federal jurisdiction. Other tests apply for office buildings, "links, instrumentalities and channels of interstate commerce," taxicab firms, newspapers, radio and television stations, telephone and telegraph systems, hotels and motels and businesses affecting national defense. There is no point in an ununionized employer checking his current status since yardsticks set by the Board may change from time to time. When the N.L.R.B. declines to assert jurisdiction, even though Congress would have permitted it, the state may step in.

In addition to these general rules, other interpretations of National Labor Relations Board policy, as currently enunciated, must be known. For example, the Board considers associations of employers as one employer for the purposes of jurisdiction. In other instances it is essential to be knowledgeable of Board treatment of businesses in operation for less than twelve months and of those interrupted by strikes. Similarly, Board rulings determine what is and what is not to be included in figuring gross sales volume or inflow and outflow for purposes of deciding if Federal jurisdiction prevails.

One non-retail business in New York was the target of an organizing drive in December of 1960. For at least five previous years their inflow of goods from across state lines was in the area of $40,000 per year; consequently, in any of those years Federal jurisdiction would not be asserted. But in 1960, before the union campaign commenced, the company had spent some $50,000 refurnishing its ofices, and fixtures representing more than half of this amount were shipped in from out-of-state. Thus by December 1960, the inflow from interstate commerce already exceeded the $50,000 minimum required for the Government to step in. The question was whether or not the Government would assert jurisdiction. On study, it was found that as a general rule the Board policy has been that jurisdiction will not be asserted on the basis of nonrecurring capital expenditures. The problem was swiftly resolved.

Other highly technical questions may arise. For instance, in borderline cases jurisdiction may hinge on whether gross or net sales are counted, or on whether or not state sales tax or Federal excise tax figures are included for purposes of calculating gross, or if discounts are deductible in computing total volume. There are cases on all of these problems and others which can be checked out so that the probable Board or court ruling can be anticipated and management can plan accordingly.

The National Labor Relations Board has the right to decline jurisdiction over certain industries as a matter of policy. At the time of this writing, for example, the Board will not step in on cases involving race tracks or most proprietary hospitals. If there is doubt about the eligibility of an employer's particular kind of business for inclusion under Federal jurisdiction, a search of previous Board and court cases will generally disclose precedent rulings which would apply. There are Board decisions on application of Federal jurisdiction to detective agencies, charitable organizations, schools, orchestras, the real estate business, a sports arena, religious organizations, a bowling alley operation, etc.

Certain employees are not covered by the act. Before labor relations law can apply, the relationship between the parties must be that of employer and employee. An agent who acts independently or a contractor furnishing services for a specific purpose is not truly an employee. Neither is someone rendering assistance but working for a third party to be considered an employee. In a downtown office building a one-man firm was hired to paint the stairway banisters. Payment was to be made for the entire job, and an agreement was entered into between the building and the ABC Paint Contracting Corporation in which the working painter held all the stock. The painter was not able to assert that he was a regular building employee. He was, in fact, an independent contractor. The cleaning personnel could not properly bargain with the building management either. The building had a contract with a cleaning service, and the charwomen, sweepers and night porters were employed by the service, not the building. Even though they worked regularly and exclusively in that building, there were not deemed employees of the building.

Furthermore, even if a true employer-employee relationship does exist, some employers and some employees are specifically exempted from provisions of the labor laws. Exempt employers include the U. S. Government, wholly-owned Government corporations, states, counties and cities and non-profit hospitals. Employees exempted from Board coverage are those working as agricultural laborers, domestic servants, supervisory personnel, etc. (It should be noted that in the transportation field Federal jurisdiction is exerted over airline and railway employers and employees through the Railway Labor Act which is separate in its provisions, administration and procedure, from the general labor acts.)

Most readers of this book will find that Federal law will apply to their own particular businesses as it does to the majority of significant business enterprises in this country. Henceforth, discussions will be predicated on Federal jurisdiction. But it must be remembered that the actual original decision must be made by the individual company, subject to possible eventual ruling by the appropriate court or agency. Problems concerning practical relations with a union are essentially the same regardless whether Federal or state law applies. However, once assured of the prevailing law, the company is in a position to judge both its acts and the acts of the union in the light of the provisions of that law. Management may then determine what can and cannot be done.

Next, it is incumbent on the company to call in all its executives and supervisory personnel who deal with the rank-and-file employees but who would not be included among the employees for bargaining purposes. These people should be advised not to take any position or to make any statements concerning unions at the plant without prior clearance from the company official or committee appointed to be the labor relations coordinator. These management officials must be told that any action or words of theirs can be imputed to the company itself. Thus, a foreman, overzealous in his efforts to "protect" his employer from the union, may decide to do his bit by warning the employees "what the company will do if a union comes in." In this context, his words are considered just as if they had come from the company itself. Supervisory personnel are deemed to speak for the company regardless whether or not they have actually been authorized to do so. When such utterances are attributed to a company, unfair labor practice charges may result. What the employer actually may say and how it may be said effectively is discussed in Chapter 7. All statements of the employer's position and policy should come only from the truly authorized representatives of the employer.

Then, the company and counsel should examine the situation to see if the union is truly within its rights in endeavoring to organize the plant. Assuming that the employer has a duty to bargain under the National Labor Relations Act, and further assuming that the employees are entitled to select their own collective bargaining representative, there may still be reasons why a union can be blocked from seeking to organize a company. The most common of these are the "one election a year" rule and the contract bar. The "one election a year" rule holds that if a union has endeavored to organize a plant and a representative election has been held in which no union won, then one year must elapse before another election can be scheduled. Organizing activity in advance of this election can be frustrated by management. Less well-known is the fact that if a union has filed a petition for an election and has subsequently withdrawn it, another petition cannot be filed for six months. The company may move to curtail organizing during this period. It cannot effectively eliminate informational activities protected by the Constitution, but it can endeavor to preclude an organizational picket line during this period.

The contract bar rule may block an election for an even longer period. In order to insure stability and harmony in labor relations, the Federal law has put certain obstacles in the way of any union which attempts to oust another. If the employer has a valid contract with a union, another union may not enter the picture during the first three years of that contract under most circumstances. This applies only where the clauses of the collective bargaining agreement are lawful. It is to the advantage of the company to see that the contract is valid. A proper agreement with a union will preclude the intervention of any outside union for three years and save the company from the unpleasant middle position in a jurisdictional dispute. Further discussion of these bars to election appears in Chapter 6.

In cases where there is a question as to what the action of the N.L.R.B. will be, some attorneys favor actual informal consultation with the Board. This is a matter of choice. Management officials should, however, know what the Board is and how it operates.

The National Labor Relations Board was created by Congress to administer the Federal Labor Relations Acts. The Board consists of five persons, each appointed by the United States' President for a five-year term. In issuing interpretations and promulgating rules, the Board, like other alphabet agencies, acts as a quasi-judicial instrument. Connected with the Board, but somewhat independent of it, is the General Counsel appointed by the President for a four-year term. The Board and the General Counsel fulfill the basic twin missions of determining the proper collective bargaining representatives and punishing management or labor for unfair practices.

The regional directors of the Board are responsible to the General Counsel. Presently, the country is divided into thirty-one regions, and regional ofices may be added from time to time. Each region is headed by a regional director. It is here, in the regional offices, that complaints are first processed, petitions for elections are filed, and hearings are held. The first contact of the company with a staff member of the Board will be on such an occasion when a field examiner or an attorney, acting under the aegis of the regional director, will commence investigating a matter. Within the regional office itself, an opinion or direction may be handed down by the regional director. He may do this upon informal agreement of the parties, or after a hearing in his offices. In more involved cases, a full-scale proceeding may be initiated before a trial examiner, who represents the National Board itself, is not subject to the regional director's authority, and may travel from office to office as his presence is required, like a circuit judge.

Provision for review, including appeal to the National Labor Relations Board in Washington, is part of the agency's established procedure. The Board's opinion may in turn be appealed directly to a Federal Court of Appeals, and ultimately to the United States Supreme Court. This is discussed in detail in Chapter 25.

Stuart Rothman, former General Counsel to the N.L.R.B., in an April 1962 speech, invited employers to seek assistance directly from the Board if they should require it. The acceptance of this offer may be of value not only to business people but also to attorneys who desire to be refreshed on recent procedural developments of the Board as it affects a specific matter. There is a pamphlet entitled "A Layman's Guide to Basic Law under the National Labor Relations Act," prepared in the office of the N.L.R.B. general counsel. This is for sale and may be obtained by writing the U.S. Government Printing Office in Washington, D.C. It yields information concerning services of the Board, unfair practices, representation elections and allied matter. The Board's Rules and Regulations also are printed in booklet form.

Understanding the Board's functions and when and how it can be called upon for help, the employer is in a position to thwart a union's demand for recognition if it is undeserved or spurious. If, however, the union's effort is not misplaced and it does have a valid claim, management has two courses open. It may evaluate the situation and recognize the union without an election (Chapter 4), or it may choose to refuse recognition and launch a campaign to convince its employees not to select a union (Chapter 7).

4

Recognizing the Union
Without an Election

The major purpose of a union's organizing campaign is to win for itself recognition as the collective bargaining agent for a group of employees. To achieve this, at some point in its drive, the union's delegate will usually approach the employer and request such recognition. He will initially demand that the employer commence bargaining on matters concerning wages and working conditions with the union in the capacity as workers' agent.

Union tactics differ as to when this approach is made. Some organizers prefer to claim recognition at a very early stage, practically as soon as the first leaflets have been distributed. If they do obtain recognition at such an introductory juncture, they have saved themselves much time and expense. Other unions prefer to wait until the campaign is well matured, and in some cases after a petition has been filed for election. At this stage, they reason that the employer who has done some campaigning will see that the union is continuing its activities, that the employees are apparently maintaining their interest in it, and that the company will, therefore, become more tractable in dealing with the union. Some unions take a hands-off attitude entirely, waiting for either the employer or the Government to take the initiative.

Usually it is a good practice for the employer to have one of his people meet the union's representatives at a relatively incipient point in developments, even before a petition for election has been filed. Some employers resist this on the theory that it shows fear at a critical time, but, more often than not, such a meeting does yield results. The top management spokesman with power to make a final decision should not personally meet with the delegate. An experienced personnel man, labor relations counselor or attorney should be present at such a meeting. The pattern of the union's argument at such a time is to speak of its strength with the employees, stress the inevitability of victory as bargaining representative in a Board-held election, and suggest that an early recognition by the employer, before further campaign efforts are made, will yield tangible and mutual benefits. These are: First, the union will consider this management "friendly" and reciprocate accordingly. Second, the company may receive certain concessions from the union—choice of the employees to be excluded from the bargaining unit, selection of certain clauses to be incorporated or eliminated from the contract, etc. These benefits are promised if the employer signs with the union at this point rather than putting it to further expense, effort and the risk of an election defeat. Third, the union will contend that the employer will be spared the cost and unpleasantness and the interruption of his business by such a full-scale campaign. Obviously, such a campaign is painted in darkest pigments, and organizational picket lines are frequently intimated, if not actually thrown up.

While the company should not shun such a meeting, it must be represented there by an experienced negotiator. At such an initial meeting, the presence of a well qualified and articulate management spokesman will convince the union's organizer that he is not dealing with an ill-defended and amateurishly-run company. Such competence on the part of management's representative can firmly scotch any erroneous union ideas that it will be able to stampede the company into recognizing the union and signing a one-sided contract through sheer irrational fear of the union. The experienced negotiator, assessing the approach, position and flexibility of the union delegate, will actually be performing· an essential reconnaissance mission. He will be obtaining intelligence data which will help him to evaluate the actual strength and basic goals of the union. This will come from an avenue otherwise closed to him, that is, the union itself. Of equal importance, the union's arguments as to why it should be recognized and its proof of majority status may be so compelling that it realistically *should* alter the course of management's conduct. Under these circumstances, recognizing the union is not capitulation, but good sense.

In one instance an attorney counseled immediate recognition of a union after such a meeting. He said, "Our client was in a business strongly dependent on the good will of unions. A vast majority of this company's sales volume came from union people, and the product was primarily marketed to those consumers who were workers in highly organized trades. The union delegate in his discussion displayed an intimate and inside knowledge of every phase of the company's operation, indicating that he had the cooperation of many key and senior employees. I was quickly convinced by the evidence he offered that the delegate did, indeed, represent the vast majority of the employees. In the face of this, I was confronted with two choices: one was to battle relentlessly against the union. The union, however, threatened and was quite capable of mounting an organizational picket line, and it was clear that the word would soon spread to all customers that the employer was unfair and refused to recognize the union. After an election, which we did not think could be won, we would meet at the bargaining table an embittered union and sit with employees who had previously picketed us. Our alternative was to turn the situation to advantage. The company knew what it wanted: a ninety-day trial period for new employees, the right of supervisors to do certain work, exclusion of certain named employees who could be described as confidential assistants from the bargaining unit, pension benefits to be excluded from the first contract, and other concessions. Management offered to immediately recognize the union. It expected to get the kind of contract the company could live and prosper with. It did. Sales-wise the firm capitalized immediately on its unionized status. Even now, several years later, particularly cordial relations exist based on the mutual give-and-take foundation established and anchored in the absence of initial friction. Without an informal early meeting between labor and management, this employer might have been misled into believing he could successfully repel the union. Had such a fight occured, particularly in this instance where the union was determined to capture this shop, the result might have been the destruction of the employer's business."

If, however, the employer believes the union does not represent the employees, if its demands are unreasonable, of if after consideration it is estimated that the union can be voted down in an election, then speedy recognition should not be granted in the absence of legal necessity. There must also be an assessment of how the union's demand for recognition can be best contested without injuring the business permanently.

Even if the employer decides to reject the union's claims, the rules of the dispute can be mutually agreed upon. For example, the union and the employer may be determined to disagree and campaign against one another but, nevertheless, may agree that the employer will allow solicitation on plant grounds, handing out of leaflets, etc., and the union in return will forbear from calling out an organizational picket line. This kind of *quid pro quo* informal agreement to set up limitations on the fervor and pitch of the respective campaign drives is usually respected by the parties. It can save both sides money and tempers, and may even form the basis for a broader accord later. Again I stress that this is not evidence of an employer's "softness" any more than it is of a union's. It is an application of common sense that saves aggravation on both sides, aids in keeping the election clean, and dampens heat and emotionalism. If the union loses, no harm is done. If it wins, there is a history of parley between the two groups, and the transition to collective bargaining is simpler. Whether such an agreement can be made often depends on the union organizer, but the qualified management representative will be able to make an informed judgment. A gentlemen's agreement to follow Queensbury rules often helps the employer more in the long run than any hard fought battle would. These methods are particularly advisable when the outcome of the election is in doubt.

When the company is convinced of the union's majority status, it must ultimately extend recognition. The organizer will request such recognition on behalf of the employees. No technical formalities need be met to constitute this a valid demand to bargain as long as the delegate makes it and communicates it to the employer. He can send a letter by registered mail with copies to half the city, or he can simply drop into the employer's office, relax in a chair and ask for recognition. For an employer to insist on a formal written demand for recognition or argue that no demand has been made, technically speaking, when management knows perfectly well that the union has asked for recognition, is usually a pointless and unrewarding tactic.

Before the employer can recognize the union claiming to represent the people, proof must be submitted that the union does actually represent the majority in the claimed bargaining unit. There are various kinds of proof, as this chapter will develop.

It is improper for an employer to recognize and bargain with a union simply because he wishes to. The policy of the law of labor relations is that the employees themselves must make this choice.

To superimpose a union upon the workers is illegal whether the employer "calls in" a union or even prematurely recognizes a union which he did not bring in, but which he feels he can deal with. Such recognition by an employer in the absence of convincing proof of the union's majority status will give rise to the inference that an illicit arrangement has been made between the company and the union to the detriment of the employees. This can lead to an investigation, often sparked by the charges of a disgruntled employee or rival union. Moreover, as a practical matter, if a company recognizes a union which its workers do not want, it may be subject to constant difficulties. The employees may refuse to accept the union as their agent, balk at its authority and resist paying the dues. If the company and union have a union shop clause in their contract, as is common, the employer may actually have to discharge those employees who demur at paying the union dues.

The acute employer can almost always determine the veracity of the union's claims through the company's own appraisal of its employees' desires as manifested by their words and actions. If the employer is thus convinced of majority status of the union he may recognize it. This is the most informal recognition procedure, but since the law does not require any particular formalities it will suffice.

Another method of recognition still short of election, but more demanding than a simple acknowledgment of majority status, is a card-check. In this case the union furnishes signed membership cards, lists of petitions which may be checked. This checking should always be done by an impartial third party, not by any employer representative. A union may be so confident of its status as to offer management or its attorney the right to check cards. Management should decline. If a management representative does check, he necessarily learns which employees are union adherents and which are not. If one of those in the former category is later fired or disciplined and the union alleges discrimination, it has an unfair practice charge against the company half-won since it can readily demonstrate management's knowledge that the individual was an early union sympathizer. So such magnanimous offers, whether made in genuine good faith or as a trap to be later sprung, must be rejected.

A disinterested outsider—often a clergyman, an arbitrator or a governmental official—should be provided with a payroll signature list by management, the cards by the union and a quiet, private room. There the card-checker should carefully compare signatures, being alert to possible forgeries or cards signed by people who are not *bona fide* employees, and then announce his decision to both parties. If he finds that a majority of employees have indicated their desire to join the union, he announces that the union is the duly recognized bargaining agent. Conversely, if half or more of the employees have not signed such documents of commitment the union must be denied recognition.

In some instances there is still another method of determining employee desires short of an N.L.R.B.-held election: an impartial private group is requested to hold the election. Only in rare cases is such a step more desirable than a formal Government-sponsored election.

Once convinced of majority status through whatever method chosen, the employer may sign a stipulation recognizing the union and then proceed to bargain with it. Whenever possible, the employer should try to have an idea of the union's true demands at this stage.

Once recognition is extended to the union, based on any of these indications of the employees' affirmative desire for the union, the employer has the legal duty to commence bargaining with union representatives that have been selected. He cannot refuse to sit down at a negotiating table. Failure to do so is an unfair labor practice. Thus, if the employer chooses to extend recognition, the union then acquires the status of duly qualified bargaining agent and negotiations must start. No government certification or stamp of approval is required to make this recognition official. If the employer chooses not to recognize the union, then he must prepare to face successfully the election campaign. The company should either recognize the union with the least turmoil, or insist upon an election and engage in a full-scale campaign. Half-way measures are pointless. For a company to insist on an election although it believes the employees want the union, and then not actively campaign to defeat a union, is compounding an error. The union victory will be almost a foregone conclusion if the company is passive. The union will feel, after winning, that the company has done nothing at all to meet it half-way, and the company will have fumbled its best chance to have neutralized particularly obnoxious union demands by failing to capitalize on the circumstances and do some horse-trading.

In summary, after careful analysis of the situation, the company should either make its peace with the union, getting the best possible contract in the process, or its executive personnel are going to have to roll up their sleeves and start working to defeat the union's campaign with all legal weapons and public relations techniques. Where a decision between the two alternatives cannot be made in the initial stages of the union's drive due to a lack of accurate information as to the union's true strength and appeal to the workers, a policy of delaying the choice, as distinguished from a "middle course," should be adopted. During the interim period, any steps which must be taken should be based on an ultimate election rather than a non-election recognition of the union. Then, when the final management decision is made, the company can either remain firm and prepared to resist or call in the union and, in good faith and spirits, set about negotiating terms of recognition and agreement. But to start with a view to avoiding an election will engender a company reluctance and, often, what is worse, a practical inability to switch policies. Furthermore, such a turnabout may well be viewed as treachery by the pro-union employees and also by the organizers who could rightly claim that the company had misled them and had not dealt in a forthright manner.

If the company determines to recognize the union, its next concern will be to negotiate a favorable first contract (Section III). If the choice is to resist the union, management must then prepare for the election (Section II).

5

The Petition for
Election

After the forces of management and labor clash over the union's right to represent the company's employees, either side may ask the Government to make the determination. When the employer does not recognize the union's claim to represent a majority of his people—because he does not believe it, and feels that in an election he can reverse the pro-union sentiment—he will welcome a vote. The employer may also find it advantageous to seek an election when his operation is disturbed due to a union's campaign. If there is an organizational picket line, particularly, such a move will be logical for the company. If a union cannot gain recognition or if it desires to be certified officially as the bargaining agent by the National Labor Relations Board, it will file a petition for election.

The petition for election serves as a request to the Government that a vote be held under its auspices among the qualified employees of the company. The election is by secret ballot, and the entire procedure is designed to implement Congress' pronounced policy that workers may exercise their free choice in democratic fashion to select or reject a union as their designated agent for purposes of collective bargaining. If the Board's requirements are met and the union receives a majority in a fair election, then, under the law, the employer must recognize this labor organization as the duly selected representative of his employees.

Advantageous utilization of the company's right to file a petition should be emphasized. When a union endeavors to organize a company's employees and does not quickly gain recognition from the employer or doubts sufficient support from the workers to insure its victory in an immediate election, the union may simply continue to campaign without seeking a vote until it feels stronger. The result is a long, drawn-out campaign which may defeat the employer by sheer attrition. Customers know the company has "labor troubles," suppliers and creditors worry and employees become nervous. Accordingly, to put an end to this "limbo," the company may, itself, request the Board to hold an election to determine the union's status. Generally, when it does this, the company is confident that it will be victorious and that the union will be defeated. This will put a ban on any further attempts at elections by any union for one year. Such an employer petition will be processed in a routine manner. The employer need not measure up to any particular yardsticks that a certain percentage of his employees do or do not want a union. However, there must be a true issue of representation in the making, and a demand for recognition must have been leveled by a union. The labor law provides that the Board should not grant a petition request unless a genuine question of representation does exist. This precludes the employer from invoking the law to force an election when no real union is actively trying to organize. An election cannot be staged by the employer for the sole purpose of keeping all *bona fide* unions away for a year after the defeat of one bogus union.

As a matter of practice, when a company experiences business disruption due to a prolonged or strenuous campaign and it doubts the union's popularity, it will endeavor to put an end to what it considers harassment by filing for an election. Before such a petition is filed, a very careful assessment must be made of the trend of thinking among the company's workers. Sometimes organizing techniques applied are not suitable to the workers a union seeks to organize and the union defeats its own purpose. When this is the case, obviously the company has no reason to push for a showdown until it is confident of defeating the union, if it can otherwise afford to wait. Conversely, if a hitherto stagnant organizing drive is beginning to make headway among the workers and time is running against the company, a petition should be quickly filed.

The employer need show in his petition only that a claim for representation has been made by a union. The employer's petition, of course, serves as a denial of the union's claim for recognition, and in effect says, "We don't believe you have a majority. Now prove it or get out."

There used to be a particularly frustrating, chaotic and damaging period waiting for the Board to function when an employer was the victim of an organizational strike by the union. The company, wishing to resist this pressure, would file a petition, and while hearings were delayed and debates prolonged, the company often suffered grievously. As a consequence, Congress made provision to alleviate this burden. It barred such organizational picketing from continuing if the union did not file a petition within a reasonable period—at most thirty days—of its start. More important still, it provided for particularly speedy special elections when a petition was filed during such a "recognition strike." The law empowers the Board to move forthwith and not take the time to comply with the more ponderous formal procedure.

If an employer does not petition swiftly when an organizational picket line is erected, the strike and attendant disruption can drag on. If he petitions for an expedited election, called an "8 (b) 7C election." (the title of the clause providing for it,) the confusion will soon be terminated. Either the union will be certified, or it will be defeated and forced to disband its picket line.

A union which has been unsuccessful in convincing an employer to recognize it as the worker's representative will file a petition with the regional office of the National Labor Relations Board. A petition by a union is tantamount to a claim that it represents a majority of the employees. Moreover, in theory when the employer receives notification of such a filing for election, this serves as an official statement of the union's desire to represent his employees. In rare cases, where a union campaign is particularly clandestine, the petition notice may actually be the first signal to the company of the union's drive; but as a general rule, the filing of a petition is preceded by a vigorous campaign. Although it is common practice that the union first demands recognition from a company before petitioning, there is no requirement that it do so.

Once the regional office of the Board receives a petition, either from the union or the company, it will assign an attorney or field examiner to the case to investigate whether an election should be held, and, if so, to determine the details and procedure. The first step is to judge if the jurisdictional standards of the Board have been met. The company will be sent a paper to be filled out and

returned. This is called the "commerce questionnaire," and in it
the company is requested to supply data which will enable the
Board to decide if, indeed, it is subject to the Federal labor laws.
The tests which the Board will apply have been discussed in Chapter 3.

Assuming that the Board will assert jurisdiction, and if the union
has filed the petition, the Government will then move to the question of determining if there is sufficient employee interest in having an election. The burden is on the union to demonstrate such
interest, and it must introduce evidence to support its petition
within forty-eight hours after the filing. This requirement is designed to eliminate the cost and inconvenience of an election when
there is no real and substantial desire on the part of the workers
for it—where no union is likely to win. The Government requires
a show of union adherence by at least 30 per cent of the employees.
While this is less than a majority, it follows that 30 per cent is a
significant segment of opinion, and it may develop that a union
campaign will succeed in retaining enough of the 30 per cent and
persuading at least another 20 per cent so as to achieve a majority.
The union presents the same type of evidence as it would at a
card-check. This may be in the form of signed petitions, dues receipts, authorization or membership cards or lists. If the Board
finds there is such interest, it proceeds. It is generally useless for
an employer who does not believe that there is the sufficient 30
per cent interest to protest. This tactic is almost always unsuccessful, as the Board treats its investigation as private, administrative
in nature, and not open to the employer's inquiries in any manner. As a rule, the Board will not disclose the evidence upon which
it bases its decision, nor favorably entertain doubts as to its own
conclusions in this situation.

If a union seeks to disclaim its interest in representing the employees after a petition has been filed, it may inform the Board
that, in effect, it is not a candidate for the employees' votes. Usually, the Board will accept such a disavowal, but the union making
it will likely be prevented from filing a new petition seeking to
represent the same employees' unit for six months.

Once the Board has received the petition, and if it finds the
requirements are met for it to assert jurisdiction and hold a vote,
the parties will then proceed to arrange for an election.

6

Arranging the

Election

When the employer receives notice from the N.L.R.B. regional director's office to come in and discuss plans for holding an election, he may assume that the U. S. Government is now interested in the company's labor relations. The Board, having decided to assert jurisdiction and, in the case of a union-filed petition, being satisfied that there is sufficient interest, commences to exercise its authority under the labor law—which is to promote industrial relations and encourage collective bargaining. The N.L.R.B., in discharging this function, acts as an umpire between management and the union, but its basic responsibility is to the employees; and its mission is to insure that the workers may exercise their freedom of choice to select or reject a union to represent them.

An informal conference with an aide in the regional office will occur at which the employer, the union, and the Government—now definitely a party to the proceedings in a legal sense—all are represented.

If the employer himself has filed the petition, he will, of course, wish to have the election as quickly as possible. But statistically the likelihood is that it is not the company which is seeking to hold the election. (In fiscal 1965, of 7,176 collective bargaining elections conducted by the Board, only 400 were petitioned for by management.) On the contrary, the company may often want to block the union's push to have the vote. There can be several key arguments the employer may wish to utilize to accomplish this, and the employer should assert his viewpoint at this first meeting in the regional director's office.

We have noted before that the so-called "one election a year rule" might preclude a balloting, and also that a valid existing labor-management contract will bar an election. Concerning the former, the Board will hold no election within a year of a previous election. In the case of an election resulting in certification, the year starts running from the date of formal certification, not the actual election. Where the balloting resulted in a defeat for the union and no certification occurred, one calendar year from the date of the vote must elapse. And in an industry (such as shipping, typically) where, due to the dispersion of the employees, the balloting occurred over a period of time rather than on just one day, the final date set for the close of the balloting is deemed the starting point of the year.

Second: a contract bar may be successfully asserted when a labor-management agreement between the company and a *bona fide* union exists. But this contract is a bar only for three years. (A contract for more than three years will, however, bar the parties to the contract from petitioning for its entire duration). That is, a contract for three years or less will block an election during its entire term, but a four- or five-year agreement will not generally serve as a bar after the third year. Moreover, to be a bar the contract must meet other criteria. It should be in written form and signed by representatives of both parties to avoid misunderstanding. If it contains provisions allowing unlawful union security or check-off procedures or sanctions discrimination against certain workers, it will not operate to prohibit an election. Nor will it do so when it appears that it was signed between the parties before the company hired-in its employees, except in the building industry, or if it is a contract for indefinite length, or when a major disaffiliation of the contracting union occurs and the workers are unsettled as a result. Moreover, if the contract was negotiated in a new unit which thereafter more than tripled in membership or doubled its kinds of job classification it probably would fail as a bar.

Third: a union which petitions for an election when the employer already has another union must file its papers within a prescribed period of time. The time of this filing, according to current Board policy, must be in the thirty-day period between ninety and sixty days prior to expiration of the existing contract.

A petition filed earlier than ninety days before contract termination is void because it is too early and one filed within sixty days before expiration is too late. An employer and his "friendly" incumbent union cannot collusively agree to block other unions from entering the picture by extending the contract between them for another year, say ninety-two days before its expiration. The Board considers this a trick, terms the extension "premature," and will not allow the contract resulting from it to be a bar to election.

Fourth: the employer may block an election if the person or group filing the petition is not a qualified labor organization. It must be an association which truly functions as a union. But the company cannot knock out a union, if such it be, on grounds that it is asserting jurisdiction over an industry where it does not belong. Steel unions may organize dressmakers, and carpenters can try to represent fishermen. As a matter of fact some unions, including the biggest of them all—the Teamsters—and the United Mine Workers, act as catch-alls and organize potential membership in trades far removed from their historical areas of jurisdiction. The employer may not like this, but he can do nothing. No law carves up industry into territories to belong to different unions. There are no assigned "hunting preserves," and any workers in private industry are fair game for any union that wants to try for them. The International Brotherhood of Teamsters, for example, represents hairdressers, stewardesses and zoo attendants. Moreover, if management does not like the principles or politics of a union it cannot protest its petition on this basis. Or, if there is a conflict between AFL-CIO unions, and one is alleging that the other has broken the no-raid agreement defining jurisdictional lines within the Federation, the election will not be affected.

Fifth: the company may successfully maintain that the election should be postponed or cancelled when the number or nature of employees in the unit does not truly represent the unit as it really is. If the plant is new, the working force is rapidly expanding, and employees with other skills will eventually be hired, the employer should insist on waiting until the employees are representatives of the ultimate, stable work force. This logic may also prevail when employment is seasonal, when a plant is drastically reducing its personnel, or if it is radically changing the nature of its operations.

Sixth: generally no election will be held if unfair labor practice charges are pending. These charges are claims of wrong-doing leveled by one party against the other. In the Government's view such allegations cloud the atmosphere, and a fair election cannot be held until after the charges are investigated and disposed of and the air cleared. This rule has an important exception. If the party charging the unfair practice agrees to sign a waiver that it will allow the election to proceed regardless of pending charges, the voting may take place. This general principle of not holding elections where charges are unresolved is utilized occasionally by one side or another to delay an election. Thus if three days before an election the union finds it is in weak shape, it may hurl charges at the company; thereupon, the Board must postpone the election. It might be assumed that certain companies not fully prepared for the election have employed this tactic also. If the charges are groundless, the Government will swiftly refuse to prosecute the innocent party. But if it concludes that one side or the other is actually guilty of unlawful conduct, it will press the charges, and in this process the election may be delayed for quite a long time. The N.L.R.B. will disregard the pending charge and hold the election where there exists a national emergency, a seasonal employment situation which creates a critical time-factor, or where the Board determines that the charges have been alleged for the purpose of obtaining a delay and are obviously and totally without substance.

If the company cannot interpose any objection to the occurrence of an election, the next step is to work out the elements of this election. This involves determination of the appropriate bargaining unit; a decision as to the eligibility of employees to vote; settlement of the details, including time and place, pertaining to the election; and resolution of other open matters.

Selecting the appropriate bargaining unit means choosing the employees who will be permitted to vote to elect or reject the petitioning union. It also identifies the workers that will be represented by the union if it wins. The company and the union will each seek to establish a unit that best fulfills their purpose. For example, Bakery "C" has 300 production workers, fifty drivers and drivers' helpers, and twenty maintenance employees—a total of 370 in its plant. If the union believes that more than 185 votes will be cast for it, organizers will argue that the appropriate unit is the entire work force in the plant, encompassing production, delivery and maintenance. C Bakery, however, sensing that the union strength is solid among the production workers, but less than a majority among the maintenance men and truck-drivers, will claim that each of the three job areas is separate and that a separate election should be held in each. If this argument succeeds, the company can anticipate having the union represent its production workers, but defeated as bargaining agent for maintenance employees and chauffeurs. Conversely, if the union petitioned only for an election among the maintenance men, feeling it had the power to win only in this small unit of twenty, the employer might contend that maintenance work was so integral a part of production and plant activity as to require one over-all bargaining unit and argue that the production employees must also vote.

The problem of defining the bargaining unit is complex, and the voting workers cannot always be easily packaged. Workers in different departments, engaged in dissimilar functions and having diverse terms and conditions of employment, may want to be divided from the other employees. Some classes of workers, such as craftsmen, have a legal right to be separate and distinct. They are guaranteed a right of "industrial self-determination." Where there is no industry-wide pattern or historical precedent, the craftsmen will often first have their own preliminary election. In this vote, called a "Globe election," they will decide whether they want to be a part of the entire over-all unit or stay out of it. If they decide to join in, then they vote in the general election with the other employees to choose the bargaining agent. And if they select to remain aloof, they become a separate bargaining unit, apart from the general group in which there may or may not be an election. Professional people, like craftsmen, have particular rights and may legally reject inclusion in a non-professional unit.

Occasionally, determination of the appropriate unit may involve a decision as to whether more than one plant, store or facility of a company is to be included in the voting or if each is to be kept separate. Sometimes the proper unit may even include the employees of more than one firm in an industry and may be constituted to take in several firms. Board policy and rulings may change. For example, for some time the N.L.R.B. held that the appropriate unit in a retail department store was all the employees. In the recent past, however, it has permitted elections in smaller than store-wide units, distinguishing between selling or non-selling employees, part or full-time employees or food service workers.

When the company contemplates its position on the question of defining the unit, it should always remember that it is dealing with a two-sided coin. What may be good for a company before an election may be bad after it. Importer "J" had thirty men who were messengers, shippers and receivers, packers, drivers and material handlers. He also had ten girls who were clerical employees in the office. The employer was certain the election would be close and he felt that if the men alone voted, the petitioning union seemed likely to win. The employer argued that the clericals were mostly billers and computer machine operators on his warehouse premises and, as such, should be deemed "plant clericals" and included in the unit. The employer was taking a calculated risk in urging inclusion of the girls in the unit. If no union was selected because of their vote, his gamble would pay off. But if there were enough votes for the union, even though the clericals did vote against the union, then these girls would be part of the unit. Whatever workers are included for voting purposes will remain in the unit and if the union is victorious it will represent all employees who voted or would have voted in the election.

In selecting the unit, certain types of employees are deleted from it almost automatically. Personnel who are supervisors or performing a management function, confidential employees and guards or uniformed watchmen must be excluded from the unit. But when it comes to determining the management position towards the inclusion or exclusion of other types of employees, careful deliberation must ensue. Proper judgment can only be made in the context of the particular fact situation. And there must be estimates of the probable outcome of the election both with and without certain employees or categories in the unit. In brief, the employer should most thoughtfully formulate his stand on this aspect of the election since it will affect not only the success or failure of the union in the voting, but also labor relations after the voting.

The N.L.R.B. in deciding its own positions on these questions examines the history of collective bargaining, Board and court precedent, the wishes of the workers, the nature and type of work performed, and, as noted, it sometimes will even conduct elections within elections. But the Board generally will try not to inject its views if the company, union and employees can agree themselves.

Once the unit has been determined, it is necessary to decide which workers in the unit are eligible to vote and which are disqualified. The general precept is that all employees in the unit whose names appear on the last company payroll list before the decision for an election is made are entitled to vote. But there are significant exceptions which the employer will do well to remember. If the industry has seasonal peaks and valleys of employment and this renders the last payroll date an unrealistic one, or if there has been a permanent reduction in work force since this date or one is contemplated before the day set for the election, the employer may request another standard for voter eligibility that will yield a more representative result.

Workers who are sick, vacationing or who have been temporarily laid off are all eligible to vote. Those who have quit, been discharged for valid reasons, or have no expectation of recall are not. Individual circumstances control eligibility of temporary or seasonal or part-time employees, but the prevailing rule is that if they have a significant stake in the outcome of the election they may vote.

Workers on an economic strike are generally eligible to vote unless the company can show that the striker has no further interest in the job and if they have been on strike for less than a year. Replacements for these strikers who have been added to the work force permanently may also vote. Casual replacements may not. Strikers who have seriously transgressed the law may not vote, providing that, on notice of the violation, the employer has discharged the workers. Rulings on issues concerning eligibility of strikers and replacements are often on a case-by-case basis, and there are so many varying decisions that generalities are susceptible to error and a check should be made in detail.

Selecting date, time and place are important. Too often management is ready to concede these points without realizing their significance. I believe that a well-chosen date or time or place may, on occasion, influence the outcome of an election. While I have no statistics to support this statement, some say that a Monday morning election is liable to be less favorable to a company than an election held on Friday afternoon. On the first work-day of the week employees are often in a low, "blue-Monday" mood. Voting for change—any change from the dismal, dissatisfying present—makes more sense than it will on Friday when the weekend is starting and a sense of well-being pervades. Other factors, such as the proximity of election day to payday, should be considered in setting the date. Most important, the company should decide if it wants the election sooner or later, and try to push for a date which accords with this aim.

The actual time of the election should be chosen so that a long pre-luncheon wait on line is avoided and so that work interruption is kept to a minimum. The beginning or end of a shift, accordingly, is often picked over a mid-working-day hour.

Whenever possible, the employer should select the plant as the site of the election. In some cases, however, the union may object to this location and the Board may uphold this contention, agreeing that the election should be held off the employer's premises. The employer must then be on guard that the election will not be held on union territory or even on ostensibly neutral ground that has been used so extensively by the union that it is considered "union terrain." The psychology of people's reactions to their immediate surroundings is evident.

If all of these issues and various other matters can be agreed upon, the parties incorporate their understandings into what is called a "consent election agreement." The regional director of the Board, pursuant to this agreement of the parties then conducts the election. In the case of a consent election if any objections are later filed, the determination of the regional director is final; there is no appeal to the entire Board itself. In the past three years about three-quarters of the elections held were conducted by voluntary agreement.

Should the informal conference fail to yield agreement, the regional office of the Board will, after issue of the notice of hearing, actually commence this proceeding. At the hearing all of the problems already discussed in this chapter are raised more formally. This is the point at which the company may officially submit arguments, if any, that no election should be held. Unions other than the union petitioning have the right to become intervenors at this time and to request that they be placed on the ballot, thus widening the choice from "union or not" to "which union, if any." Both the company and the union or unions present their viewpoints by argument and the testimony of witnesses if they desire. A Board examiner presides at the proceedings. When both sides have concluded their presentations, the record of the hearing is given to the Board's regional director for determination. If it is decided that the election should be held, an order titled "A Direction of Election" is issued by the N.L.R.B. In this order all of the problems presented at the hearing are resolved. The description of the voting unit and criteria for eligibility to vote are set forth, and the date, time and place set for the election are stated.

Even after the election is scheduled, the employer may recognize the union if he wishes to do so and is convinced of their majority status. But if this is not the choice and the company proceeds to election, it should intensify its efforts at this time to convince its employees of its views.

7

The Employer's

Campaign

The first shock of the union's organizing drive has worn off, a compromise settlement based on recognition of the union without an election has been turned down, and the employer is ready to fight back. For several days now, and perhaps weeks, the company and its officers have been the victims of the union's charges and the butt of the organizer's humor. Most employers, having seen the whites of their eyes, are usually ready to damn the torpedoes and steam full speed ahead against them. The torpedoes, in this case, are the unfair labor practice charges that will be alleged against the company if it makes statements which are deemed to block the employees in their free choice. This can be damaging artillery. A company is best advised to chart a course carefully so as to avoid the court and Board decisions on which it could founder and yet to obtain maximum effectiveness from the counter-campaign. A union's conduct during a vigorous organizing drive may be distressing to an employer, but it will be all the more painful if he finds that, due to his indiscretions, the powerful machinery of the Federal Government is lined up behind the union.

The employer who decides that his workers do not want the union must set about to convince them of this through a campaign which is within the bounds of the labor laws. There is a wide scope of protected freedom of speech that can be utilized. The trick is to do so effectively and carefully. And while the employer is conducting his campaign he must be alert to see that the union campaign does not transgress its boundary lines. Just as the union will police the employer's statements, so too the company must check on the organizers. First we shall discuss the area open to the employer, then the measures which he must take to guard against union unfair labor practices and disruption of the company's operations due to the organizing campaign.

The law provides what the employer can and cannot say. Close adherence to this is important to avoid charges against the company. In the broadest sweep, the picture the law paints is this— an employer may not use threats to persuade workers not to vote for the union and he may not make promises to them contingent on their voting against the union. In other words the whole constellation of contingencies is barred to the employer. Statements such as "If a union wins the election I will see that this plant will close its doors," or "If you vote for the union and we find out, you'll be fired from the store," or the promise "The day the union is defeated I'll raise the pay of every worker in this hotel," or "If you vote against the union and defeat it I'll institute Blue Cross and H.I.P. benefits for all of the workers on the staff" are clearly statements containing threats or promises. These are taboo.

But there are many constructive remarks that an employer can make which are covered by the freedom of speech provisions of our Constitution and which are not deemed to be an unfair labor practice. An employer is well advised to point out certain facts of life. A statement: "We're paying the best that competition will allow and no union or anyone else can change that" is proper, and so is a prediction or prophecy that the establishment of a union might "result in a reduction of hours worked for all you people."

An employer is permitted to point to his previous record. Consistent wage increases, well-rounded benefits, fairness and impartiality in treatment of personnel should be reviewed in detail.

In many companies that are being organized, management stresses the negative factors concerning unions. Thus the employer will point out that the selection of a union will result in payment of dues, initiation fees and assessments. This added cost to the workers, it may be stated, will, in the employer's opinion, bring them no new benefits. One employer observed that in his opinion the turning point in his successful campaign against a union was when he found out that the union seeking to organize the employees charged the workers fines for failure to attend meetings. He stressed this to his people. "You'll be working for the union," he said, "not for me, not for yourselves." This approach apparently was telling.

Certain employers will attack the union on grounds that are not directly related to the issue of wages and working conditions. In the South, many large companies have stymied organizing drives by injecting racist tactics and by arguing that unions are a force for integration and that the advent of a union in the plant would mean an end to segregation and job preference for whites. Recent Board decisions indicate that such incitements will be curtailed. In other areas, unions have been attacked as Communist dominated.

If a union is controlled by irresponsible elements or unsavory characters, employers often consider this to be an advantage to them and do not hesitate to use such information in their addresses and pamphlets to the workers. For example, in one situation several organizers for the union seeking to win recognition had recently been arrested on assault and attempted extortion charges. The employer had a copy of the newspaper article reporting this blown-up, duplicated and distributed to his people. "Do you want these men to represent you?" was the caption.

These are usually unique situations. It is the opinion of most responsible labor relations counselors that "red herring" attacks often boomerang. A union with a good previous record can disprove the employer's charges and then all of the employer's other statements are disregarded. Moreover, if the union does succeed in winning, there exists a personal resentment which is not easily healed.

Many employers successfully appeal to the "company family," and the sense of "togetherness." The union people are pictured as outsiders who do not understand "our" problems. Other executives claim that management is doing what it can for its people, that a union will only cost money and mean outside regimentation and control and that the union will not be able to improve conditions.

In summary, the scope of speech which the employer may exercise is wide. The company must always take precautions to avoid threats and promises. It is preferred practice to have all employer's speeches and statements reviewed in advance by counsel so as to avoid this. No one set speech or group of statements makes a foolproof pattern. To a great extent the outcome of the election will be decided not by what the employer says when the union is organizing but by what he has done before it came into the picture.

Canned or form speeches are not always effective. There are

examples of statements that have been made and deemed permissible by the Board on file, and employers can be supplied with these. The dividing line between protected speech and that which is not permissible is narrow. To say that "If the union is voted in, the plant will close down," is improper. But to state that the union will mean increased costs and that the company cannot cope with any increased costs may be allowed. There is a blurred region between clearly legal and obviously illegal speech and only a trained scout can negotiate this no-man's-land successfully. Moreover, if a charge is filed against the employer, the Labor Board investigator will view the criticized speech not as an isolated bit of verbiage but as one mosaic tile in an entire context of employer behavior.

The employer can best get his points across to the employees by speaking to them and by the publication of bulletins and leaflets. Contrary to much popular belief, it is perfectly lawful and proper for an employer to campaign in an endeavor to defeat a union at an election. To this end management may make its views known but cannot put pressure on the workers. Accordingly, calling men into the office of a supervisor and talking to them and asking their opinion of the union has been held to be not permissible if there is any hint of a threat by the company. The safest rule is for the employer to deal with his employees as an entire group, or in large public units, and not to button-hole individuals or small groups or visit their homes to question them. It is too easy to allow a charge of unfair activity to creep up this way, and at a hearing it often becomes a question of the word of one man against another.

The employer may be deemed to act in bad faith if he suddenly gives increased wages or benefits to his workers just after a union petition for election has been filed. As a practical matter also it is not advisable to grant such extraordinary benefits for several reasons. If the union is defeated, the workers have learned that they need only bring in the spectre of a union to cajole improvements from a reluctant employer and this can be expected as a regular occurrence; and if the union does win, it will proceed to negotiate for increases over and above those just given so that the end result may well be a double cost. If, however, an employer has followed a certain pattern of conduct, he need not change this conduct just because of a union's petition. In one plant the manager handed out merit increases to workers every September just before the start of the busy season. A union commenced an organizing campaign in August, filing a petition for an election early in September. There was a hearing on the petition and a consent election agreed to on a Wednesday in mid-September. On Thursday the election date was announced to the workers and on Friday the employer's annual unilateral increase was promulgated. The union charged that this was violative of the law, but the National Labor Relations Board upheld the company's action. The raises, the Board ruled, were part of a regular pattern of conduct. Moreover, they were being processed by the bookkeeping department prior to Wednesday. The criteria of the Board was whether the action was a proper exercise of management's prerogative or was calculated solely for the purpose of coercing the employees. This is still the standard which is applied, and any new benefits which management plans to give should be measured in this light.

We have discussed here what the company may do. What it cannot do is to discriminate against pro-union employees or engage in "union-busting." This is discussed in detail in Chapter 26.

Management also has a right and a duty to itself to see that a union organizing drive does not disrupt plant discipline and orderly production. To this end reasonable rules may be enforced. Companies may have regulations banning any solicitation within the plant during working hours or littering of work-benches and rest areas with pamphlets. These rules may be applied to a union organizing campaign provided that they have been uniformly enforced against other solicitors. Outside organizers generally need not be given access to the premises; their task does not have to be made easier by management. Employees on payroll may properly be forbidden to give out handbills in the plant during working time. While the employer cannot fire a worker for engaging in union activity, he can insure that it is not done at company expense. There is no obligation to permit workers to discuss the union on company time, and no reason to tolerate any interruption of the regular work schedule during working hours. Further discussion of rule-making and employer pre-election conduct follows in Chapter 8.

Normal discipline should not be suspended. A worker has a guaranteed right to select a union, but he has no guaranteed right to be insubordinate to a foreman or loaf on the job during a union's organizing drive. Too many employers, fearful of a charge of anti-union bias, abdicate responsibility in their companies during a representation campaign. This is unnecessary. Sensible and proper rules may and should be maintained.

Congress allows the employer to express his views on unionization of his company. This right can only be implemented when these views are expressed articulately. Considerable effort should be devoted to this, as recent statistics show that in nearly two-fifths of all elections held, the employees vote for no-union. The employer does have close to an even chance of winning the election. He can increase his chances of victory by effective campaigning.

8

Holding and Appealing
the Election

The election day is the day of reckoning for management and the union. On its outcome will hinge the company's industrial relations pattern for at least one year. In the privacy of the voting booth, and by secret ballot, the employees will engage in the ultimate expression of America's labor relations policy, their right to economic self-determination.

After management and the union have agreed to a consent election, or after the formal hearing procedure resulting in a directed election, the regional director's office will mail out notices of election. The notices state the date, time, and place of the election, the voting unit, the choices which will appear on the ballot, the eligible voters, and those specifically excluded from voting. A sample copy of the ballot is sent with the notices. These announcements will be in English, and may also be in any other language appropriate to the ethnic complexion of the voters. On receiving the notices, the company should follow the regional director's instructions and post them on the bulletin board or some other conspicuous place where all employees can easily view them.

There are other requirements with which the company must comply in order to prepare for the election. Management must furnish to the regional director a list of employees on the payroll as of the eligibility date. The company will be asked to name observers (in smaller units, usually two), corresponding in function to the "watchers" in a regular political election, to represent it at the polls. The right to name observers is actually a courtesy extended to each side by the N.L.R.B. and the employer should accept the invitation to do so promptly. The company may not select managers or executives to act in this capacity, the theory being that their presence at the polls might intimidate the voters. Non-supervisory personnel such as clerical employees in non-voting departments may act as observers. The employer is also free to designate employees in the voting unit, voters themselves, to act as his observers.

The duty of the observers is to be at the polls before they open until after they close, to assist generally in the election and to aid the Board agent in ensuring that orderly procedure is followed. Observers have the right to challenge persons who try to vote but who, in their opinion, are not eligible. The company's observers should be alert to challenge unqualified voters: people who are not in the unit; strikers not entitled to vote; employees who were discharged or quit before the cut-off date; and "ringers" who may drift in trying to stuff the ballot boxes. The union's observers will challenge those they allege are really supervisors and try to block their voting. The observers may not electioneer during voting, help voters fill in ballots, nor leave the polling place during the election. After the election, observers from both sides will remain with the Board agent while he counts the votes. It is their duty to double-check him. When observers have been named, the Board will send to them a standard instruction form setting forth these duties.

Observers can play an important role in elections, and management should be cognizant of its responsibilities. In a close election, victory or defeat can turn on a small margin, and the correct exercise of challenges can be the critical factor. The ancillary jobs of the observers are also important. Accordingly, the company should select its representatives with care and discernment. Several factors enter into the choice. Foremost is their loyalty to the company. In addition to this, however, it is important to choose people who remain calm but will speak up and assert their rights when necessary. The observers should know the individuals voting wherever possible so that they can check the face of the voter against the name on the payroll list. An effective combination of management observers, in smaller shops, often consists of a person from the office clerical staff (either a bookkeeper well acquainted with the payroll, or a mature secretary) and a voter in the bargaining unit who knows his fellow employees. In selecting observers in larger units, the requisites for the proper performance of their duties should be kept in mind.

The election area is generally set up in a manner that will facilitate prompt and orderly voting and subsequent dispersal without danger of fire or the hazard of a milling crowd. Usually there is a line formed outside the polling area. The employee walks into the place where the balloting is taking place, identifies himself to the Board agent and observers, receives his empty ballot and steps into the voting booth. If his right to vote is challenged by either side, the ballot is put in an envelope which is sealed, marked and impounded separately. If no question, his ballot is dropped into the box. This voter then should leave promptly—preferably from an exit separate from the entrance—and the next voter should come in.

When voting is over and the polls are closed, the Board agent who has been sent in to supervise the voting may up-end the ballot box and, under the watchful eyes of the observers, immediately start to count the ballots. If there is a clear-cut majority, one way or the other, the results will be announced then and there. However, two occurrences may preclude this. If there was a second union on the ballot and the workers had the choice of voting for the petitioning union, the intervening union or no union at all, none of these three alternatives may have received a majority of the votes cast. In this case, a run-off election between the two choices which received the largest vote will be held at a later date. This way a clear majority of votes will elect one of the two remaining selections. In the case of run-off elections, particular attention must be paid to the questions of the voter eligibility date although usually the date utilized in the first election again applies.

The number of challenged votes withheld from the counting may be sufficient to swing the election either way if the margin of victory is slim. For example, 200 votes are cast: ninety are for no-union; ninety-five are for the union; and fifteen ballots are challenged. If ten of these fifteen are deemed valid votes cast for no-union, the union will not have received a majority and it will not be certified. In such a case, then, it becomes necessary to decide about the challenges. No official announcement of results is made, and the regional office of the N.L.R.B. determines the validity of the votes in question. If a challenge is deemed valid, the envelope and the ballot inside are thrown out. If the challenged person's right to vote in the election is upheld, the envelope is opened and the ballot is counted. Challenges are considered on an individual basis. Each envelope bears the name of the voter so that the status of each may be discussed intelligently. The vote itself, however, remains secret—sealed inside the envelope unless it is decided that the vote is valid and shall be counted. When decisions on challenges are being made, both sides should be present to argue in support of their observers. The actual judgment, however, is generally made by the regional director.

If the election returns demonstrate that a union has won a majority, this does not necessarily mean the company must accept this mandate as final. The company has a right to protest the election results based on the contention that the union's conduct before the actual election or during it was unfair and prejudicial to an honest and true election. The union also has a right to object to the outcome. Such objections to elections must be filed by the objecting party within five days after the tally of votes has been announced. Copies of the objections must be served on the other party (or parties) which then has a limited time in which to file its answers to the objections, assuming it wishes to try to uphold the election result. The objecting party, on occasion, may request a meeting with Government officials to orally argue the issues. Hearings may actually be held after the regional director's investigation of the situation. Ultimately, the decision is rendered by the Board's regional director and the election returns are sustained or voided. The parties then have ten days in which to file exceptions to the regional director's report or ruling with the full Board. The Board may uphold the director or order a full hearing at which its examiner will preside in what is like a trial.

The employer must be aware of all of the possible grounds for objecting to an election. In the category of objections based on the conduct of the election are complaints that the polls closed too early; that the ballots were not secret; that the Board agent interfered and was not impartial; that there was coercion in the polling area; that the ballots were not freshly tallied; or that there was insufficient notice for the election. There is no specific requirement that a minimum number of eligible voters in the unit must vote to validate the election returns. But if the percentage participating is so small as to indicate to the Board that the results are not representative of the wishes of the unit, the election can be voided.

Moreover, elections have been set aside due to a union's improper campaigning before the election. An election may not be set aside because of the union's "over enthusiasm" in campaigning even if the electioneering involves exaggerations, vilification, and errors. It will be voided if the union engages in trickery, forgery or other types of gross fraud. In a case actually decided by the Board an election was set aside where the union based its campaign on incorrect statements of the minimum wages and conditions which it had obtained for other workers in factories in the same industry where it was the bargaining representative. In reality, wages were lower and conditions less favorable than claimed. Management maintained that the workers were so grossly misled as to make a mockery of their right to exercise their discretion based on their estimate of the facts. This position was upheld and the election was set aside.

In rare cases one party or the other may move to void an election based on interference not of the other party, but by some outside person or agency. On occasion "set asides" have resulted when such a third party, such as a local chamber of commerce or citizen's committee, has been guilty of fraud or skulduggery.

The company must be on guard that it does not do or say things which will enable the union to set aside a no-union vote. To recapitulate, if the company engages in coercive surveillance or interrogation of its employees, it will be deemed to have interfered with the election. Management should not make lists of employees who accept union leaflets, nor should it watch those who stop to talk with union organizers, or photograph these people. The law bans attempts at ascertaining the employees' views "unofficially" before an election and the employer should not conduct a "private poll."

As was discussed in Chapter 7, employer promises contingent on union defeat, or threat based on union victory, are conduct which may result in negating the election results if the union objects after the election. Increases in wages or fringe benefits, announced or granted by the company between the time a petition is filed and the actual day of voting, are often held to be objectionable.

The employer's conduct of his campaign and his restrictions on the union's campaign can also figure in a union's successful plea to reject unfavorable election results. For example, an employer may not address a captive audience of his workers within twenty-four hours of the election. A company spokesman may speak to employees during this last crucial day if the workers choose to listen and do so on their own time, but the audience may not be addressed and compelled to listen on company time. Speeches on company time are allowed prior to twenty-four hours before an election, and literature may be circulated by the company even during the twenty-four hours preceding the election.

As noted, the company may forbid soliciting on its premises during working hours and include the union in this ban. To extend this rule to nonworking time, such as during lunch and rest periods, an employer must show that such stringency is essential for the efficient operation of the business. For example, in a department store, where it is recognized that such organizing activity even during "off" hours on the selling floor would disrupt customer service, the Board will permit such a rule. In cases where this rule is allowed, the employer is generally on the safe side if the union is given equal opportunity to reply to a speech given a captive audience. When solicitation is allowed during nonworking hours, the rights of the union to reply to the company are not so carefully guarded. The employer should not enforce a "no solicitation" rule against the union and then campaign himself during working hours, particularly when it is hard for union organizers to find a nearby place to address the workers.

Supervisors may not instruct employees how to vote against the union, nor can the company post sample ballots already marked for no-union on its bulletin board.

These principles cannot be taken as permanently accurate. Broadly speaking, the N.L.R.B. will try to maintain fair opportunity for both union and employer to publicize their viewpoints to the employees. But the laws regarding the entire area of campaigning and company rules concerning union organizing are particularly intricate and constantly changing. As each case is decided on the facts by the National Labor Relations Board or the courts, new opportunities are opened or closed to management. Consequently, it is essential that the instances cited here be viewed only as examples and that a careful survey of the latest developments be made by the company's industrial relations advisor or attorney immediately prior to the campaign.

The Board and its officials will sustain objections to an election if they believe that the conduct was serious enough to preclude free choice. The interference must be of a substantial nature, and all the surrounding circumstances in a particular case will be considered; therefore, a company can in certain cases remedy a mistake it has made. To illustrate, when a foreman unlawfully threatens the workers and this is one isolated incident, if the company promptly, publicly and effectively disavows these utterances, it may save itself from a sustained objection based on interference.

The company may base its objections on conduct occurring after the election petition has been filed, but not on episodes that transpired before this. Moreover, if the company knows of improper union conduct before the election occurs, it should immediately charge unfair labor practices against the offender. It should not hoard the offenses, like cards to be played after the election if the outcome is unfavorable. Naturally, if it does not learn of unfair pre-election conduct until after the voting date, it is not stopped from objecting to this conduct. But if it can be shown it knew of unlawful conduct well before the election and did nothing about it, the winning union may have powerful grounds on which to urge the Board to ignore the employer's objections.

In a later Chapter, 26, we will discuss employer's unfair labor practices. This conduct may also be the basis for objections to election, but both are dealt with separately and the criteria applied by the Government is not always the same. In one situation, the union complained of a certain employer's conduct prior to an election by filing both unfair labor practice charges and objections to the election. The incidents were deemed grounds to set aside the election by the regional director, but, on hearing of the charges before the Board's trial examiner, no unfair labor practice charge was upheld against the company.

Whenever a union wins an election, the employer should carefully comb the events leading to and including the election to see if grounds exist for objection. The employer should be careful not to engage in campaign conduct which will enable his adversary to successfully set aside an election which the union has lost. When this happens and another election is held, the union has powerful ammunition to use against the company, and clever organizers may even cite the actual wording of the report that holds the employer is guilty of objectionable conduct in their renewed campaign.

Negotiating the First Labor-Management Agreement

Preparing for the First Negotiation

Opening Negotiations

Techniques of Bargaining

Contract Provisions:
Wages and Other Issues

Contract Provisions:
Fringe Benefits

9

Preparing for the
First Negotiation

The outcome of the first negotiated settlement between the company and the union may well determine if the business will remain alive and profitable or if it will wither and die. Concessions which management cannot realistically afford will ultimately spell conclusion as surely as a hearse. And conversely, extreme management "absolutism" may result in a disastrous debacle.

Every statement made during the negotiating sessions, consequently, may take on great importance. It would be both melodramatic and inaccurate to state that the opening minutes are the most crucial. Indeed, it is folly to generalize at all, in advance, that one or another particular step in the bargaining process is the turning point. The very nature of collective bargaining is continuous. Key moves in certain directions will naturally vary with each individual negotiation. Like any dynamic process that involves human beings, some moment will tend to be of prime significance and other times will constitute a period of "treading water" with little or no forward motion. The important fact to remember is that at no time can the company afford to risk relaxing its alertness.

Seemingly innocent statements or admissions may be the basis on which major aspects of the settlement can later be built. A misspoken word can be a snare for the unwary. Attempts to convince the other party of the correctness of one's position are important. But the results of oratory must be kept in perspective. Collective bargaining sessions are not essentially exercises in semantics. It is not always the most cogent argument or the most eloquent advocate that wins. The outcome of negotiations is very much determined by the needs of the parties and by their strength.

The company has work to do before the first bargaining session begins. It must select its negotiating team. Detailed advice on this is given in Chapters 20 and 34 of this book. Suffice to say here that the team must have adequate authority to negotiate independently. The union's negotiating committee will conduct its bargaining and take a final position subject to ultimate ratification by its rank-and-file membership. In a similar manner, management's negotiating committee may state at the outset that its authority is limited by the necessary eventual approval of the board of directors, certain stockholders or the corporation's president. In fact, at times this necessity to refer to the highest authorities may even be skillfully used to the advantage of the company. It demonstrates that the negotiators must "sell" any settlement to the company's owners. This can point up the necessity of achieving a rational compromise. Generally speaking, the company's negotiating committee should be sufficiently responsible and conversant with the company's needs and desires so that formal approval of its board or other top echelon group should in fact be little more than a rubber stamp process. A committee with insufficient authority to negotiate can only waste time and will cause a deterioration of relations.

In addition to having authority to bind the company and skill to negotiate for it, management's spokesmen must be prepared to know just how much they can offer. With rare exceptions the company's cost for labor will be higher after it concludes its first contract with the union than it was before the advent of organization. Recognizing that the initial negotiation will probably result in such an increase is nothing more than dealing with reality. But practically every company will be choked out of existence if it simply yields to the union's total demands unstintingly. Consequently, there should be a determination, in advance of negotiations, as to just how much of a labor cost increase the company can absorb.

This factor can be determined by the firm's comptroller or accountants in conjunction with production, sales and administrative personnel. It is basically an economic mission which must be accomplished, and while such a calculation cannot be rendered accurate to the last dollar, a workable and meaningful computation can be made. The company must figure its costs as compared to the costs of its competition. It must also determine various other factors: Can expenses be trimmed elsewhere? Can volume or price be increased? Is the company getting adequate labor at presently-paid wages? What are competitive firms paying for labor? Are reserves and expectations sufficient to warrant operating at a deficit for a period? Does market research and forecasting show an upturn or decrease in business?

Even where a company enjoys a "natural monopoly" it may find that an increased cost will price its product or service out of the market for its customer. For example, if all taxi drivers received an increase and all fare rates went up in a certain city, even though not a single competitor had the advantage of a lower wage rate, and all cab labor costs were uniform, still it is possible the taxi company could not afford the increase. In this case the true competitive picture would include not only other cabs, but the cost of buses or other forms of transportation and the expense and ease of downtown parking and garaging. Cabs compete not only with other cabs, but also private cars, buses and other modes of public transport. And people can still choose to walk. It is a fallacy for the union—particularly in industry-wide negotiations—to argue that all competitors will be equally affected and therefore no harm will result in a large raise. The increased taxi costs may result in less taxi rides over-all just as increased industry-wide steel costs can result in less consumption of the domestic product and more importation; and higher building costs, causing larger rents, may mean less occupancy.

A management that knows how to manage will generally be able, with the aid of a competent staff, to assess the competitive economic picture and determine its own "point-of-no-return." This means that up to "X-dollars-per-year" of increased costs the company may continue to function (and "X" may be any figure from zero up or down). Above "X" dollars the continued life of the company is in jeopardy. Any union pressure to obtain a settlement substantially beyond "X" will present the company with four alternatives. First, it may refuse the demands and accept a strike. The second choice is that it can close down. Third, the company may sign the contract because it is too weak to take a strike and then plan its future in accordance with the theory that its days are numbered. And fourth, it may radically change its method of operation by plant relocation, automation, subcontracting out, cut-back in certain areas of production or service, or other major change in policy.

If the management negotiating team is appraised of the "X" point in advance of the sessions it can break "X" down into cents-per-employee-per-hour and proceed to design initial package offers which it calculates will lead to a settlement on the safe side of "X". Moreover, if it sees that a settlement will not be achieved within this acceptable framework it can begin preparing for the alternatives well in advance. Anything less than this kind of pre-agreed limit is dangerous. A negotiator with no sense of his own maximum flexibility is like a blind bullfighter—with anything less than unbelievable luck he will get badly hurt.

The negotiating sessions will occur after the union has been certified or otherwise recognized. There is no particular time in which a contract must be concluded as there would be if this were a renegotiation of a presently expiring agreement. It is usually wise for the employer to hammer out and sign a contract as soon as possible so as to avoid prolonged expenditure of time and effort by his negotiating executives and minimize the period of employee distraction. But often he is quite content to let the negotiations drag. The union, on the other hand, is generally anxious to conclude negotiations as quickly as possible. They have "steamed-up" the workers in their organizing drive and want to deliver promised new benefits swiftly. Only after the increases are settled will the situation simmer down and permit the union's organizers to devote their time to other important fields of activity. As a result of this it may develop that the union is pushing to a show-down and the employer is delaying. Comprehension of this union psychology will enable the company to act more effectively.

Physical arrangements should be made for the negotiations which will best create an atmosphere for business-like conferring. The classic bargaining arena is a long table with seats for the key negotiators of labor and management on each side, and rows of folding chairs for the committees and staffs of each party behind their principals at the table. In negotiations where the committees are small, a simple dispersal around chairs in an office is now in vogue. This often develops an atmosphere conducive to sensible give-and-take. Negotiations, if few people are involved, may be held in the plant or an attorney's office. It is sometimes not advisable to hold first negotiations on the union's premises. For larger groups, public rooms should be hired. Most hotels in major cities are equipped with adequate space for this purpose and can provide the necessary public address systems, stationery, supplies and adjoining rooms for separate caucuses. Moreover, convenient eating and sleeping facilities are provided in the same building. While it is desirable to have telephones conveniently near, phone service in the actual negotiating room should be discontinued as it is distracting and disconcerts the speakers.

The negotiating committee, if it is not comprised entirely of professionals, should be carefully briefed in advance by their counsel or labor relations advisor as to their attitude. The context of the first negotiations is usually somewhat less than entirely friendly. An air of mutual distrust and suspicion often prevails. Some may feel it is like negotiating a peace treaty after a war. There are enough problems without the additional super-charging of the atmosphere that will occur if management's representatives enter the room with an antagonistic bearing and chips on their shoulders. The company's committee members must accept the change in circumstances—they are not there to defeat or embarrass the union, they are there to negotiate a contract. International diplomacy decrees that a nation send in a new ambassador to represent it when its policy changes; often it is wise to exclude from the negotiating committee the company executives who most publicly and vigorously spearheaded the company's campaign against the union. The new faces of negotiators less committed to an "anti-union" policy may serve the company in good stead. And the "tough" executives can subsequently be used when the company desires to take a particularly strong and forceful position. In smaller businesses where there is one key executive or principal who must cover all labor relations functions, it may be true that the man cannot be changed—but his outward attitude can and should be modified.

Throughout the actual conduct of all the negotiations—both initial and subsequent—the employer's representatives should act with courtesy and dignity. Politeness alone does not win points at negotiations, but the employer must always remember that the spirit forged at these sessions will remain for some time. Abuse of employees or rudeness will engender resentment not only at the table but later on as well. The employer must recognize facts about the negotiating employees and union delegates. The rank-and-file employees on the negotiating committee probably have never bargained before. This is usually their first experience as "leaders" representing their fellow employees. It is also the first time that most of them will be sitting down for discussions at the table with the company's top management. This is a novel role in which they are cast, replete with newly-won importance. Moreover, often for the first time they are publicly identifying themselves in front of management with the union, and this can result in a mixed attitude of bravado, fear of reprisal and probing to see how far they can go. The rank-and-file employees on the committee may also be flushed with their recent victory because their union has been recognized or has won an election. These committeemen who were probably the union's staunchest adherents inside the company have promised much to their fellow workers, and they come negotiations feeling a duty to consolidate their gains and clinch the triumph by "bringing home the bacon" in the form of fulfillment of their campaign promises.

Some of the individuals on the committee will be aspiring to higher levels of union leadership, either as volunteers or paid workers. The negotiations will present them with an excellent opportunity to demonstrate to their fellow workers their solidarity with the union, and their capacity for argument, oratory, courage, perspicacity and leadership.

The union agents will often talk particularly roughly and toughly to management in the opening sessions of the first negotiations, directing their words more to their own partisans on labor's side of the table than to management's representatives. The point of their belligerence is to reinforce the belief of the rank-and-file in the potency of the union. By comprehending what is behind these words, and understanding the words themselves, management will do a more effective job. These aspects of the negotiating table as an intramural forum must be recognized. Certain statements may be discounted and others deemed particularly significant in the light of this insight.

All of the points in this chapter should be discussed by management with its labor relations advisors prior to opening negotiations. Thus prepared, the company is well armed for the commencement of the actual negotiating proceedings.

10

Opening Negotiations

Most negotiations are relatively informal sessions, yet even the most casual have a pattern to them. At the start, the parties will each indicate a single designated spokesman who, in turn, will introduce the members of his negotiating committee. A member of the company's team should act as secretary, taking note of attendance and keeping minutes of the meeting. Various preliminary announcements may be made by each party. Rules of procedure should be established and the duration of the first meeting may be agreed upon. Then it is time for the actual business of the meeting.

Too many employers think that the first session is a "warm-up" period during which their negotiators can relax, and often management's second team is put in to bargain. Many companies indulge in the costly luxury of allowing junior officials to represent them at this opening session, later to find that they have erred. It is true that little actual bargaining will occur at the first session. There should be, and generally is, a statement of position by both parties. Regardless of the union's introductory remarks, I believe that is essential that management open the meeting by making such a keynote speech. Content and also tone are crucial aspects of this statement. It is imperative that the company demonstrate to the union bargainers, the shop negotiating committee and, through them, the entire staff of employees, that management is effectively organized and decisive. It must be established that the company will, at the very least, play the role of equal partner with the union in determining the outcome of negotiations. Any thought on the part of the worker's committee that the company is the victim of drift or that the union can dictate the terms of settlement due to the company's default can be effectively, quickly and crisply dispelled by this initial statement.

In the first moments of the proceedings it is good policy to have the employer's spokesman make clear the basic position of the company towards the union. At this "premiere" negotiation, after recognition or certification, employees will obviously be concerned with the company's attitude towards them. In disclosing this and expressing its viewpoint, the company should usually steer between the two opposite poles. On the one hand, the company might look foolish if it announced that it was welcoming the union with open arms and was certain that its presence would improve the situation for all concerned. In most cases the company has just concluded an election campaign against the union, or it has reluctantly and, after delay, recognized the union, bowing to the inevitable. In either event a sudden pro-union pronouncement would make it look as if the company had intentionally misled the workers when it delayed recognizing the union or electioneered against it. Such a reversal of policy might be regarded as hypocritical and as a demonstration of fear of the union. The few firms which have voluntarily embraced the union should certainly feel free to announce this, but it ill befits those which succumbed only under pressure to endeavor to gloss this over.

On the other hand, stating that the union's victory cuts no ice with management and that the company is, and will continue to be, totally indifferent to the union's demands and will ignore its entry into the picture serves only to enrage the employees who support the union, strengthen their loyalty to the union, stiffen their determination and may lead to an unfair labor practice charge based on a refusal to bargain.

As a rule, the most practical course lies between these two alternatives. A moderate approach will yield management the best results both as a philosophy of labor relations and as a public position to be articulated to the workers, the Government, stockholders, customers, and other interested third parties.

After a bitter election campaign, opening comments may follow a typical pattern, recapitulating the company's opinion that a union will not serve the employees better than the company itself has and demonstrating that the company is still consistent with its stand taken during the organizing drive. Moreover, management's remarks should graphically serve notice on the union's committee and organizers that just because the union has won the election, the company is not now making an unconditional surrender, nor is it afraid to repeat directly to the union the criticisms that it has earlier leveled.

Then management may affirm that, since the employees have selected this union as their bargaining agent, the company is committed, for better or worse, by Federal law to bargain with it and intends to obey the law and bargain in good faith. It is appropriate to state that the company will not be stampeded into committing suicide by giving in to unreasonable demands at any time, but that it will always listen with interest and study fairly and carefully any proposal the union might make. Because the earlier hard-fought election may have created bad feeling, it may be noted that management is looking forward to mutually fruitful and co-operative relations with the union. At this point, management spokesmen should emphasize that the company will always treat the union, its organizers and its members honorably and in accordance with the laws and will live up to the spirit and letter of any agreement with it—and that the company expects the union to do the same. Differing individual situations will, of course, require additions to, or subtractions from this description of opening comments.

Furthermore, it may also be wise at this time to comment on the future of day-to-day relations in the plant, shop, hotel, ship, store, warehouse, or center. Often it is announced that in view of the workers' selection of the union to protect their welfare, the company will no longer feel the same degree of obligation and responsibility which it previously exercised. Consequently, the inception of the union may result in cancellation of pay for workers absent with minor illnesses, curtailment of advances against salary, discontinuance of discretionary wage increases based on merit or productivity, etc. Many employers feel that this type of statement is necessary in order to make clear that the advent of a union is not an unmixed blessing, and to demonstrate that the union has its disadvantages as well as its good points. These employers and their advisors believe that such pronouncements will set the scene for the subsequent curtailment of previously granted management benefits and allow the company to recapture some of the dollars which it will presumably spend as a result of the union's demands. Moreover, they also opine that such a "tough" approach at the beginning will yield additional psychological dividends as the labor-management relationship develops.

Some management representatives, on the other hand, judge that the first negotiation is not a propitious time to express this. They fear that such frankness may only whet the appetites of the committee for negotiated contract increases, in anticipation of offsetting the changes that management threatens which would reduce the worker's benefits. Discretion must be exercised and the ultimate judgment made concerning this aspect of approach depending upon an assessment of the facts and background of the particular situation.

Often an effective conclusion to this "keynote address" is a statement that management's team shall endeavor to negotiate a settlement which is satisfactory to all parties, but that the basic responsibility of management's negotiators is to the company. As a result of this it is made abundantly clear that, while management's spokesmen will be equitable and bargain in good faith, they do not propose to preside over the dismemberment and downfall of their principal—the employer. The frankness and firmness of this statement is appreciated. The negotiator who states that he will try to be so "fair" as to become a dispassionate mediator rather than a committed advocate will immediately be distrusted. Truthfulness on this point will create an atmosphere in which the company's negotiator's statements will be given credence. Any statements short of such complete honesty and smacking of a false altruism will be greeted with suspicion and resentment. The union's negotiators, it may be assumed, are quite capable of representing it, and management's men need only worry about the company's future.

Having clarified the company's position, it is well to move on to the economic factors which will shape the company's bargaining posture. The chosen position may be that the company must hold the line and cannot increase its cost if it is to survive. Or, particularly in the case of a publicly-owned company where a good profit picture has been widely publicized, it may be that the company will be in a position to make moderate upward adjustments. However, it must be emphasized that the company's ability to make such increases is controlled by competitive factors, its need to accumulate profit to provide for new plant and equipment, research and development, repayment of corporate indebtedness and a fair yield on investment to corporate stockholders. Accordingly, while not denying that there is a profit, it is well to demonstrate that like a pie at Thanksgiving dinner, wedges must be cut for differing recipients—allowance must be made for reserves, debt payment, dividends, internal capital investment, executive compensation, increased benefits for non-unionized employees, etc. as well as for the members of the collective bargaining unit.

One basic problem that arises here is just how frank the company should be in disclosing its economic position. In almost all instances when the company is doing badly and making no profit or posting a loss it usually has few hesitations to state this. In the rare instance where fear of competitors, the potentiality of corporate raids or vanity disinclines top management to make public confession of their plight, the fact is usually already well known. The problem then in essence is: should a company plead poverty when this is not the case. Obviously, publicly-held companies cannot persuasively argue this since their statements are a matter of record, and the union usually can obtain copies of their annual reports. But there is a strong temptation in most closely-held corporations, partnerships or single proprietorships to do just this. In my opinion this tactic serves little purpose. As a general rule, acute union leadership has a pretty fair idea how the company is doing. And the company must remember that it will probably have repeated negotiations with the union so that if it cries "wolf" too often it may find that its bid for help, sympathy and cooperation when it really needs it, will fall on calloused ears.

Moreover, the company negotiators must recognize that the frame of reference of the workers frequently is different from that of executives or owners. Several years ago at a plant in New Jersey, the committee was negotiating in the executive conference room on the ground floor. The company's principal made a dramatic summation to the effect that he had come up specially from the company's office in New York to tell the union negotiators that he put the last of his personal money into the business. The clear implication of his talk was that if he had to sign a contract with a raise in it, the next paper he would sign would be an application for relief at the welfare office. When he finished, the shop chairman said quietly, "I don't believe a word of what you said." The employer, more in sorrow than in anger, and surprised at the lack of effect his eloquence had engendered, murmured, "Why?" And the shop chairman rose and silently pointed out the window to the parking lot where the owner's chauffeur was lounging against a late model Cadillac limousine in which he had just driven his employer up from the city.

Now, the owner may well have been telling the truth. Obviously, the car and driver were no proof of the company's profitability. He could have been living on his wife's money, or the bank's, or creditors, or money from any one of a dozen other sources. The point is that the committee concluded that it was *their* work that was paying for *his* car, and they believed that if he could afford this kind of transport he could afford to give a raise. It is important to remember this difference in values and outlook. A worker in a shop once told me that in his opinion anyone who wore a tie and jacket on a weekday was a rich man. This is something to bear in mind in negotiations.

Certain things, ranging from the employer's car, chauffeur, and custom tailored suits to a lot of overtime, will be taken as indicative of profit. The company's negotiators must recognize this and plan their strategy accordingly. A good negotiator says that a company is losing money only when it actually is. And then he is able to offer the union a certified statement of an independent auditor to this effect. Whether or not the offer is accepted, the statement, thus backed up, can be given credence.

If a company states it cannot afford to give a raise, the union has the right to demand an inspection of its books, and failure to yield them may result in a Board order that these be delivered to the union. Having union committees pour over management's ledgers is usually undesirable, and as a consequence great care should be taken not to fall into this trap. In one case, it had been stated that the company was in bad economic straits and did not feel an increase economically justified or financially defensible. The union's business agent, rephrasing the words a bit, talked to his committee and then shot a question back to the comptroller of the company. "Since you said you cannot afford to pay a raise what do you plan to do?" The management committee, instead of quickly responding to the query, waited for counsel to do so. This was wise. Any reply to this question, in the context of that afternoon's negotiation, could have resulted in a requirement that management show their books. Instead, counsel corrected the union leader, restated the position that the company would not accept a raise in pay and carefully noted this wording down. The business agent took the defeat cheerfully and much later admitted that he had been probing, and had hoped to get management in a position of opening its accounts or at least enabling him to say, as he bluntly put it, "You claim you can't afford it. We want to see your books. Now put up or shut up."

When a planned opening statement of the company's position is delivered to the committee, management can count on its soon being relayed to all employees. With decks cleared, management representatives can devote themselves to the give-and-take of negotiations and constantly employ the techniques that will lead the company to a settlement which is simultaneously realistic and desirable.

11

Techniques of

Bargaining

Builders need tools. The techniques which management's negotiators employ in collective bargaining are the tools they use to build a contract favorable to the company. From the employer's viewpoint, successful collective bargaining is a process wherein the union negotiators are convinced of management's needs to the extent that they agree to a settlement with which the company can live fruitfully.

As the previous chapters have shown, the company's spokesman should first make his "keynote speech" which specifically deals with management's reactions to the newly instituted union. The next step is to ask the union's spokesman to discuss in detail the demands which he is making. Management generally is given a copy of these demands prior to the negotiating session and will, of course, have studied this list in advance of the joint sessions. Nevertheless, these proposals are often lacking in clarity and can frequently stand elucidation. In the course of hearing the union's explanation, display, support and discussion of its requests, acute management representatives often receive clues as to the relative emphasis which the union itself places on particular proposals. Those demands which are carefully detailed and substantiated with data and dwelt upon at length can be regarded as more urgently desired than the requests which receive a cursory airing. Very skilled union negotiators knowing that this "run-down" on demands can serve as really useful reconnaissance to management will be careful to avoid just this type of emphasis or de-emphasis, but not all are this sophisticated. In some cases, this discussion serves as a good opportunity for union bargainers to underline those issues that later will be stressed, and even to indicate to the company what they consider absolutely necessary as a minimum for settlement. Additionally, hearing this explication of the proposals, management may often be able to construct cogent rebuttals from the very logic used to advance the propositions. And in detailed discussion it is often possible to see more clearly the true implications of certain requests which, on their face and before careful study, may appear innocuous.

After it has heard the union's demands and before a detailed rejoinder to each request, it is generally desirable for management to acquaint the union's shop committee with the financial facts of their joint business life. Previous chapters have demonstrated that it is important that the company analyze its own enterprise, its ability to grant increases, if any, and if so, the extent to which it can safely allow its costs to rise. The very processes which the company undergoes in arriving at the answers to these questions should be discussed with the bargaining committee of the union, although in simplified and edited form.

The economic factors that will shape management's policy are seldom static and will vary from time to time. It is certainly relevant to discuss, often in sequence, business conditions in the entire United States; the situation in the particular industry in question, both nationally and in the local geographic area in which the company is located; and finally, the business of the individual company represented at the bargaining table. All these topics are germane and may prove of importance to the union's people in helping them adopt a realistic perspective.

An investigation of national business conditions and particularly of developments in labor relations, even though not directly related to the specific negotiation at hand, often plays a direct role in achieving a settlement. For example, during the Spring of 1962, many management negotiators correctly emphasized the stock market plunge. Forecasters of commerce all viewed the drop as a harbinger of recession, and many business people were revising estimates downward, cutting back on inventory and retrenching in anticipation that the poor market performance pointed to bad times ahead. As a result, prudent employers during that Spring necessarily had to anticipate a decline in profit margins since all economic indicators suggested this. Not to project this thinking would have been sheer folly, and the gloomy expectations were properly shared with union committees. With tough sledding ahead, possible imminent depression and probable skidding sales, it was often pointed out to union negotiators in those months that management would be less than responsible if it granted major increases.

The national trend in labor-management settlements is often significant. In the Spring of 1962, the United Steel Workers Union had settled its pattern contract with the major steel companies for no wage increase and improvement only in fringes. This was partially a result of the pressure of the late President Kennedy and Arthur Goldberg, then his Secretary of Labor, who pushed for a policy of "non-inflationary" collective bargaining settlements. The administration formula, to which both steel labor and management adhered, was that increases should be given only insofar as they reflected actual gains in productivity. Not content with this generalization, the Government was even more precise and suggested that the over-all average national productivity gain was about three per cent. This then became, in effect, the Capitol's officially endorsed yardstick to be applied to each settlement. Certainly management spokesmen would have missed a golden opportunity during this period if they failed to make this Government position clear to labor's negotiators when the latter's demands exceeded the three per cent formula. After all, it was a labor-endorsed and union-supported administration which had made this recommendation, and if management was willing to adopt it, certainly organized labor could not, with good grace, balk. Astute management negotiators used the three per cent formula as only a point of departure in their efforts to contain labor's demands. If it could be demonstrated that productivity in the actual company in question had not increased by the three per cent average, then by Washington's precepts, a settlement of less than three per cent was indicated.

In recent years Government efforts to avoid inflationary settlements have continued. In the 1965 steel negotiations, official Washington suggested that an increase amounting to 3.2 per cent was the "right" settlement. It now seems likely that a government guideline may be urged on both parties when significant or major contracts are negotiated. However, many union leaders are growing restive and have flouted the government recommendations. They argue that price stability has not been maintained and that the cost of living is rising and they assert that their members will not accept such recommendations. The settlement in 1966 after an airlines strike resoundingly shattered the guidelines despite efforts to retain them. Nevertheless, continued governmental intervention in collective bargaining will, no doubt, have some impact on the settlements.

In many cases it is advantageous for management negotiators to discuss economic current events. This can include the cost of settlements in other situations, the average amount of increase and the shifts in industry locations and the labor market.

Conditions in the entire industry should often be discussed. If it is a weak sector of the economy, this should be indicated and the problems considered. When all manufacturing firms engaged in a certain line of production—for example, rolled steel plate, fine surgical instruments, cheap cameras, plastic eyeglass frames, or compact automobiles find their future endangered by foreign products that are flooding the American domestic market, labor should certainly be apprised of this. Dramatic disclosure of the dangerous situation will focus attention on the problem of saving companies and jobs rather than on pie-in-the-sky demands for increases from an industry that may be dying even without any wage betterments. Moreover, in this situation one might try to enlist union cooperation with management in endeavoring to convince appropriate governmental agencies that their liberal tariff policies are jeopardizing an entire industry's existence and can result in loss of high standard jobs and invested capital, a decrease in union membership and the undermining of our national defense effort should an emergency arise. Management and labor, each for its own good motives, may join hands to protest low import duties which have all of these unfortunate aspects and which serve only to subsidize substandard labor rates in certain foreign countries.

Industry-wide difficulties may be relevant in many other cases too. A trend in public taste away from a certain type of finished product —be it chewing tobacco, buggy whips, spats or walking sticks—may threaten an entire industry. Government action against a product— liquor or cigarettes—or against an industry—drug or automobile or aluminum or steel or electrical appliance manufacturers—will be relevant also. Antitrust proceedings or activities of the Federal Trade Commission, Federal Communications Commission, Interstate Commerce Commission, Food and Drug Administration, or Congressional investigations might well be discussed. Developments among competitors certainly have a bearing on individual companys' problems. When other firms in an industry are becoming increasingly automated, displacing labor, a representative of the negotiating firm would certainly be remiss if he did not point out that it was incumbent on the union to "go easy on him" since his plants had higher labor costs than his competitor's. He should also note that his plants provided many jobs and employed many more dues-paying members than these relatively unpopulated automated factories.

The state of a segment of the industry in a particular geographic area should, in many cases, be discussed with the union. In September of 1966, "A," a labor relations attorney, was negotiating a contract for a number of concerns in the textile processing industry, most of which were located in the metropolitan New York-New Jersey area. "A" contended that the future of the plants was seriously menaced by competitors from out of the area, basically, the South. Costs of operation, exclusive of labor, may have been the same with lower rents and electricity costs in the South offsetting the freight differential for shipping goods to the New York converters. But in the mid-Atlantic States, New York and New Jersey primarily, the mimimum rate to general helpers was $2.40 per hour, while Southern competitors were paying drastically less than this. Thus "A's" concern was the future of the textile finishing industry in New York, Southern Connecticut and Northern New Jersey. The disadvantage under which these firms operated compared to Southern competitors was the key to "A's" attitude at negotiations. The employers could not afford to widen the already dangerous disparity.

Industry conditions may be unique in certain particular localities. If a particular port is steadily losing freight tonnage, it is a joint problem of longshoremen and stevedoring concerns which the industry in other areas does not share. In fact, in certain fields only local industry conditions are materially relevant. This can be true in building construction and service industries and among local transit and communication companies, retail stores and wholesale depots, banks in certain metropolitan centers, laundry and dry-cleaning establishments, hotels, restaurants, barber shops, etc. If spokesmen are bargaining for a group of newly-organized firms in a single industry, this "local industry-wide" approach is particularly significant.

Finally, management negotiators should consider the economic position of the particular concern involved in the negotiation. In many *bona fide* cases the particular problems of a company, even internal difficulties, should be brought to the union's attention.

Example: In a publicly-held company, an overly-generous settlement may result in a proxy fight against management which would be considered by some shareholders as too pro-labor. The union, which got on well with incumbent company executives, has a right to know that too hard a push on its part might result in the firing of its management friends. Example: In a partnership, one of two partners had just bought the other out, working capital was short, and a major account had just been lost when a principal customer decided to cease contracting out and to take over the operation himself. The company's future was uncertain—it needed a period of time without the pressure of increased costs to consolidate its position. The union had a right to know that too much pressure could force the company over the brink. Example: A company, the largest in its industry on the Eastern seaboard, was paying the highest wages and granting the best fringe benefits already. Any major victory by the newly organized union would have merely widened the existing and serious gap in labor rate between this company and its competitors. Management's fear was that even with its particular know-how the broadened gulf of labor costs would force it out of business. "Keep our costs in line with our competitors," they said. If they had not told the union this, the result might have been a defunct company. The consequent loss of many jobs paying better-than-average rates would have seriously damaged the union's ability to organize other employees in this industry.

In summary, management negotiators do not convince a union with abstractions, nor do they successfully bargain collectively in a vacuum. It is often profitable for the employer's spokesman to dwell on relevant facts and situations in the nation, parallel industries, competitive businesses, and the particular economic situation of the bargaining company.

Following this, management's representatives should rebut in detail any of the union's proposals that the company deems unreasonable or excessive. Management should also, as it threads its way through the labyrinth of demands, consider the acceptance of some. Obviously, it might be foolhardy at first blush to embrace publicly all of the union's requests which management is privately prepared to grant. Nevertheless, the dividends in good will may be high if management acknowledges at an early stage that a particular demand is worthy and that it has no objection to it. For instance, to nurture the spirit of forward motion and potential agreement, management should frequently be willing to agree in principal to

the articles providing for grievance, arbitration and no-strike procedures. When the company recognizes that it will have a union shop,
maintenance of membership, and dues check-off provisions, it may
be sensible to agree to these as well. These kinds of concessions
may cost the employer nothing, but will bring the divergent sides
closer together. When the employer concedes such things, the union,
recognizing the good faith nature of management's bargaining, may
itself eliminate or reduce certain demands. In successful labor relations management will often have to say "No," but it should seldom
do so without a purpose.

After discussion of the union's demands, management will
probably note that, with a few exceptions relating to union security,
grievance procedure, etc., all other demands either directly or indirectly amount to a cost item. It is often useful to total the cost of
all the union proposals. The same discussion of the problem of
increasing costs, which management has privately considered earlier,
should be paraded across the table in joint session. It is sensible,
after dissecting the demands, to examine the anatomy of increase
and to tick off the possible sources from which the company can or
cannot derive the necessary additional revenue. It may well run like
this: "There are four places from which the money can come to
cover the raises. First we could increase the price of our product."
(If this is not feasible, it should be explained that this cannot be
done because the laws of supply and demand and the forces of
competition—or a Federal or state regulatory agency—determine
what can be charged. The company cannot operate independently.)
"Second, we could increase volume thereby lowering our cost per
unit." (If this avenue is closed because the company cannot afford to
increase the advertising and merchandising budget or expand plant
or storage facilities, this should be told.) "Third, the company can
take increases from current high profits." (The addenda to this usually is that profits are not that high.) "Fourth, the increases might
be taken from our reserves, the 'pot of gold' in the bosses' safe."
(There seldom is such in small, closely held companies and in larger
firms part of reserves are needed for expansion and other items.)
Other appropriate possibilities should be mentioned also at this
time.

Management negotiators for their convenience will soon divide
the union's demands into five categories—those which the union
absolutely must have; those which will be compromised; those which
management will positively not accede to; those the company must

have and those which both parties find innocuous. In a recent negotiation with a newly recognized union in New York, demands exemplary of each category existed. It was obvious that the company would have to agree to a union shop, dues check-off and maintenance of membership. Wage increases were negotiable as were pension and welfare benefits. The union, in turn, would get no contract if the company couldn't get the right to departmental seniority and the privilege of suspending seniority for several months until the plant could be reorganized—nor would management under any circumstances agree to the demand barring outside maintenance contractors. Finally, management could and did speedily agree to routine arbitration, grievance and no-strike clauses.

Knowledge of the union's goals can be gained in several ways other than at the bargaining table. Particularly where the union has been recognized without an election, informal exploratory talks can be held between the parties. And if the union has contracts with other companies in the industry, these firms can be contacted and their agreements studied. Moreover, the union's own statements in other contexts, such as their publications or newspaper reports of their convention proceedings, will yield insight into what they will seek to achieve in negotiating.

The following two chapters contain a discussion of the substantive issues which management must consider. The dynamics of labor-management negotiations, which are equally applicable to the initial negotiations as to subsequent encounters, are further discussed in Chapter 21.

12

Contract Provisions:

Wages and Other Issues

The president of a company which was about to commence negotiating a collective bargaining agreement with a union that had just
won recognition asked his attorney: "Is there anything sacred?
Can they negotiate with us on how we run our enterprise, what
products we make, whom we sell to, what supervisors we hire?"

These are important questions. According to law bargaining issues
may be divided into three categories: issues that must be negotiated; issues that may be negotiated, and issues that cannot be
negotiated.

The duty to bargain collectively and in good faith has been
interpreted to mean that the company must negotiate on certain
things. These subjects include wages, hours, and terms and conditions of employment, such as the duration of a contract, procedures
for interpretation, modification, and administration of a contract,
the no-strike clause, all types of increases, bonuses, holidays, vacation pay, guaranteed wage plans, termination of employment, lay-
offs, transfers, reinstatement of strikers, recall, seniority, changes in
working hours, work schedules, free time during working hours,
welfare, pension, health and insurance plans and union security
provisions that meet Labor Management Relations Act requirements. Even subcontracting or plant relocation, when the change
would seriously affect the employees in the existing unit, are generally considered to be subjects for mandatory bargaining. Failure

to discuss union proposals dealing with these subjects is unlawful for the employer and can result in charges that he is committing an unfair labor practice.

In the so-called permissive area where management may bargain, but cannot be compelled to bargain, are such issues as the location of new plants, the product to be manufactured, general business practices, schedules and processes of production, methods of operation and wholly internal union actions. For example, the company may want to institute a requirement that, before a strike can be called, the union must submit management's final proposal to a secret vote by the rank and file employees. If the union and the company both wish to negotiate on this, they are free to do so. But if either party refuses to discuss such an issue, it is entitled to abstain and will incur no liability. Conversely, the union may demand that all foremen be graduate electrical engineers. The employer can maintain that the hiring of management personnel is strictly a management prerogative, and as such, is not within the purview of the union. Here again the Board will not chastise management if it refuses to bargain on this. Like the question of a strike vote this is deemed a matter of internal policy, not required to be discussed with the opposite party, and the participants may reserve this right not to debate such issues.

Finally, there are nonbargainable subjects. For example, the union may not bargain about a union shop in those states where a union shop is prohibited, nor may it bargain for a closed shop arrangement in any state. The union may not negotiate for hiring halls that are discriminatory. It cannot insist on provisions that would violate federal law relating to hot cargo movements or secondary boycotts. Furthermore, the employer cannot state that he will bargain about the right of the union to represent the employees. The union, having been certified or recognized, has an absolute right to be considered the duly authorized bargaining agent and the company cannot demur at this.

The four general areas which are most frequently the subject of collective bargaining are wages, union security clauses, personnel management provisions and fringe benefits. The first three are discussed in this chapter, and the fourth in the next.

Those businessmen who think that negotiating wages with a union at the first bargaining session amounts only to achieving agreement on the size of an increase are generally quite mistaken.

The actual dollar increment for all employees of the company, or those in certain major categories, is called the across-the-board increase, and represents only one aspect of negotiations on the problem of wages. These negotiated increases are added to the hourly, daily or weekly rate paid the employees.

In many cases the union will seek to negotiate with the company on job descriptions and categories of work. Thus, in a single factory there may be press-operators, welders, polishers, tool and die-makers, utility men, porters, packers, shipping and receiving help and truck-drivers. The union will endeavor to have written into the contract all of these different job classifications, often with descriptions. Then it will try to negotiate, in addition to the across-the-board increase, the minimum "hiring-in-rate" for each category and the maximum pay. Between the beginning figure and the ceiling are usually graded steps, which are based on length of service with the company.

It is not always necessary for management to grant additions in minimums and maximums that equal the across-the-board increase. The company spokesman may quite logically say: "We are willing to give an increase to the people working for us, but we do not favor increasing the minimum rates. We are already paying enough to get good people and more than competition pays. We want to concentrate all our improvements for those already working for us." This reasoning may impress the union as being fair. And, a refusal to increase minimums does not directly affect any of the people who are already hired by the company.

In larger companies the wage and salary administrators or other members of the personnel staff may have already established wage classification standards and rate progression ladders. The incoming union may accept these in whole or in part. In smaller firms where hiring was done on an individual basis before the advent of the union, and no formalized tables of organization prevailed, the classification must be built up from scratch. In these latter cases, if certain particularly skilled employees are receiving more than the top rate for this job as negotiated by the union, the likelihood of the union's agreeing to a reduction for these people is remote. Their wages which are truly "super-scale" are generally kept intact as individual stipends called "red-circle" rates. These are maintained as long as the favored individuals remain, but when they leave, their successors get the regular wage scale.

The general principle adhered to by most unions when they

negotiate wage scales is that all people doing the same work receive the same wage. The only widely practiced exception to this is agreement to periodic wage boosts based on longevity in the company's employ, that is a form of progression raise. Thus, provisions are not made for the more proficient or more productive worker. Uniformity of compensation rather than payment for individual efficiency is the rule. Many may argue that this puts a premium on mediocrity, but it is, nevertheless, the fact in most contracts today.

An employer may, however, reward particular workers if he sees fit. This may be accomplished by awarding merit increases over and above the standard rate called for in the contract. But the employer must protect his right to do this. When a collective bargaining agreement states that the company will pay $1.95 per hour to all sales clerks, a change in this rate—whether up or down—is subject to collective bargaining. If the management wants to reward a particularly able and attentive salesgirl by giving her an extra twenty-five cents per hour, a union can argue that such action may not be taken unilaterally and is a proper subject for discussions. The company may find, under certain circumstances, that this contention will be upheld. However, if the contract clearly states that the $1.95 is the minimum compensation that the employer can pay the employee, or specifically arrogates to the company the right to make merit increases in its sole discretion, then the union cannot contest a unilateral increase.

As in all contract provisions, the actual wording of the clause is essential. A company contracts to pay filing clerks $70.00 per week to start; $75.00 after six months employment and $80.00 after a year of employment. The term "employment" becomes critically significant and must be defined. If an employee is laid off for nine months in that first year, or takes a three month maternity leave, does her upward wage adjustment come after six months of continuous work or automatically on the sixth monthly anniversary of her service with the company? The answer should be in the contract itself, the former provision, of course, being more advantageous to the employer.

Connected with the issue of straight wages are such matters as premium pay for work on the second or third shift, provisions for extra pay if work is performed on contract holidays, Saturdays, or after certain hours, and arrangements regarding overtime pay. In many companies, there is additional pay over and above the basic wage for work that is done on shifts other than the first shift. This premium pay may be computed as a percentage figure or in dollars or cents. It may be the same for the second as for the third shift, but is often higher for the latter. Work performed on contract holidays generally involves double pay or triple pay.

Time worked over 40 hours in a week must, by law, be compensated for at 150 per cent of the straight-time rate. However, unions can bargain for more than this and may ask for provisions for double time for all overtime, or for overtime pay for all hours in excess of a certain number of hours per day. This can cost an employer more than he pays if only the federal statutory requirements are followed. A worker can work 10 hours a day for 4 days and have the 5th day free and yet receive 32 hours pay at straight-time-rates, 8 hours per day for 4 days, and 8 hours at time and one-half, 2 hours per day at overtime rates. If the union did not prevail on this, the employer could fully comply with the law and still pay no overtime for such a four-day week. Similarly, if Saturday pay is at double time, a man can be absent for two days during the week, say Monday and Tuesday, work straight time Wednesday, Thursday and Friday, at premium rate on Saturday and for the 32 hours still receive the equivalent of a full week's pay.

Incentive pay is another issue which may arise in a contract. Compensation may be geared to the piece-work of an individual or extra pay may be given based on the productivity of a team of workers. In setting such rates, attention must be given to selecting the standards and establishing modes of changing them to accommodate new operations or changes in production method. In other specialized contracts it may be necessary to consider a guaranteed annual or monthly wage; or to set scales of commissions which the workers can earn in addition to their straight wages.

In many union contracts today labor's negotiators will ask for and get a cost-of-living "escalator" clause. This means that the employer is obligated at stated intervals, usually once every three, four or six months, to give employees covered by the union contract an adjustment on their salary dependent on any change in the cost of living between the base period and the adjustment date. The actual figures are computed and maintained by the Bureau of Labor Statistics of the United States Department of Labor.

For those employers who do not have such clauses in their contracts or who are negotiating intial contracts, effort should be made to avoid the introduction of such obligations. (Concerns which do have the requirement are often well advised to get rid of it, even if it necessitates a sizable across-the-board increase to provide the momentum to blast that imbedded provision out of the contract.)

The escalator clauses are unfortunate for most employers for several reasons. One of the principal advantages of a collective bargaining agreement is that at least for the term of the agreement, for better or for worse, the employer knows what his labor costs will be and can set up his price list taking this into account. The escalator clause cancels this advantage since it means that on one or more occasion during the contract period increased payroll may become necessary, and no advance planning as to the impact of this is possible since the amount cannot be predicted. I speak of increases with little thought of apology to those who point out that escalator clauses can mean decreases also; because the law of "what goes up must come down" does not seem to apply to the cost-of-living indices of our economy. This has been particularly true since the advent of big, modern unionism in the 1930's. Since 1940, the cost-of-living has moved steadily upwards and nothing in the present complexion of our economy indicates that the trend will be halted, much less reversed. The employer who faces reality and will not gamble on deflation and depression must recognize that escalator clauses mean raises. The presence of the escalator clause in some of today's major collective bargaining agreements actually provides some of the impetus for the very inflationary spiral which in turn results in a higher re-evaluation of the cost-of-living a few months later.

Escalator clauses, it is submitted, are not truly advantageous to the employer for still another important reason. The increases which the employees receive under them are not truly satisfying to the worker. The employee who receives the adjustment does not think of it as a real wage increase or of any substantial benefit to him. He feels it is more in the nature of keeping him even, but not helping him to get ahead. It does not take the place of an across-the-board increase and in the opinion of many employees does not actually appear to be a concession on the part of the employer. The employee feels he is getting nothing.

The individual employer who gives the adjustment, on the other hand, may find that while the cost-of-living has gone up generally and he is obliged to increase his payroll, he cannot increase the prices of his particular goods or services. Such an increase can be particularly harmful to him. An employer who has absolutely no control over the national cost-of-living, and often little control over his own price list because of competitive market conditions, can find the escalator clause will prove a particularly bitter pill.

Those employers that have these clauses and foresee scant prospect of removing them or who find it impossible to avoid including them in contracts negotiated in the future can endeavor to modify them in several ways which many responsible unions will accept and which, to a certain extent, can alleviate hardship to the company. The employer should attempt to have a maximum set on the amount of increase under the escalator clause. The union may retort that it wants a minimum. From this, a clause would develop such as there was in some contracts in the New York City area which provides for semi-annual adjustments with an increase of not less than fifty cents per week nor more than $1.00 per week. In this context the union's demand for a floor, is a fair trade for a ceiling. It makes future wage costs more predictable, and limits intangible cost factors.

It is also helpful to key the cost-of-living increase to the city in which the firm is located. This is primarily useful in that it often enables certain employers with local unionized competition to stay closer to their competitors. And it eliminates the possibility that a company will have to give a cost-of-living increase despite an actual drop in the index in its own locale. This is a safety device particularly suited for recession-prone areas. A wise union should appreciate its utility, since the ultimate consequence of forcing an individual employer to pay above the local market for competitive skills can be the removal of the plant to another area or its shutdown entirely.

There is no mystery to obtaining the actual index figures. Local offices of the Bureau of Labor Statistics are generally glad to oblige and will answer a telephone question. Inclusion on a mailing list can be assured by writing to the Bureau, a part of the U.S. Department of Labor.

The typical contract, in addition to wage and fringe benefit provisions, has clauses which cover other terms of employment. A list of these conditions could extend for many pages, and would include paragraphs relating to safety and health provisions, workloads and size of working crews, management prerogatives, veteran's re-employment rights, leaves of absence, grievance, arbitration and no-strike provisions, union security and seniority. All of these items can be of significance to the employer. For purposes of discussion here we will first consider the area of management rights and then the question of union security.

The general principal governing the seniority system is that the first person hired in is the last to be laid off. In other words, as length of employment increases, so does job security, and the long-employed workers increasingly are insulated from the vicissitudes of the business cycle. Before a company is unionized the criteria of whether or not to retain an employee when a reduction in work force is necessary or to recall an employee when additional places open up is best summed up in one word—"ability." After the typical contract is instituted the key word will change to "seniority." As a corollary of this the company must carefully develop its position on seniority before the negotiations open. It must be prepared to determine such issues as whether seniority will be company-wide, plant-wide, job-wide or department-wide. Where there are provisions that senior employees "bump" junior people who are laid off by moving down into their jobs, it is essential that there be a phrase asserting that seniority only prevails where the more senior man can do the work required of him. Provisions must be made as to pay scale for employees who are temporarily or permanently moved up or down to positions carrying different rates. Departments and job descriptions should be precisely defined.

In view of the fact that workers with tenure are hard to dislodge, it is essential that the company exercise care in its hiring policies. The right to lay off indiscriminately is suspended when seniority is instituted. Most contracts provide for a probationary period of two weeks, thirty days, or some longer period for new employees. The longer probationary period the company can get the better. Supervisory personnel should be instructed to scrutinize new employees carefully during this trial period so that the weak performers will be weeded out before they get on the seniority ladder and gain tenure.

Union representatives may request provisions having to do with workloads and work assignments. They may seek to freeze workloads and work assignments at current standards or to change them. The result of negotiations on this issue will have an impact upon the efficiency of the company's operations.

Almost all contracts include provisions for grievance procedures. In the event of a failure to settle a dispute through company-union discussions, arbitration is usually provided for. The grievance procedure can be established in a general way or in considerable detail, where each separate step is prescribed, as successively higher echelons of company and union officials confer.

The scope of the arbitration provision is something that must be determined at negotiations. Will this remedy cover all disputes arising out of the relationship between the parties or simply specified ones? For example, if it is stated that recourse to arbitration will prevail only when differences concerning discharge and discipline arise, then it follows that, if the company introduces a new machine and the workers refuse to work on it and the dispute cannot be resolved, the union has a right to strike.

But, if the arbitration clause is all inclusive, it means that any disagreement between the parties arising from the contract or otherwise will be taken to arbitration. A corollary of the broad arbitration clause is generally a no-strike no-lockout clause, obligating the union not to strike during the life of the contract, and the company not to engage in a lockout, but to choose arbitration instead.

The management-prerogative clause defines the extent to which management will unilaterally be able to control and direct its operations, without the need to consult the union and obtain its approval. A well-written management prerogative clause, for example, may preclude a union complaint that automation has taken a job away, if the right of the company to introduce new techniques and machinery is preserved without qualification.

Some old time labor negotiators who represent management tend to scoff at the management-prerogative clause. They feel that management either will manage or it won't, and that, if it won't, no clause in the contract will give it the power to do so. However, the doctrine of the inherent right of the company to automate, sub-contract, move, or merge has been eroded by many court decisions. Increasingly, it appears that, to be safe, a company must bargain about matters once considered wholly within its own sphere.

How far the company can go in making its operations more efficient without bargaining during the life of a contract and how much the union has to say about company policy are complicated problems. As a result, negotiators are turning to the relative security of a management-prerogative clause, if they can obtain it, since it can clarify questions that might otherwise be hard to answer.

Unions usually demand a protection of their status. Whenever they can achieve it they request the establishment of a union shop. This means that all employees must join the union and maintain membership in it. Coupled with this may be the check-off which provides that the employer shall deduct dues from the worker's pay and remit them directly to the union. The terminology used in these provisions can spell the difference between a valid contract and one that is void. The law prescribes that definite requirements be met if these clauses are to be deemed legal. For example, a union security clause will be ruled unlawful if it does not provide that both present and future employees be given at least thirty days before they must join the union. In the states where a union shop is legal, the union may legitimately bargain for this. Under Federal law, individual states may ban a union shop. Where the union shop is prohibited, a request for it need not be entertained by management. Union shop prohibitions are also known as "right to work" laws.

Less helpful to the union is the agency shop, allowing a worker not to join a union but nevertheless requiring that he pay dues to it. A maintenance of membership clause is still another provision bolstering the union's security. Check-off regulations are stringent. The employer has no right to check-off dues and pay them to the union, regardless of contract provisions, unless the individual employee has signed a card which specifically authorizes the company to take this action. The employer should keep these cards on file in a safe place. When there is a check-off provision and a union shop called for in the collective bargaining agreement, the company should offer this card to each employee at the time he starts employment or joins the union.

Other negotiable arrangements can increase union (and job) security. For example, a union may demand a clause that bars the company from moving its present location. Union and company can agree that the latter will not subcontract out any work that is presently being performed by members of the collective bargaining unit. And unions may get the company to purchase and attach union labels, or to give their members first notice of a new job or to grant top seniority to the union shop steward.

Employers should consult their advisors on other aspects of union security including the "hiring hall," and about exceptions to the general rules which pertain in certain particular industries. In fact, all clauses which are proposed by either side for inclusion in the contract should be carefully examined by management to anticipate the results of such provisions in practice.

13

Contract Provisions:
Fringe Benefits

One of the most disturbing problems which confront those who professionally negotiate labor contracts is the amazing lack of concern that many employers and company negotiating teams show toward fringe benefits. Many executives feel that after the actual dollars-and-cents increase has been settled the other union demands —and the company's counter-demands—are just details to be mopped up by the second team and do not merit the consideration of management's top talent.

There are few contracts where fringe benefits run less than twenty per cent of the straight wage costs and many in which they run over thirty per cent. A safe rule-of-thumb average is that fringe benefits cost the company about one-quarter of the actual wages. Included in fringe benefits are all the items which cost the employer money but which do not go into the employees' pay envelope in the form of take-home pay for hours actually worked. Some are required by law, such as workmen's compensation, social security, unemployment and disability insurance, etc. And there is a long list of costly items, some seen in all contracts, some appearing in only a few, including holiday and vacation pay, hospital, medical and other welfare benefits, life insurance, sick-leave, pension contributions, wash-up time and coffee-break time, work-clothes allowances and reserves for technological unemployment, severance-pay costs, etc. Two items alone, vacation for two weeks, and paid holidays, generally average close to one-twelfth the total wage cost.

More than 90 per cent of plant workers receive six or more holidays, two weeks' vacation after five years service, life insurance, hospitalization and surgical benefits. About 70 per cent of plant workers and 80 per cent of office workers have retirement pensions. One-third and two-thirds of plant and office workers, respectively, have some form of major medical or catastrophe coverage.

There is only one professional, safe and sound way in which to negotiate fringe benefits. This is to convert all of the benefits demanded into actual dollars-and-cents costs. In the case of the majority of significant items, this can be done quite simply and accurately. Pension costs and welfare plans underwritten by an outside insurer such as Blue Cross, Blue Shield or a commercial carrier can generally be precisely computed based on the company's estimate of premium. If these benefits are not based on insurance, then the cost is the percentage of salary or dollar amount demanded by the union in contributions to the welfare or pension plans. On the items which are more difficult to figure—how many employees will take up to five days sick-leave requested for inclusion in the contract and at what cost to the employer—experienced labor management contract administrators can generally give a satisfactorily close estimate. In this example, simply multiply the average number of employees by five days individual pay and you have an accurate figure of what sick-leave will cost. Even other items, apparently less tangible, can ultimately be translated into monetary equivalents.

The company should resist contracting to give benefits which are not based on the actual dollars and cents to be paid. For example, if the company commits itself to pay a $15.00 monthly insurance premium for hospitalization and surgical care, it can figure its cost for the duration of the entire contract. But, if it promises to buy expanded Blue Shield or Blue Cross benefits without specifying cost, it may find itself paying increasing figures during the span of the agreement as the insurance company raises rates. The employer's cost projections, therefore, are subject to unpredictable variations, and when he does pay higher rates, the employees do not recognize or appreciate the increased burden. Where the union will not agree to clauses specifically limiting costs, provision should be made that if medical or hospital insurance companies offer more expensive plans during the contract's duration, the employer may continue with the least expensive plan that resembles his original commitment. Or the employer should include the right to have free choice of insurance carrier, so that he may obtain the required coverage for the workers at the lowest premium price.

Once the cost is ascertained, management is in a position to sensibly negotiate a contract. The company can calculate what it is able to give as an over-all package increase and, during the negotiations, can determine just what items will fit into that package. This determination is not something which can be done on a hit-or-miss basis. Each and every fringe benefit should be viewed from several points of view. There are three categories of fringe benefits which employers should be most inclined to give.

First, there are those concessions which will actually help the company. Reasonable vacations, for example, are not to be resisted because the employees come back refreshed and relaxed and again ready to work. For this reason, as a general practice, employers are advised to insist that their people take vacations rather than just collect the vacation pay and go on working fifty-two weeks a year. Some other fringes also can actually increase plant productivity and the granting of them can be turned to advantage.

Second, are the fringe benefits which management judges will "sell" its entire settlement offer. In this connection it is a matter of isolating certain segments of the union's negotiating team and tailoring elements of a package satisfactory to them. Professional union leaders are generally very much in favor of welfare and pension benefits that go into funds administered by joint boards of trustees on which they have representation and over which the union actually often has considerable control. The rank-and-file worker is more often concerned with actual take-home pay and tends to minimize fringe benefits. As a practical rule many negotiators find that it is the leadership that pushes in the direction of these fringes while the rank-and-file hang back. Pension benefits to a thirty-year old worker seem like pie-in-the-sky and the complicated advantages of tax deferred compensation are difficult to explain. But union leadership, backed by their research, education, information and legal departments, recognize the advantages of these items both to the rank-and-file and to the union as a going and continuing organization. And they stress these benefits. On one occasion when an employer, tired of computing myriad fringe benefits, converted all the fringe benefits into cents per hour and told the negotiating committee that they could have everything they had asked for in fringe benefits in the form of a straight wage boost, he threw the union committee into civil war. It was only the full pressure of the leadership that forced the committee to reject the offer and finally insist that the dollar amount be split between wages and fringes.

The wise employer will "beam" his offer to diverse elements within the union so that, when it comes to union acceptance of his final offer, he will have partisans on labor's side of the table willing to take the whole because of the part that they, in particular, have won. Recently, a contract was negotiated in which four cents an hour was granted for the pension fund. The negotiating committee consisted of senior shop employees with many years of service. Two, in fact, were within a year of retirement. This sold them on the contract which involved only a five cent straight wage increase. Had the four cents for pensions not been given, the committee would not have endorsed the settlement and the employer would have been faced with the necessity of giving a straight wage increase of much more than nine cents if he wanted a contract settlement. These important union spokesmen on the committee wanted agreement so as to ensure the pension benefit. To include as a part of management's package offer something for each "special interest" within the union requires both good judgment and informed understanding of the particular union, from its international policies to its shop politics.

The third type of fringes which the practical negotiator does not object to granting are those fringes already given but not as a matter of contractual right. For example, in small shops most employers grant their older employees one, two or three days off in the event of a death in the family. If this is, indeed, the practice and the union wants a clause guaranteeing these benefits to any employee with three or five years' seniority, management usually should have little objection. The granting of this should be traded for a concession from the union or can help to break the ice.

The tragedy about fringe benefits is that often, just as the employer is unaware of their cost, the employees do not recognize their importance. It is imperative both for improved productivity while a contract is in force and in preparation for negotiation of a new agreement that management make the work force aware of what their benefits are and what they cost the company. Simple and direct information in this connection and honest reporting to employees can have substantial significance. In some situations it may be advisable to consider ways and means of graphically demonstrating to the employees both the value of the benefit to them and the expense to management. A definitive program can be established to achieve this. One approach is to prepare and circulate booklets containing a resume of all benefits; or this information may be posted on the bulletin board; or a one page discussion of each different advantage may be distributed periodically in pay envelopes.

It is essential that management be careful in agreeing on the contract wording. Precise language can save dollars. A prime example is the criteria of eligibility for benefits written into the contract. Three employers, each with 1,000 men earning the same wage, can agree to grant nine holidays with pay in the contract year. But the cost will be different to each firm. Company A, the least astute, will agree to give the day's pay to all workers employed when the holiday falls provided they have worked the month within which it occurs. Company B, the intermediate company, gives the holiday only to men who have worked during the week in which it falls. Company C, the hardest bargainer of all, pays its employees for the eight hours provided they have a record of thirty days of service with the company and work the day before and the day after each holiday. While the substance of the benefit is the same, the phrasing surrounding it can mean a cost differential of thousands of dollars.

The same principle is equally applicable to arranging vacation terms. Suppose an employee with over five years of service is entitled to a three-week vacation with pay. The contract should define the entitlement. If a man works only three months in his seventh year of employment does he get the full three weeks or only a portion of it? If the contract is silent on this, the man will certainly claim a right to the entire vacation pay, and a controversy may spring up. However, if the collective bargaining agreement provides that the 120 hours of vacation pay should be pro-rated on time worked, that is "ten hours of vacation pay accrues for each month of employment during the past calendar year after the fifth year of employment computed as of July 1," then the problem is alleviated. Confusion can be even more thoroughly avoided by including other precise definitions in the contract. In this case, to continue the example, a "month of employment" would be defined as any "month in which a man works at least fifteen days including holidays, sick leave and vacation as days worked." It would be established that the commencement of a man's service, for the purpose of computing seniority on which vacation pay is based, would be the first day he started working for the company, providing such tenure was continuous. Provision should be made to determine the date in the case that employment is broken due to a lay-off for a long period, a leave of absence, the resignation of an employee who is subsequently rehired, a prolonged illness, and so forth.

With regard to vacation the company might wish to specify its right to close the entire plant down for a vacation period. Conversely, for competitive reasons, some companies might want the right to stay open and merely furlough groups of employees at a time. The safest clause is one permitting a plant to remain open or shut at the discretion of management.

It is unrealistic to suggest that every detail can be set forth in a contract or that all imaginable contingencies could be covered in advance by the agreement. However, the more tightly worded the provisions are, the fewer difficulties will arise. There are books available which contain sample contract clauses on a wide variety of topics. Also, existing collective bargaining contracts may be checked. These sources may profitably be consulted by management representatives when drafting their own labor-management contract.

It would be naive to imply that unions are unaware of the significance of precise phraseology or that they would permit management, unhampered and unfettered, to choose the wording it prefers. Obviously the terminology selected is not just window-dressing but does substantially determine the fringe benefit to the worker and the cost to the employer. Management, therefore, when it makes a proposal or accepts a proposition must base its stand on the actual wording of the provision and not deal in abstractions. Example: six days of sick leave per year means one thing when the employee is entitled to it effective as of his first day of employment during the contract year, and quite another thing when it is earned one half-day per month worked. Example: three days of paid time-off in the event of a death in the family is less costly if family is defined as "parents, spouse or children," than if it can be stretched to include remote cousins, great uncles and aunts. In negotiations, therefore, the company should hinge its offers or acceptances on already-worded paragraphs, not on intangible principles susceptible to diverse interpretations at the time when the verbal agreement is being reduced to writing, or when the contract containing only the bare outlines is actually in force between the parties.

Most employers will grant certain economic benefits as supplements to wages, such as welfare provisions including costs of hospitalization, doctors' and surgeons' care and other forms of medical treatment. Management will also frequently contract to make stipulated payments for the purpose of securing pension benefits for their employees. The administration of these funds may, in many cases, be either in the hands of management alone or of a joint controlling board comprised of both management and labor. Pursuant to the law in force now, no new welfare or pension funds can be set up over which unions have total jurisdiction. The direction of these funds generally is in the hands of boards composed of an equal number of representatives from management and labor. Unions which controlled such welfare or pension plans prior to 1946 are exempt from the requirement that they share the helm with management and are often loath to voluntarily negotiate away this right. Often unions try to move in on welfare or pension funds which are wholly run by management and demand an equal voice. From a management viewpoint, strong arguments can be made that whenever the employer can retain sole control over trust funds set aside for the purpose of paying these benefits, it should do so. There are several reasons for this. The first of these is that management, which has to bear administrative and operating expense as well as the cost of purchasing benefits, can make successful efforts to minimize expenditures. Though control is joint and direction comes from both parties, the money still comes from only one—the employer. Management will find that lower overhead means that more real benefits can be bought and the ultimate cost to the employer is less.

Second, experience has shown that when joint funds are administered by union and management, the union will often dominate the picture. Where the pension or welfare plan is an endeavor of one company and one local union, equality of influence may be achieved. But in cases where dozens and sometimes hundreds of business firms participate with one international union, such a result seldom emerges. The union is, as its name implies, unified; all of its representatives on the board are subject to the internal discipline of the same international union and are often full-time professional labor men holding down jobs within the union. Management's delegates, no matter how conscientious in fulfilling their obligations, usually do not represent directly all of the included companies. Moreover, these trustees do not have power over the various competitive firms which are parties to the fund and management representatives are frequently not "full-timers," having other responsibilities or business interests. As a practical consequence, the day-to-day administration of a joint fund usually falls to the labor delegates.

Third, the employer is paying for the benefits and his employees should know it. When applications are made to a "joint fund office" on union premises, secretaries and clerks working partly for the union and partly for the joint fund do the processing, and checks are mailed out from the union office with a letter of notice signed by the union chairman or secretary. All too often this leads the recipient to believe that the benefit has been paid for by the union, not the employer.

Fourth, labor-management joint trust funds are becoming an increasingly substantial factor in our economy. Dollars contributed by the employers flow into the coffers of the fund. Until benefits must be paid, money accrues and has to be invested in stock, bonds, banks, government obligations, first mortgages and real estate. This capital finds its way into the money market both as debt and equity financing. The influence of these funds in our modern society is certainly burgeoning. The eventual consequence of the power to be realized both in the economic and political realm remains yet to be seen. The potential influence of these vast funds in the money market must be considered by those who direct or who may direct their activity. Management must work to retain meaningful control of any such funds which it presently holds and should redouble its efforts to obtain co-equal status in the direction of funds which have previously been administered, for practical purposes, mostly by the union. This goal is translated into actual words, sentences and paragraphs when the collective bargaining agreement is written. It means also that management must concern itself with the personalities of those who will represent it on pension and welfare fund boards to ensure that these people are responsible, conscientious and aggressive.

A more detailed discussion of joint funds and their administration is included in Chapter 38, which deals with management's function. Labor union leaders often assert that pension and welfare fund money is something that the workers bargained for and won; and, as such, something that belongs to them. Following this logic they believe that it is entirely appropriate that unions dominate the management of such funds, and, in fact, some believe that the law should be amended to permit unilateral union administration of pension and welfare funds.

Management should insure that the contributions will be to a pension plan that has been, or will be, qualified with the U.S. Internal Revenue Service.

If the business is contemplating contributions to a multi-company pension fund that has already been established, it should investigate the trustees representing other contributing employers. Management's attorney or other representative should speak to these people before making a commitment to join this plan.

If there is no pension plan in the industry and one is being started, management should actively take part in the initiation and development of the new plan. This approach to pension fund administration applies equally to other fringe benefit plans that are to be jointly administered by labor and management.

One can hardly emphasize enough how essential it is that management take great care in negotiating specific contract wording. The offhand approach of agreeing to certain benefits with the proviso that the details will be thrashed out later simply does not work. The gap between general agreement in principle at the table and the actual article in a written contract can involve thousands of dollars.

Moreover, arbitrators' awards can construe vague or incomplete wording in such a way as to cost management money. A contract provided that workers who were laid off got their accrued vacation pay at the time of lay-off. It made no reference to workers who quit or were discharged. An employee resigned his job. The company refused to give him accrued vacation pay on the theory it had no obligation to do so. On arbitration, it was held that vacation was a compensation that accrued as the man worked, and that he could not be deprived of vacation pay earned (but not paid) in September and October simply because he left in November. The employer would have been much better off with wording in the contract that defined and the employees'rights.

Fringe benefits are a complicated and costly matter for management. As such, the employer's representatives must negotiate these issues with concern and caution.

Living
with the Union

14

Changes in
the Company

It was a particularly steamy day in August, and a new client had come into lawyer "A's" office. Even the air-conditioning was not effective in cooling him down and it was soon apparent that it was not the noonday sun, but rather a freshly recognized union which was responsible for his high temperature. This chap was a partner in a new and thriving business. When the work-force approached fifty people, a union organizer approached the work-force. In very swift order, in late July, the organizer came, he saw, he organized, and his union was recognized by the company as the collective bargaining agent. It was a fortnight later that this employer came to "A" and asked that "A" negotiate his initial contract. This was done and just before Labor Day, after the contract had been signed, "A" spent an hour with this client discussing the need for changes in the shop to gear the company to living with the union.

At first he seemed surprised to find that "A," who had bargained so long and hard with the union and resisted so many of their demands, characterizing them as unreasonable and unrealistic, could even suggest that peaceful co-existence could prevail. Perhaps it was as if Mao Tse Tung had praised capitalism. The point was then, and is now, that for better or for worse this company, like many others, now had a union and its problem was to continue a profitable earnings record despite the union's demands.

One alternative is to enter into one of those long drawn-out feuds of attrition which so often end in a Donnybrook with victory for none. The other more practical alternative is to try to live profitably with the union. For an hour "A" spoke with the company representative trying to convince him that this was the wisest course. This was not urged out of altruism or weakness or appeasement or to make the employer's life easier. It was advocated for only one reason—because in this case it was the most profitable way to run the company.

Months later, sometime after Christmas. this same client called and arranged to come in to discuss a new field that the company was branching into. After they had talked about this, he said: "You know, having a union has been less painful than I thought it ever could be. In fact it has certain advantages."

What then are these advantages and how best can management capitalize on them?

With a union there is one negotiation to cover wages and benefits for all members of the collective bargaining unit. In many smaller plants where there is no union, every single wage increase is, in effect, the result of a negotiation between the employer and the employee. Any man in the work crew is free to come to the employer as often as he desires and request an increase. It is too costly to say "yes" each time, and it is embarrassing and damaging to morale to say "no" constantly. In a unionized plant, collective bargaining occurs periodically—every one, two or three years as a rule. From the end of one session to the beginning of the next, no bargaining need be engaged in, and, in fact, it should not be. To grant any increases over and above the union contract opens the door to having every employee in the plant trying to strike his own bargain with management. Moreover, granting increases will inevitably make the union bitter against the employer who gives privately more than he would grant when the union asked. As a result the union will be more militant toward the employer in an effort to recoup lost prestige and it may, in special circumstances, level charges against the company. Finally, morale in the shop will deteriorate when some employees get raises and others do not. Every employer should have a form answer when any employee asks for a raise in the midst of the contract: the employee selected the union to bargain for him; and the company, respecting this choice, will not engage in *selective,* but only in *collective* bargaining. The employer will find in this way that actual wage costs can be held down, that expense for labor can be accurately calculated for periods of at least a year, that managers are spared the annoyance and saved the time previously spent in handling numerous wage-increase requests, and that the work of the bookkeeping department is simplified.

A labor-management contract sets up machinery for the airing and settlement of grievances. Resentments that once festered underground can now be resolved. As a result, spirits and morale in the shop often are improved.

The collective bargaining agreement has brought systematization and regularity, and as such it is a management control and aid. It may be followed to advantage and disregarded at peril.

In some instances the advent of a union in a company yields particularly unique advantages. Where competitive conditions in an industry are chaotic, the uniformity of wage cost that comes when the entire industry is organized may lead to more rational behavior and a greater awareness of pricing based on costs. And a union's victory, dues collection, and maintenance in one shop often will enable it to organize another.

A contract provides standards for treatment of people that are predicated on certain criteria. Pay and benefits are based on skills and length of service. These standards do not differ with the individual. In non-union plants the company alone must make decisions about each person. For example, when a man is sick, should the company pay his hospital bill or part of it? Should it shoulder his medical expenses or a fraction of them? Does he get compensation for time away from work, and if so, on what scale? In smaller plants where the employer has to make these decisions, it is usually done on an individual merit basis. The decision is often an agonizing one, usually leaving the worker feeling that he got too little and management feeling that it was giving too much. Management is always fearful of setting a precedent, and worries lest it be accused of favoring one worker over the other. In larger plants, where management unilaterally sets the standards, the company alone is to blame if the benefits are less than the employees looked for. Collective bargaining contracts generally cover sick-leave with pay, hospitalization, disability, medical or surgical payments, early retirement and other aspects of these problems. The wise employer lets the contract work for him. He gives what the contract calls for; no more and no less. He spends no time over such decisions and takes no blame. The union will work most closely with the company that follows the contract this way, and bother it the least.

The attitude of paternalism which may have existed before the shop was organized should be eradicated completely. In many shops, for example, the company lends money to its employees. The consequences are often bad. Some men quit when they owe the company money—others are kept on when they should have been fired because the company has loans outstanding to them that it wishes to recoup. Still other workers forget to pay back and require constant dunning. In one company where loans were repaid on a payroll deduction system, the debtors nearly always asked for increases to cover the deductions so they could have the same take-home pay.

When a union represents the employees, practices such as loans should be eliminated. When a worker votes to select a union, that vote says, in effect, that the worker does not look to the employer to solve his problems. This should be accepted by the company, and it should not place itself in the role of an unwanted father. The employer can avoid many headaches this way.

A union can affirmatively aid the employer in increasing his sales. With recognition of the union comes the "union label." In many cases, particularly among producers of certain products and those who render certain services, this can be a significant asset. "Buy union-made goods," can be a telling selling point. If this is important, arrangements should be made to obtain use of the union label at contract time. Often just the knowledge by potential purchasers that the product is union-made is advantageous. One large bakery, for example, prints on its packages of rolls that their product is "produced under union shop contract with the United Bakery Workers pursuant to National Labor Relations Act as amended." One can only conclude from this that there are consumers who have a particularly hearty appetite for union-made rolls.

In certain cases where a union has organized many shops engaged in similar operations in the same industry, it has its fingers on the manpower pulse. It can act as a particularly efficient employment agency since it intimately knows both the employer and the prospective employee. Moreover, if a union appreciates the friendly attitude of certain employers, it will channel to them the best people who come along. In one situation, a union actively recruits personnel for an industry which has a chronic labor shortage. The organized employer in this industry has a distinct advantage over the non-union employer because of this union activity. Moreover, the standard union wage rate results in a fair distribution of key people to all employers in the area and prevents companies bidding-up wages in an effort to compete with each other for personnel.

Sometimes a union aids in spreading and applying useful knowledge. A union business agent calls on many plants engaged in the same activities and the manner in which certain problems are solved in one plant often applies in another. In some instances a business agent will even suggest to a company that it go after certain business when another firm has dropped the account. It is true that it is not conventionally within the purview of unions to solicit sales for employers, nor should their representatives engage in "espionage" or bearing tales, but they can and sometimes do serve as useful channels of communication or sources of knowledge.

At times, unions will aid in improving morale and enforcing discipline in a plant, although it is not their job to do so. It is not good management practice, but in some cases—particularly in small plants, where the company is lax in running the shop—the union will step in to fill the vacuum. It may "ride herd" on employees who are getting a free ride, or those who slack off to the detriment of the whole team. The union does not do this for the employer's good but for its own. The more productive a plant, the more profit, and the more profit the better the chances of getting an increase. Regardless of motive, unions can and do help management. Most frequently this aid is unsolicited and not officially recognized, but sometimes it is directly requested.

The workers in one industrial plant, members of a militant union, were simply not producing up to their capacity. Any effort by management to force higher production standards would have been labeled a "speed-up" or "sweat-shop technique," and the union would have fought it. There was not sufficient time for the gradual introduction of production improvements to raise the morale and tighten the discipline in this shop where these elements had so far been absent. The company could not survive in business long enough for this. As a result, a meeting was called with the union. It was explained that a production increase of ten per cent must be achieved or the company would be forced to close the plant and lay off all the workers permanently. This was no bluff. The labor delegates were invited to inspect the company's cost account sheets and other financial data. The union, knowing the condition in the plant, agreed at once that a problem existed. It was suggested that this crisis could be solved only by management and labor working in tandem. The union agreed to cooperate, recognizing that the alternative was the shut-down of the entire operation. It took the position that an employee who was hurting the company by being chronically absent, late, inefficient or lazy could cost all of the workers their jobs. The union then helped management to run an efficient plant through the joint efforts of management and the union, which in this case did management's work more successfully than the company itself could have. The business was saved.

Management should be alert to situations such as these where the union can be called upon for aid or can be used to advantage. The wedding of a union and a company is usually a shot-gun marriage. And like all marriages it is for better or for worse. Wise employers will make the best of the situation, for divorces are not easy.

15

Work Rules

People become confused without rules to live by. Rules range all the way from the laws of the land where violation results in imprisonment to the principles of common courtesy enforced only by the need to live as part of society. All social organizations—schools, churches, armies, countries—have rules. Any firm that employs more than one worker must also have rules to provide the "laws" which will govern people during their hours at work.

When there are only a few employees with long terms of employment the rules can be verbally explained to each. But as soon as there are new employees or a sizeable number of people working, written rules become necessary. In written form there can be no misunderstanding of the rules and no defense that they were not published. Printed rules are the guide lines for all employees to follow.

Rules should be simple, understandable and available to all personnel. They should either be printed in booklet form and handed to each employee or posted on several well-placed bulletin boards. Newly hired personnel should get the rules as part of their "employment kit," and be advised to study and abide by them.

If a large number of employees speak a language other than English, a translation of the rules should accompany the English version. It is absolutely essential that the translation be accurate. A New York area plant owner, some years ago, thought he had a "revolution" on his hands. There was a wildcat strike brewing which had all the elements for a riot. On investigation, it was found that the trouble stemmed from dissatisfaction on the part of Puerto Rican employees who made up nearly half of the work force. Their reason proved quite justifiable. The English language version of the plant rules decreed temporary lay-off for a certain infraction. In Spanish the punishment was discharge. As soon as word of this had gotten around it was decided that this was an evidence of management's discrimination against Puerto Ricans. It did not occur to anyone that the discrepancy was a mistake. The plant owner, a thoughtful chap, had purposely printed a Spanish translation to accommodate the Puerto Rican workers. But the translation was carelessly and quickly done by one of the Spanish-speaking employees who was unschooled in English. A double-check with Berlitz could have saved a lot of man-hours of production.

Plant rules in a unionized company differ from those in a non-union organization. In both they deal with the do's and don'ts of conduct. But in the plant without a union there should be included in the rules many of the provisions that normally would be in a collective bargaining agreement, such as holidays, length of vacation and sick-leave provisions. In making up these rules, the non-unionized employer's quickest and surest guide is to adopt and follow provisions from the labor contract of a similar unionized company. These conditions may, of course, be modified to suit the company's convenience to a certain extent, but provisions which are too much in favor of the employer and written without regard for fairness will simply serve as a magnet for union organizers and draw the employees' resentment. In a unionized shop it is not necessary to regulate these matters, but there is a wide range of problems that can be dealt with in rules.

Generally rules for all kinds of companies fall into two categories. First, there are those rules which are universal in application to all kinds of enterprises. These include provisions covering lateness, absence and reporting change of address and family status. The second kind of rules are those which apply to certain kinds of establishments. For example, in factories there are requirements that ensure that safety equipment is used, insist on reporting of accidents at once, rule that racks and tools are checked out and replaced, hold that all employees punch their own cards in and out, and only their own cards, etc. In retail stores, the rules will prohibit smoking in restricted areas, serve to stop abuse of coffee break and require courtesy to customers. In the case of outside salesmen, the regulations may prohibit these employees from drinking while on company business and department store buyers may be forbidden to accept gifts from firms they deal with. In restaurants and hotels, sanitary regulations are particularly significant.

An effective method for formulating rules is to have management supervisory personnel list any employee activity or behavior which bothers them. These should be culled, considered and edited by the plant superintendent or another top management man. Ultimately, senior management will decide what problems need to be dealt with. Many rules will require important policy decisions. For example, frequently it is asked if there should be a rule against drinking and alcohol on the premises. The answer can only be that this depends on the employees involved. In a heavy industry shop where there was a history of drinking on a badly supervised night shift it was quite reasonable to include such a rule. Failure to do so coupled with the number of previous infractions might even have been considered by some a green-light, and would certainly give trouble if it came to an arbitration on a firing for drinking in the plant. In a non-unionized clerical office, staffed with girls in their late teens working under the close direction of mature supervisors, such a rule would only serve to annoy and insult all of the workers. Rules against fighting, stealing and narcotics should similarly be very carefully considered since the adverse reaction may outweigh any possible benefit.

Management should also discuss inclusion of a rule requiring work standards both as to quantity and quality. In one textile printing shop a rule had been instituted banning negligent spoilage of fabric. What the floor foreman could previously only nag about and the careless workman shrug off can now be more effectively dealt with. Carelessness is documented, the union notified, and with a minimum of bickering, action may be taken in the case of a chronically sloppy and negligent "spoiler."

In states which allow a garnishee to be placed on the employer for a worker's debts, careful consideration should go into determining the position of management when it is notified that an employee has a garnishee. It seems particularly heartless to fire an employee when and just because he is in debt. But failure to do so can cost a company money. In New York State, for example, when a company is notified that there is a judgment against one of its employees and a garnishee for him has been served, the bookkeeper for the company must deduct up to ten per cent of the employee's pay until the garnishee is off. Failure to do so renders the company

liable. At the very best a garnishee means extra bookkeeping for
the front office. At worst, in case of a slip-up or failure to deduct,
it can mean that the company must make good the employee's
debt to the creditor—something even the most generous are reluctant to do. Many shops give employees a week to clear up these
wage attachments and, barring that, discharge them.

There is a trend among state legislatures to curtail the employer's
right to fire for wage attachment and companies must be alert to
see that their rules do not violate the law. In New York, commenc-
ing January 1, 1967 it is unlawful to discharge an employee
because an income execution has been served upon the employer.
However, this restriction will not apply if more than one such execution is served within twelve consecutive months after January 1,
1967. If the employer violates this law the employee may sue for
wages lost not to exceed six weeks and the court may order his
reinstatement. Since different states have different statutes the
multi-plant or multi-store employer may have to modify his company rules on a state by state basis to conform to local legislation,
and the laws with respect to discipline for income executions should
be closely watched since they are changing.

After it has been decided what to cover in the rules, the firm's
attorney should draft the actual language. Then, key company
officials can meet with their lawyer to review his draft, and, if
necessary, to revise it. Subsequently, the rules can be promulgated.
These regulations should be as clear and concise as possible, but
not wordy or abstruse. Nor should rules be designed to curb behavior that is unlikely to occur.

The important thing to bear in mind is that all regulations must
be impartially enforced. Severity to one man and leniency for
another results in accusations of favoritism and prejudice. Worse
still, it can cause chaos in a shop. Most arbitrators are reluctant to uphold discipline where uniformity has not been followed.
One of the soundest union defenses in an arbitration is to demonstrate bias and unequal treatment by management. Thus rules
become meaningless and, like any ignored laws, worse than useless.
The bitterest pill for an employer to swallow is when a key man
who is usually conscientious breaks a rule. As much as management would like to make an exception, it should be reluctant to do
so because of the threat posed to the discipline of the entire plant.
The only way to avoid this problem is to consider the penalties
carefully when making up the rules. The supervisory personnel must

review the consequences of enforcement with the best workers in mind as the potential violators, and not just assume that infractions will be committed only by the worst and most expendable employees.

The penalties or sanctions for each offense should be deliberately thought out by management. First, as any lawmaker must, management should make the punishment fit the crime. Neither over-strictness nor extreme liberality are compatible with a well-run company. Common sense, the general labor market, and the particular nature of the skill required in the business operation are determinants of the sanctions to be imposed. Obviously a first offense of lateness is not a fair ground for discharge, whereas an assault or theft may well be. Intermediate between no punishment and firing (which in the industrial situation is the supreme penalty) are other appropriate penalties such as suspension from overtime, disciplinary lay-off for a day, or a week, etc. Short of this warnings should be issued. The penalties for breaking rules should be defined in advance and distributed with the rules so that everyone knows them. However, the company should not defeat its own purpose in prescribing penalties. For example, many firms found disciplinary lay-offs were impractical. The employee enjoyed a few days of rest and the company's production suffered. In an area where skilled or experienced labor is hard to get and productivity important, such a punishment will likely require the company to schedule overtime, and the result may be more inconvenience and monetary loss to the company than to the offender.

In enforcing the rules it is important to "build a history" in connection with any worker. For example, in a store where four unexcused latenesses in any three-month period were grounds for discharge, a routine was adopted. On the first offense the employee received a warning slip. The second occurrence occasioned a letter to the employee with a copy to the store union steward. When the girl was late for the third time the personnel manager signed and mailed a registered letter to her with copies to both the steward and the local union. In the letter it was clearly stated that this was the final warning and another lateness would result in discharge.

The reason for this formality and detail is to insure that the discharge will stand up on arbitration and reduce the opportunity for excuses. Furthermore, when there is such a formal, documented record, management minimizes the likelihood of a dispute. The union will be discouraged from filing a grievance against the discharge when it knows that all employees are dealt with in the same manner and that adequate warning steps have been taken. Thus a file of warnings should be carefully retained. Form letters for use in case of routine infractions may be mimeographed or printed in larger shops and used repeatedly with only the names and other particular information having to be filled in for each incident. The form should be approved by the company's counsel or trained personnel experts before duplicating however.

In a non-union shop, management is free to post rules when it desires. In some cases this is true in a union shop. But in others the union may rightly argue that rule-making is a function of collective bargaining. Informing union officials that rules are about to be posted, showing them the rules in advance and discussing rules with them is good policy. But it can be a mistake to insist that the union publicly and officially approve such rules. The business agents are not working for the company but rather for the workers for whom management is making the rules. It is management's responsibility to manage. Rule-making is a prerogative of management. The company must see only that the rules are fair and just in scope and equitably enforced. This assured, they need not apologize for rules.

16

Administering
the Contract

Almost inevitably a union's initial contract with a company causes an increase in labor costs. The company can partly counteract this added expense, as we have seen, by turning the union's presence to advantage and by maintaining and raising the standards of discipline, morale and production in its operations. The management can achieve further cost reductions by careful and successful administration of the collective bargaining contract. There should be a systematic program for dealing with problems of contract interpretation and issues of labor relations policy as they arise.

Specific key company executives should be charged with the fulfillment of the labor relations function. This job must be pinpointed so that both company, union and employees are aware of whose responsibility it is. This position may be occupied by the production manager in factories, the personnel director in stores and retail establishments, the general manager in hotels, clubs and restaurants, the captain of a ship and the operations chief in transit companies and utilities. In major companies it will be the vice-president or director of industrial relations; in the smallest concerns the "inside partner" or single proprietor. The important thing is that company management recognize this function and assign someone to it The person assuming this position should have a knowledge of the field of labor relations generally and must know the specific contract or contracts which he is charged with administering. And it is essential that this executive be given the necessary authority to implement his decisions. Wherever possible, management should arrange for depth in this department, so that others equally familiar with the contract and empowered to act may substitute with facility when the key man is away at another company installation, sick, on vacation or otherwise unavailable. In larger companies, staffs will, of course, be available to support the industrial relations chief this way. But even in small firms arrangements should be made so that the factory manager is back-stopped by a principal or another executive. Problems arising from the contract do not necessarily burst into full bloom at convenient times. No manager can accurately foresee when trouble will break out. But when problems do occur it is inexcusable if no solution can be found because there is not a company representative at hand with technical know-how and sufficient authority to represent the management. Small problems, left untended, can swiftly burgeon into large ones and often develop confusion, irritation and business interruption that would not occur if they were dealt with in a speedy and decisive manner.

Knowledge is power, it is often truthfully said. And in this case the basic source of knowledge is the contract itself. This is the text from which all sermons must be preached. There is no substitute for specific knowledge of the contract. The most extensive background in labor relations including familiarity with precedents and practices in other plants can often be rendered meaningless by a short but precise sentence in the contract. The contract prevails over generalities. It is usually not difficult for these senior management officials to familiarize themselves with the contract. Having most likely played a role in its negotiation, the agreement will probably be familiar ground to them. If, however, questions do arise, counsel should be consulted and all possible sources of misunderstanding ought to be anticipated. The agreement should be duplicated. Usually the union attends to this and provides management with sufficient copies. If it does not, the company can have the contract printed or mimeographed. The contract is not a confidential document, and security measures are not necessary for its safeguarding.

The collective bargaining agreement should be given to all members of management's team who will be concerned with its provisions. All supervisors who direct the workers in the collective bargaining unit should particularly acquaint themselves with provisions concerning work-week and hours, shared time, grievance procedures, wash-up time and/or coffee break, work rules and management prerogatives. Maintenance and engineering department executives must be aware of sanitary and safety requirement, shift rules, etc. The paymaster's office or bookkeeper needs to have a thorough understanding of the contract to correctly compute worker's take-home wages, vacation pay and entitlement, the holidays due, compensable sick-leave rights, etc. All these officials should meet with the company's top labor relations executives who can explain any points in the contract which require clarification. In companies where more than one union represents the workers and additional contracts exist, parallel procedures should be followed.

In addition to knowledge of the contract, top management must see that all supervisory personnel be made aware of the significance of the union. First, it must be made clear to all personnel—management and workers alike—that the union has cost the company money, and that spoilage, wastefulness and carelessness are luxuries that can no longer be tolerated. This approach will not work if it takes the form of a drastic crack-down. It will succeed if sensibly and gradually instituted. Second, all levels of management must realize that the advent of a union has injected a third party into the normal, everyday relationships in the company. Each of the factors in the labor relations triangle—management, employees and union—must be aware of the other. Lower echelon management frequently has a harder time adjusting to the union than do the company's senior executives. The reason is that the customary prerogatives of these men—foremen, floor supervisors, route supervisors and department managers—are often severely curtailed. No longer can they make decisions unilaterally. What could once be handled by spontaneous order may now have to be the result of a conference. These management representatives must understand that henceforth their actions will be governed not only by company policies, as previously, but also by the provisions of the prevailing contract. Violation of the collective bargaining agreement by a foreman is deemed to be a violation by the company. And subsequent company protests that the foreman did not have authority to disregard the contract will not be very persuasive.

By Federal law, an employer has a duty to bargain collectively with a union which is the properly recognized agent of his employees. Court and N.L.R.B. rulings hold that this duty does not cease after the contract is negotiated. On the contrary, it continues during the life of the contract. The union's representation is not an occasional function—a one-shot deal—but is a constant matter. The union has a right to be consulted by the employer on many items. For example, if the employer is setting up a new operation requiring a skill category not previously assigned a wage rate, he cannot determine on his own what the pay will be. Although this new operation is instituted during the term of the contract, employer and union must meet to negotiate the specific matter.

Even tighter restrictions may be imposed by management. A company comptroller once incredulously asked, "You mean to say we can't even raise wages without the union's approval?" The answer was: "No, you can't." Unilateral wage increases, or the addition of benefits such as an extra holiday or longer vacation, have been deemed an unlawful practice on the part of the employer and companies have been condemned for by-passing the union. There are certain special circumstances which do permit this, but the employer is best advised to consult with the union before attempting to institute any major mid-contract changes in wages, benefits, working conditions or operations.

An employer can avoid this duty to bargain with the union in two ways. If the union's complete inactivity is deemed a waiver of its rights, the employer is freed of the responsibility. This is rare. What can be done, however, is to incorporate wording in the contract during bargaining sessions which does give the employer a free hand. Thus some contracts state that wage rates are minimums only and any increase is management's exclusive right. Other agreements provide that new operations or installation of equipment will be within the company's sole jurisdiction. Without such wording it is potentially dangerous to ignore the union. Good management ensures that all supervisory personnel understand this.

Foremen should not argue issues with union representatives. Instructions should be given to all line personnel that when a question about the meaning of the contract or its application arises, this should be taken up with either their superior or the appropriate staff executive of the company charged with this responsibility. This will minimize the possibility of erroneous interpretations by personnel not trained in contract administration. Even more important, however, it will ensure uniformity within a company. If all foremen could make their own interpretations of the contract, the result would be that company policy would differ between departments and perhaps even from shift to shift.

If there is difficulty in interpreting provisions of the contract at top level, then, of course, professional outside counsel may be called in. If the contract itself is actually ambiguous, precedent, procedures and practices in other companies will carry weight. A labor relations advisor or attorney should be conversant with these and be able to apprise the company accordingly.

An effort should be made to have a uniform and stable company position on all uncertain issues even before a dispute actually occurs. Executives charged with developing these rules should bear in mind always that whatever interpretation the company makes in one case must later apply to identical fact situations. A consistent view will be required; accordingly, each stand taken by the company should be considered both in the light of the current problem and in terms of ultimate consequences.

Company interpretations should be made in the same way that an arbitrator's decision is formulated. This approach is based first on what the contract says, second on the intent of the parties who wrote it, the precedents in the company, practices in the industry, decisions of arbitrators, the fair and equitable thing under the circumstances, the record of the individual or individuals concerned, if relevant, and other factors. Interpretations of vague or unsettled aspects of the contract should be determined at the highest company levels.

All problems that arise should be systematically recorded. Wording which is unclear must be noted along with those clauses which are precise but difficult for management to live with—in short, all trouble spots warrant this attention. If nothing can be done within the duration of the current contract, there is always another negotiation. It is then that those items which the company sees as weaknesses in the contract can be repaired and defects in its construction can be rectified.

It is often valuable for the firm to have periodic management conferences attended by supervisors, the labor relations official, the bookkeeper and others concerned with labor policy. At these sessions the operation of the contract should be reviewed and problems pinpointed. Recent management decisions on issues can be reviewed. New company programs can be explained. Such meetings will serve several purposes. There will be an effective exchange of information. Management can see where the collective bargaining agreement is, from its viewpoint, inadequate or confusing. And the company will discover areas where more effective management action is needed. As a result of this it may change work rules, improve employee communications, or take other necessary steps.

An efficient administrator sees that the union gets no more than it bargained for. Just as the quality of goods from a supplier is checked when received, so too the employees' actions must be watched in terms of the labor agreement. The expense to the company must be only what the contract requires—no more—and the union must live up to its obligations. Should it fail to do so by claiming for itself or its members more than its due, the company must take action to assert its rights. Efficient contract management cuts company costs. It is essential that all employers develop able and effective contract administration.

17

Grievances

Telephone books are larger than labor contracts and more comprehensive in covering their field. It might take a volume the size of such a directory to include the solutions, negotiated in advance, to every problem which could arise in the course of a three-year relationship. In fact, during the pressures of negotiating a contract, particularly the first contract, some provisions are often omitted intentionally by one or both parties. Even in cases where a company and a union have had contractual relations for many years, new problems crop up which the contract simply does not cover. The very nature of human beings, the dynamics of collective bargaining, and the changing forces of our society indicate that this will continue to be the case.

Completeness, though desirable, is almost impossible to achieve. As a result, contracts must provide methods for settling problems during the existence of a collective bargaining agreement. Two major types of trouble can occur in the administration of a collective bargaining contract: the parties may differ on what the contract means, or they may agree to the meaning of a clause but one side may argue that the other fails to live up to the agreement. In the event that either kind of dispute cannot be settled informally, one side or the other may file a grievance.

All contracts should set forth a procedure for processing grievances. The formality of this procedure will depend primarily on the size of the enterprise. In large companies there are various "steps" in processing the grievance. Each step involves a meeting between officials of the company and the union to discuss the problem and endeavor to reach a settlement. If agreement is not reached, the complaint is passed up to the next rung of the ladder.

The representatives of the parties who meet are counterparts of each other; that is, generally of equal status. Thus, department foremen meet with the union's departmental stewards; general foremen with shop chairmen; industrial relations manager with local business agent or business manager.

In smaller companies the grievance procedure is less formalized. A misunderstanding is discussed informally between the worker, the shop chairman and a company official. If the difficulty is not resolved, the company's principals meet with the union business agent and often the entire shop committee in the attempt to arrive at a solution.

The grievance itself, in a smaller company, may be merely a verbal statement. Generally, however, an employee's grievance is filed in written form with the company by a union official. Management then has a certain number of days in which to consider the complaint and formulate its position. It, too, generally is required to reply with a written answer. If management does not acquiesce to the union's demand, the grievance is discussed first at the lowest level and then is passed on up the chain of conferences.

A grievance is filed and prosecuted against the company by union representatives rather than by the individual employee who originated the complaint. In some cases, unions screen grievances submitted to them by workers before presenting the dispute to management. Theoretically this filters out claims which the union will not endorse on grounds that they are frivolous, unjustified, unworthy, or otherwise bad policy. Unfortunately such selectivity is exercised less than it should be. Too many union leaders take the position that they will not "stick their neck out," and automatically adopt any complaint as the union's official grievance.

The case law indicates that generally it is up to the union's discretion to decide whether or not it will process a member's complaint. However, in situations where the union refused to do so the aggrieved member has filed an unfair labor practice charge against the union claiming that it did not fulfill its duty of representing its members. In some instances the Board's regional director may order the union to process the grievance. These directions may be appealed, since the union leadership often feels that it, not the Board, must have final say-so over what matters are to be processed.

Management should be aware of these background pressures on union leaders.

The company, too, should submit grievances when it feels advantage is being taken of it. If lower-level supervisors cannot obtain satisfaction by discussing the problem with departmental stewards, they should consult with top echelon management officials. A grievance which is deemed justifiable by these executives should then be presented in written form for discussion and settlement.

The company should, of course, exercise judgment—not permitting every minor irritation or foreman's gripe to be exalted to the status of a formal grievance—and should be prepared to substantiate its grievance with facts. But too often, through management's default, grievances become the exclusive tool of the union. Companies can and should utilize the grievance process where appropriate. When they do not, they are chronically on the defensive. Experienced management realizes that grievance procedures are a two-way street. Alert employers will tax a union with a grievance charge when it is violating the contract or when workers do not concur with management on an interpretation. A formal grievance can often strengthen management's position. In addition to resolving the issue on which it is based, the grievance proceeding establishes the fact that management is aggressive and is willing to defend its prerogatives from infringement. Moreover, the union which may be reluctant to put a damper on a shop activity which it knows is wrong can be prodded into action by management's use of grievance procedures.

Regardless of who initiates a dispute, there are certain effective grievance-processing techniques which should be followed by management. The grievance meeting usually—but not invariably—should be held soon after the problem arises. In labor relations, real problems which are ignored seldom disappear, they almost always get worse. Informal procedures should make it feasible to hold a meeting within a day or two of the filing. The company's position should be decided before the meeting by all management representatives who will attend. Settlements may be achieved; but if the cost is appeasement or retreat from the specific provisions of the contract, such weakness can develop dangerous precedent.

Management must always remember that a grievance meeting is not a negotiating session. Though they are similar in form, their functions are not identical. Basic policy is determined at a negotiation session—that policy is clarified and implemented at a grievance proceeding. Serious problems occur when this distinction is forgotten. One company that was in the habit of making substantive concessions at grievance meetings was giving without any return. Faced with myriad grievance sessions, it was, in fact, maneuvered into engaging in marathon contract negotiations which continued weekly for the duration of the contract.

In plants where there are frequent grievances or a history of disputatious relations, it may be advantageous to schedule regular grievance meetings. At an isolated mill in an eastern state, grievances and arbitration demands were coming in with appalling frequency. To deal with these as they arose would have practically required the installation of resident counsel, and the company did not have the financial resources for this. Instead, consciously violating the principle that grievances should be quickly aired, the company was urged by counsel to schedule grievance sessions with the union once every two weeks. This technique had several advantages. First, trained counsel could travel regularly to the plant for each meeting appointment and was able to discuss with company executives the position to be taken on each of a number of problems immediately prior to the joint grievance session. The piece-meal approach was banished, and the positions taken were consistent with the contract and with each other, giving the company the advantage of a solid and coherent approach to grievance discussions. Second, some imagined or petty grievances tended to expire because there was no heat to nurture them. The two-week "cooling off period" froze out many grievances which should not have been issued to start with. Third, settlement could be achieved with greater ease because more issues were at stake and consequently there were more areas for compromise. Both sides had greater maneuverability. Fourth, the formal bi-weekly sessions, replacing the previous hurried "coffee conference" showed the union that management was finally taking its labor relations problems seriously. Fifth, the very nature of this systematic processing presented an opportunity for give-and-take discussions in an informal forum not charged with the tension of a negotiating session.

Many companies could profitably take advantage of this periodic settlement method. In the particular mill mentioned, the grievance rate declined sharply after six months. The joint committee continued to meet, however, to discuss problems which might become grievances in order to head-off trouble. These conferences are still continued—now on a monthly basis or less often if neither side has business to place on the agenda. Considering the decrease in complaints with no other major factors changed, it can be concluded that these scheduled sessions have succeeded in clearing the atmosphere.

Companies having a heavy load of grievances might consider this technique. They should be careful, however, not to feel pressured to settle every grievance at the meetings. If a grievance has been placed on the agenda in advance, management will be rightfully expected to have formulated a position with respect to the problem by the time of the conference. But, if new issues arise in the give and take of the session, company executives are justified in postponing a definitive statement of their position until they have had an opportunity to consider the matter carefully. It is desirable for the company to have its labor counsel present at these meetings, particularly when this program is being initiated. After a while, however, as the relationship between the parties matures, it may not be necessary for this advisor to be present at every grievance session with the union, a brief pre-meeting talk or telephone call sufficing.

These inter-negotiating sessions often open opportunities for the shop committee to make suggestions about improving various aspects of the labor-management relationship and the business generally. Moreover, at these meetings management can present some of its problems outside of the crisis atmosphere of bargaining. The company may find that when it finally does get to the negotiating table, it is given greater credence and a more sympathetic and understanding reception. Certain major industries—notably steel—have adopted the practice of continuous meetings between company and union committees to discuss developments and problems, albeit not specific grievances, between negotiations. The theory behind this is that the deadline pressures and public concern surrounding negotiations are absent and a less partisan and more rational attempt can be made to solve problems in the more temperate climate of meetings between negotiations. At this point there is still a question as to how successful these endeavors have been. But there is scant evidence to show that in small or medium sized companies such sessions can do harm and, indeed, there are those who believe both company and union will benefit.

The question arises in an employer's mind, "Should the company pay the men for sitting in on grievance meetings?" As a general rule workers should be paid for their time when they are in joint grievance meetings with management but not when they meet among themselves to discuss the grievance. The money expended usually is well-spent by the company. To insist that these meetings be held off company time usually encourages a non-cooperative attitude on the part of the committee members which can cost the company more than the hour or two of pay. A warning must go with this general rule, however. Where it appears grievances develop because the men prefer grieving on company time to working, management must reappraise its policies in this regard.

Agreement should be reached in advance about payment for time after normal working hours. When the regular work shift ends at 4:00 o'clock p.m. and the meeting starts at 3:00 o'clock p.m., provision should be made if the conference runs one or two hours past usual quitting time. The company may maintain that this should be on the worker's own time; it may pay them at straight time rates; it may give them compensatory time off; or it may pay them at overtime rates.

The company cannot dictate to the union who will be present at the grievance meeting to represent the union viewpoint. But it can and should see that the committee's size be kept in proportion, and its composition reasonable. In one small plant where the grievance committee approximated the size of a symphony orchestra, management consented to pay the committee only after the union agreed to pare its membership down to three. Similarly, the union should be prevailed upon to avoid selecting several committee members from one specialized segment of the company's operations when the absence of these men from their jobs will jeopardize the firm's ability to carry on its normal commitments. Committee membership should be chosen from diverse work areas so that operations continue while disputes are settled.

If the grievance cannot be satisfactorily settled through the procedures discussed in this chapter, the alternatives presented in the next chapter remain.

18

Arbitration

In the third act of "Measure for Measure," Shakespeare holds that "Virtue is bold, and goodness never fearful," and in "King Henry VI" he advises "Fight to the last gasp." Both adages may be adopted by a thoughtful employer as sound principles when the grievance procedure is stalemated. After the dispute has been discussed at all levels of union and management representation and the final "summit conference" has failed to yield agreement, a deadlock exists. Its resolution depends on the parties involved and on the contract. Three alternatives generally exist.

First, one party can give in. As a general rule, when a grievance has been discussed at all steps including the highest without achieving a settlement, the company's position on an issue must be vital. If the company's experts believe there is a favorable chance of winning the arbitration, the choice to arbitrate should usually be made.

There are, however, good reasons for management to decline to insist on arbitration of a grievance it has authored or to accede to the union by dropping its demand for arbitration on a complaint initiated by the union. It is dangerous to arbitrate with a weak case since losing it may mean setting precedent. It may be unwise to allow arbitration of a case if the company's victory would be a hollow one. Employee reaction to such a decision might well outweigh any benefits. For example, a company had rules that on the third offense of drunkenness on duty the employee would be fired. Smith, the riveter on the night shift, was clearly intoxicated. But when the company gave him his discharge slip, the union lodged a grievance.

It urged that Smith be given one more chance. The company refused and no agreement was reached. The union issued a demand for arbitration of Smith's case. Top company management backed down in the face of this and Smith was reinstated. Why? Smith had twenty-seven years of service with the company. If an arbitrator ruled against the company purely on the basis of sympathy, all the company's rules would be weakened as a consequence and contesting of them would be encouraged. And if the arbitrator followed the letter of the contract and the rules and permitted the company's action, resentment in the shop at Smith's dismissal would smoulder unabated. The union suggested transferring Smith to the day shift where the temptation would be less, and the company accepted this proposal. Whether this is termed surrender or strategic retreat depends on the observer and the circumstances of the individual case.

Sometimes it may be good policy not to push arbitration if it will unduly embarrass shop chairmen or union business agents and embitter them on a personal level. These consequences should be considered in the occasional cases where they may result.

Arbitrations are an expense item; therefore, if the matter involved is not important for management and if the issues are insignificant, it may not pay to arbitrate. Similarly, if the chances of winning an arbitration are remote, the company may choose not to arbitrate.

The second alternative which may be selected, if the company does not choose to compromise, is a strike or lockout, the ultimate weapon in the economic "hot war" between management and labor. This is a possible alternative when the collective bargaining agreement does not provide for arbitration of all disputes between the parties. Many contracts do contain this broad provision, directing that when no settlement is reached the parties must accept arbitration. However, some agreements contain less inclusive arbitration clauses. There are clauses which provide that only disputes arising out of the contract, as distinguished from the entire collective bargaining relationship, will be arbitrated; clauses calling for arbitration only when matters of discipline and discharge are involved; clauses specifically exempting certain problems from arbitration such as those concerning work loads and automation. Finally, there are those few contracts making no provision for arbitration.

When there is an arbitration provision in a collective bargaining agreement, there should be, and almost always is, a corollary provision, usually termed the "no-strike, no-lockout" clause. This prevents either party from taking such action. The union cannot legally pull a strike because it is unhappy about a dispute nor can the employer shut down the plant for this reason. Instead, both have traded these rights for the right to arbitrate. Furthermore, most contracts provide that the parties must abide by the arbitrator's decision and, no matter how distasteful this decision may be, the provision forbidding a strike or lockout prevails.

I believe that the incorporation of the broadest possible arbitration clause in the contract will prove beneficial to the company. The clause should provide that all disputes between the employer and the union will be subject to binding arbitration. One of the purposes of a collective bargaining contract is to provide stability for the company. This is seldom gained where there is always the possibility that a dispute can erupt into a full scale walk-out with the employer powerless to avoid this. The right to strike or lockout during a contract's term is usually more favorable to the union than the company. The strike has proved to be an effective weapon of economic pressure which can be used to force an employer to alter his position. The lockout, on the contrary, has been less successful and is not frequently resorted to by management. Saying that "all bets are off" if a dispute cannot be settled and that the parties each have a right to fight it out is often like agreeing that, in the case of disagreement, a boxer and a one-armed man may step into the ring. The boxer may sign such an agreement, but the one-armed man seldom will.

There are some who, no doubt, would disagree with this advice that management seek a comprehensive arbitration clause. They would argue that there is greater independence or self determination if management is free to force a test of strength. They would maintain that workers would gladly arbitrate many an issue that they would not consider important enough to strike over. Lastly, and perhaps most persuasively, they would say that when a company is economically much stronger than the union and can afford a lockout better than the employees can a strike, that an arbitration clause benefits the union more than the company.

Recent Federal court decisions and laws enacted in many states indicate that arbitration is favored by public policy and that the Government will make every effort to support it. This, too, is quite logical because arbitration promotes stability in relations between employer and employee and avoids economic unsettlement, both of which are desirable public goals. The United States Supreme Court has ruled that when the parties have an arbitration clause in their contract, a parallel no-strike provision will be implied, even if it is not specifically written in. Strikes will be barred over any disputes on which the parties have agreed to accept compulsory arbitration. Moreover, the trend of decisions indicates that the courts will rule in favor of compulsory arbitration on as many issues as possible if they can support this position with even the most general wording in the contract calling for arbitration. Companies that wish to purposely exclude certain issues from the scope of arbitration should see that these areas are distinctly spelled out.

Unions, as a general rule, will go along with arbitration provisions. Their leadership has come to have faith in the caliber, judgment and justice of arbitrators. For them, also, it provides an economically civilized method of settling disputes and saves them from striking against an employer during a contract period, which a responsible union will try to avoid whenever possible. Arbitration enables the union to obtain redress for grievances which are not pressing enough to warrant a strike and to avoid bitterness, cost and disruption. If a union demurs from incorporating arbitration and no-strike, no-lockout provisions in a contract, all these arguments should be presented. Thus, arbitration should be mandatory, not discretionary.

The third alternative for settling a dispute is to arbitrate. Barring the exceptions discussed above, if and when a company feels it has a just cause and "virtue" on its side and the issue is of significance, it should press to arbitration and arbitrate to win.

Arbitration should not necessarily be avoided even when management feels victory is improbable. A dispute arbitrated and lost can sometimes do management more good than knuckling-under without resorting to the last recourse. In plants where management has been lax in enforcing standards of production and performance and discipline and has never challenged the union's say-so, one of the best ways to signal a return to a responsible and efficient company labor relations policy is to insist on arbitration of an issue that involves principle. As a shop steward once said of a company that followed this policy: "When they stopped playing dead and insisted on arbitration, we knew they meant business again."

Once it is determined that a dispute will be arbitrated, the parties must obtain an arbitrator. There are various ways in which this is done. Some contracts provide that a company and union, or several companies in an industry and one or more locals, will have a permanent arbitrator. This individual, often termed an "impartial chairman" or "umpire," will be named in the contract to serve for its duration. Sometimes he is paid a set yearly retainer by both parties, sometimes a fee per case, often a combination of both. Some contracts will not appoint an arbitrator but rather will name the impartial agency that will perform this function. Either a state or city mediation or arbitration service, the American Arbitration Association, or the Federal Mediation and Conciliation Service may be named. Frequently this is the case. These agencies maintain panels of arbitrators whom they deem qualified. A list of three or more names is sent to each party after a request for the naming of an arbitrator is made by one. Each party may cross out the names of nominees it specifically wishes to avoid. From the remainder, an arbitrator is chosen. These arbitrators are paid by the parties either equally or as apportioned by the arbitrator.

There are pros and cons which can be argued for many hours on whether to have a separate arbitrator for each case or to retain a permanent impartial chairman. Proponents of the latter idea point out that regular umpires know the industry and its problems best, are fully conversant with the contract, will be consistent in decisions, save the time of selecting an arbitrator and serve to reduce costs.

Many management advocates prefer not to have an impartial chairman. They argue that there is perhaps an unarticulated inclination on the part of arbitrators who are permanent third parties to "split" decisions over the course of many arbitrations. For the employer who goes to arbitration with an affirmative "prepared to win" approach, this can be detrimental, Moreover, it is sometimes claimed that permanent chairmen may be the victim of predispositions, prejudices or personal feelings about the parties, developed over the years, which creep into their decisions. When there is one arbitrator in an industry for a city or a locale, still another difficulty may arise. Fifty or a hundred or more shops join with one union in selecting the arbitrator. One, two or half-a-dozen dissatisfied employers can do little to end the arbitrator's tenure, but if the union is displeased with this impartial chairman, it can force him out at the end of his term. This may even operate at a subconscious level to adversely affect the employers' chances of winning. Where a single company and union select an arbitrator, that umpire is responsible to both equally and this particular problem does not arise.

Before agreeing to a permanent arbitrator the company should carefully consider the individual suggested. Even if an acceptable

person is available, it may be best for the company to refuse a permanent designee, retaining instead the right to choose arbitrators
when the need arises.

In some contracts three arbitrators are specified to function jointly.
Because of additional costs and complications, this is only practical
in larger bargaining units. Selection problems are generally the same
in any event.

Once the arbitrator is selected, the parties determine a mutually
acceptable time and place for arbitration; usually the offices of a
governmental or arbitration agency, sometimes the arbitrator's office
or specially hired premises. The arbitrator will open the session by
explaining the rules to the parties if they do not already know them.

The collective bargaining contract is the "private law" which both
union and company have agreed will govern their relationship. When
one party thinks that "law" has been broken or is not being followed, that party will call for a strike, a lockout or a decision by
a higher authority. In this case higher authority often is not the
courts, but rather the arbitrator, who functions like a "private
court" for the parties.

Labor arbitrations, it is claimed, have advantages over court proceedings for both parties. The problem comes to issue quickly and
the long delays associated with the judicial process are avoided.
There are seldom grounds for an appeal of the arbitrator's decision.
This also serves to save time and, additionally, to cut costs. Arbitration procedure is non-technical and less formal than a court trial
and the contestants participate more directly. Hearings are private.
The arbitrator has specialized knowledge of his subject. The proceedings are relatively inexpensive. Some of these reasons for
arbitration are particularly valid. Concerning others, particularly
the claim that arbitrations are inexpensive, persuasive counter-
arguments could be advanced.

An eloquent and sophisticated minority regard the arbitration
process with distrust. These views, which run counter to the U.S.
Supreme Court decisions bolstering arbitration, were expressed in a
book written by Judge Paul Hays, a former arbitrator and law
professor and now a judge of the U.S. Court of Appeals. In the
volume entitled "Labor Arbitration   A Dissenting View"
Judge Hays asserts that many arbitrators are unqualified for their
quasi-judicial function. He complains that the arbitrator is beholden
for his job to the parties that he must impartially judge! It is suggested that an arbitrator may not want to offend a "customer" that

supplies business. Moreover, the Judge charges that many arbitration awards are actually rigged in advance by the parties.

It is undoubtedly true that a significant group of labor arbitrators are less concerned with the concept of absolute right or wrong than they are with promoting industrial harmony. Consequently, their decisions are often in the nature of a compromise. For example, Corporation X fires an employee for lateness. The union contests the discharge. Attempts to settle the grievance fail, and a month later the case is heard. The two obvious choices are to uphold the disciplinary action of management, or to rule it acted unjustly, in which event the employee should be reinstated with back-pay for the time lost. But frequently arbitrators will select a third alternative and issue a decision that neither party has asked for. The award will direct the employer to rehire the man but state that his time off the job was a valid disciplinary suspension and that he is not entitled to back-pay. This tendency to "split decisions down the middle" is viewed with disfavor by some; but others believe that compromise decisions and even rigged awards can, in the long run, promote labor peace.

Arbitrations vary in tenor from "cracker-barrel" informality to quasi-judicial proceedings. The parties may simply sit, living-room-style, with the arbitrator and discuss the problems. On other occasions a stenographic record is made, witnesses are called, examined and cross-examined and written briefs are requested by the arbitrator. In some states arbitrators may administer an oath and swear-in witnesses so that false testimony constitutes perjury. They may subpoena witnesses, records and documents and have their awards confirmed in the state courts. The general trend is towards vesting arbitrators with these powers in more and more states.

There are those that say the best way to keep the peace is to prepare for war. Preparation is the best way to win arbitrations, too. The company's advocate should have his case thoroughly analyzed and his presentation planned. "Perry Mason-type" courtroom tricks don't impress arbitrators much nor does the sound and fury of a windy argument. Facts and fairplay do.

The contract is the first line of defense. The "equities" of the situation, or what the policy "should be," comes into play only in border-line cases. Counsel may request permission to render written statements in support of witnesses and oral remarks. This is particularly effective when sympathies and equities are on the union's side but the contract supports the company. Written matter can state this with unemotional clarity, disassociated from the personalities at the hearing. Also the submission of such briefs is advisable at the close of the proceeding, if the arbitrator seems unconvinced. There is usually nothing to lose and everything to gain.

Assuming the arbitrator accepts jurisdiction, his award cannot be appealed successfully except in unusual circumstances. The courts are growing increasingly reluctant to interfere in the arbitrator's exercise of his judgment or to question whether or not the decision was "fair." Judges will void arbitrator's rulings only where fraud, corruption or duress is involved, where the arbitrator's actions are palpably capricious and he is guilty of misconduct or partiality, or where the arbitrator exceeds his powers or gives a final award that is so imperfect as to amount to no decision at all. In the great majority of cases, once the award is made the parties will have to abide by it. Failure to do so may result in Federal court action under the Labor Management Relations Act against the party which fails to adhere to the decision or enforcement of the award by state courts.

The extent to which the Federal courts and the Board exalt arbitration is illustrated by the latter's position when its jurisdiction collides with an arbitration award. The Board will not step in to hear an alleged unfair labor practice if the matter is being, or has been, fairly arbitrated. For example, Manager Jones suspends his shop chairman for a week. The union believes that in doing so Jones is motivated by anti-union bias. It can file an unfair labor practice charge against the company or it can contest the discipline before an arbitrator. It chooses the arbitration and loses; then, shopping for another chance, it goes to the Board and files charges. The Board will probably not entertain this. If it did so and came to a conclusion different from the arbitrator's, there would obviously be difficulty. The Board's opinions clearly point out that the Board has jurisdiction in such cases, but that it will abdicate this authority so as to encourage the arbitration of disputes. However, this principle only applies if the Board considers the arbitration fair and regular. When it does not deem the arbitration a proper one, or if the proceedings are unfinished or imperfect, it will assert its jurisdiction and refuse to defer to the arbitration. Where the parties do not avail themselves of their contractual right to arbitrate and a charge is filed with the Board, recent rulings indicate that the Board will entertain the matter and make a substantive determination.

The United States Supreme Court, as noted, stands squarely behind arbitration. It has ruled that a federal court may compel arbitration. And in a 1960 opinion rendered in *Steelworkers v. Warrior and Gulf Navigation Co.* the high court said: "The labor arbitrator performs functions which are not normal to courts. . . . The labor arbitrator's source of law is not confined to the express provisions of the contract, as the industrial common law—the practices of the industry and the shop—is equally a part of the collective bargaining agreement although not expressed in it. [The arbitrator's] judgment of a particular grievance will reflect not only what the contract says but, insofar as the collective bargaining agreement permits, such factors as the effect upon productivity of a particular result, its consequences to the morale of the shop, his judgment whether tensions will be heightened or diminished. For the parties' objective in using the arbitration process is primarily to further their common goal of uninterrupted production under the agreement. . . ."

In summary, the employer must always remember that the best place to appeal a lost arbitration is the next contract negotiation. At the bargaining table, the arbitrator's award can be negotiated out of existence. Employers should keep a list of unfavorable awards and endeavor to reverse these at subsequent collective bargaining sessions. Between contract renewals, arbitrations won can greatly benefit the company.

19

Dealing with
the Union Delegates

Jeremiah, the Old Testament prophet, spoke of "a man of strife and a man of contention" and some employers may think he was describing their business agent. But management must recognize that these men have a job to do. If his job, as the union delegate sees it, often means bedeviling the company, irritating foremen, aggravating supervisors, and annoying executives, it is not necessarily a consequence of any personal enmity on his part. In too many companies, mutual distrust and dislike between company man and union man have repercussions which are bad for the enterprise. To avoid this, an understanding of the union delegate, his job and how to get along with him is necessary.

The delegate works for the employees of the company—or, more concretely, for the union. He is chosen to be the workers' spokesman and is supposed to solve their problems by negotiating for them, processing their grievances, arbitrating their cases, and in many situations acting as a sort of combined social service and referral agency for union members who have medical, legal, financial, social or family problems. He is often their intermediary in dealings with the police, housing authorities, welfare officials or the agents of other governmental agencies. The delegate works for the members and is paid by them. Most important, he is chosen—directly or indirectly—by them. The business agents, or "organizers," as they used to be called, are either elected by vote of the rank-and-file union members or appointed by senior union officials who are themselves elected by the membership. The Landrum-Griffin Act, signed into law in 1959, was aimed at strengthening union democracy; and periodic union elections must be held pursuant to its provisions.

The secret ballot which is provided for in the Landrum-Griffin Act and aimed at promoting union democracy also makes politicians out of union representatives. Like all elected officials, first and foremost they must please their constituents. Taunting the British and "twisting the Lion's tail" were popular political tactics in the early days of our Republic. Similarly, there is often a temptation for the business agent to be vigorously anti-company since it pleases the voters. In unions where the leadership is entrenched or is backed by a powerful machine with henchmen or "yes men," the need to attack management is not as great. Thus, paradoxically, as the Government's effort to make unions more democratic succeeds, the leadership may be more extreme in its anti-management posture, and union leaders may find that they increasingly risk their jobs if they counsel patience and moderation in dealing with management.

As is discussed in Chapter 36, it may be easier for union leadership to allow a matter to go to arbitration and let the arbitrator rule against the union's position than to try to convince the workers in the shop that the company is right. And sometimes a union leadership will not insist that the members take a management offer even if they think it is the best that can be obtained. Every unhappy union member means a vote against the leadership. Responsible union representatives can and do lead, but the company cannot expect these men to side with management. Management must fight its own battles.

Union representatives are usually workers who have come up through the ranks, first as employees, then as people with an active amateur interest in union affairs who often serve as shop committeemen, then shop chairmen and finally as full-time, paid business agents and delegates. This, in turn, is the springboard to bigger jobs —local business manager, president, international representative, city, state or joint board official—and ultimately to top positions in the international union. This is the general pattern. There are, of course, exceptions. Representatives for one union may be hired from another union's staff, or agents may be enlisted from outside the labor movement. But this is rare, and few unions actively recruit and run training programs for agents fresh from college and other fields of endeavor, as a company does for its management.

Businessmen often are surprised at the ability of the union delegates with whom they come in contact. They should not be. There are two significant reasons for the high level of union representation. The first is natural selection. The general pattern—promotion up from the ranks—means that the agent must have intelligence, skill and qualities of leadership to get his job and to hold it. The second reason is that the business agent usually spends as much time with his contract as with his wife. Company officials in smaller plants are often concerned with other problems, but the business agent's only business is labor relations. Large enterprises have executives hired solely for this function; other companies can obtain counsel or labor relations specialists when necessary. It can be fatal to match amateurs against professionals, and most business agents are professionals.

Some businessmen think of all union representatives as corrupt or gangster-like. Not only is this obviously silly, but this attitude can cause difficulty for a company. At a session a few years ago, one employer whose labor force was already organized told another whose plant was in the process of being organized how the union officers had unionized his shop with threats of violence. A third employer was incredulous. "I know that union," he said. "I never believed they were like that." The first employer affirmed they were. "Just a minute," a bystander said, "You've had a union for years now. How could this have happened to you?" "Oh," replied the old-timer, "It did. Back in 1937." The story had been told as if it were a fresh occurrence, and, but for the question, everyone present would have assumed the incident was current.

Today, by and large, union techniques are different. There are crooks in the labor movement just as in every place where power and money appear to be easily attained. Congressional committees, newspapers and television have dramatically demonstrated this. But, as labor relations professionals engaged in day-to-day contact with unions will point out, there are many honest, dedicated union leaders. These have not received the publicity given the dishonest, and consequently the general public tends to relate unions to racketeering rather than recognize the great number of union officials who are honestly and properly doing their job. The company must not prejudge the union or the union representatives with whom it deals.

No matter what kind of union local or representatives a company faces, it can and must avoid illicit financial dealings with the union's delegates. "Payoffs" are a violation of Federal law and carry stiff penalties as noted in Chapter 28. The exceptions which allow a company to pay a union or its agents are specifically set forth in the law.

Any payments other than these are taboo. Unless he is an employee of the company, the delegate must not personally receive any company funds. And a payoff by any other name is just as wrong. The laws and court decisions are broad enough in this respect to cover loans, gifts, lost bets, and other subterfuges. Even the sale of a company product or service for less than the regular price is deemed a violation. Scrupulous adherence to the law is essential to avoid disaster.

After the union contract has been negotiated and signed, the company will, of course, see less of the business agents, but they will still be around. Dealing with grievances in the shop will be the main duty of the agents between bargaining sessions, and their responsibilities will include liaison between the local union and the company's employees. The union representatives will, according to contract provisions, be granted access to the shop during business hours in most cases. Some clauses even provide them with bulletin boards for posting notices. The employer should insist that whenever possible the union delegate notify him in advance of a planned visit. Moreover, the business agent should not be permitted to hold union meetings in the shop or to disrupt operations by taking large groups of men off production or operating jobs while he is present. And the union representative must abide by the safety regulations while he is in the shop. In effect, the company should treat the union agent as a business guest on its premises.

Management may in some cases utilize the visits of the union delegate to discuss company problems with him. Very often these men will have experience due to working with production men and operating personnel, and they can be helpful.

Good union representatives will know—others must be told— that they, too, have a stake in successful company operations. Where a company does well and makes profits, pay increases are negotiated for its workers; the union agents have satisfied constituents and a sound base for organizing new shops. When the business fares poorly, it cannot raise its wage expenses and the employees become disgruntled. Furthermore, if bad times become the rule rather than the exception, the company may be forced to cease operations. This means loss of jobs for the workers and loss of membership, dues and prestige for the union. Union leaders who wish to avoid this grim alternative can often be prevailed upon to cooperate with management to attain better results for all.

In order to live harmoniously with a union, it is good practice for management to win the respect of the union representatives. One way to achieve this is to tell them the truth. It is pointless to present inaccurate facts or figures to union representatives. They usually have a pretty good general idea themselves how the business is going. And, under current law, the union has a right to some information from the company's records—seniority lists, payroll and wage-rates, for instance—and the management can be compelled to disclose this. Moreover, falsifying information is often judged an unfair labor practice.

Barring special circumstances, it is usually good policy to "build up" the union leader's status with the employees wherever possible. For example, if the company is going to give in on a dispute, the compromise should be made because the union delegate asked for it. This way the union representative has *delivered* something for his constituents, and his position is relatively secure. Too many employers want to be the "good guys" and hope to undermine the union. They try to do all the giving themselves and give the union representative only a hard time. In most cases, the result is not to weaken the union but to strengthen it. The business agent has to build back his prestige, and this is best done by pressing management. Most of these union agents know this part of their business well. It is a form of self-preservation. An inexperienced employer should think carefully before adopting techniques designed to belittle the business agent.

Employers should overrule any temptation to play politics within the union. They should avoid backing one faction or the other, both within the shop and on higher union levels. Most often such interference can boomerang. "The boss' " support may be a kiss of death for his favorite and result in the election of an official who is particularly antagonistic to the company which tried to defeat him. Meddling in internal union politics is dangerous.

If the company finds itself with a union representative it simply cannot get along with, it can appeal both to the shop chairman and to senior officers in the union for a change. Many local unions have several business agents on the payroll, and if personalities make coexistence impossible in a particular case, the local business manager or president may substitute one agent for another.

If the business agent cannot or will not help with specific problems, the employer should feel free to tactfully suggest that higher union authority come into the picture. Provided this is done so that the regular agent does not feel that the company has gone over his head, no bad consequences need result. The senior union officials, usually more secure themselves, may be in a better position to take a long-range view and to be more sympathetic to a company's legitimate problems.

A final word must be said concerning the shop chairman and his committee of shop stewards. Unlike the business agents, these functionaries are serving two masters—their employer and their union. Often there is a conflict. The employer should be aware of their sensitive position. They should not be discriminated against because they are union spokesmen nor should they be treated as if they were "biting the hand that feeds them." However, shop stewards are employees and must do a day's work for a day's pay. Chairmen and committeemen may be paid for time spent at grievance meetings with the company. They should not be paid for time spent away from the plant on union business, nor should they be allowed to disrupt operations to conduct union business. Shop chairmen and committeemen are governed by the same rules as other workers. The chairman, and sometimes vice chairmen, are protected by seniority when it comes to layoff, but they have no free hand regarding their conduct and can be discharged or disciplined for infractions just as other workers. As a practical matter, the employer should have a particularly strong case when such disciplinary action is taken since some will always suspect the company of anti-union discrimination. Charges against union committeemen must be amply documented.

Fighting a "cold war" takes time and money. It should be avoided wherever possible. If the points discussed in this chapter are followed, a good relationship between the employer and union representatives can be achieved and maintained. And the fruits of such understanding will benefit the company.

Renegotiating the Contract

Planning for Negotiations in Advance

Renegotiating Know-How

Telling Management's Story

20

Planning for Negotiations
in Advance

Planning in advance of actual contract renewal talks is just as essential to a well-run business and to the successful outcome of negotiations as the planning of all other phases of operation. Too many employers feel that a bargaining table is like a dinner table— they start the activity when they sit down. An off-the-cuff and informal approach by management's negotiator may appear a good impression to convey, but negotiating is not a spontaneous art. To be effective, careful preparation is necessary.

The executives of a business responsible for its personnel functions should confer well in advance of the reopening of contract negotiations and work out an integrated campaign. The time to start such planning depends on the size and nature of the enterprise. In very large-scale operations with funds to support an extensive industrial relations program, preparation for the next contract negotiations should start on the first working day after the current contract is signed. One large employer group has a labor relations attorney who, discussing this, said:

"We literally start preparations this way. We go over the record of the negotiation just concluded, examining it in detail. We solicit impressions, reactions and comments from our employers' negotiating committee and make note of strong and weak points, good and bad tactics, persuasive and poor strategy on both sides. We re-evaluate the union's demands in light of what they finally got, gauge what they wanted but did not get, and anticipate what they will push for when the next contract is negotiated. In effect, we develop a thorough analysis of what transpired, and formulate a critique of the techniques of both parties. These *"post mortems"* are profitable when we evaluate and anticipate subsequent labor-management sessions in their light."

"During the term of the contract we continuously consult with employers, ascertaining what clauses in the agreement create a particular burden for them and what provisions need clarification. We follow carefully the utterances of the union and its positions in other relevant negotiations. Finally, we try to absorb all information which may affect the labor-management relationship, including competitor's contract settlements and all governmental activities, business developments and current events which are pertinent."

In smaller businesses this same degree of thoroughness cannot be economically supported. Nevertheless, there should be at least one "morning-after" session at which the company's negotiators and principal managers examine the negotiations in an effort to learn from them. At least six months before the termination date of the contract, intensive thought and discussion should be given to preparing for the approaching contract bargaining.

One of the first jobs of the top management in this regard is to select its negotiating team. In single companies, the size of the company will dictate the number of company negotiators. Different viewpoints should be represented. It is important to have a man with a financial background, such as a corporate comptroller, treasurer or vice-president for finance, or, in a smaller firm, the partner charged with administration and the managing of "the front office." An individual with technical comprehension of the jobs actually being performed—an operations manager in a retail store, or a production supervisor in a factory—is a valuable addition. Naturally, the personnel and industrial relations department should be included. In some cases it is desirous to bring in a management official not directly connected with the operational or production functions, such as a sales manager or purchasing agent. These people may provide an objective and refreshing viewpoint to the management committee from time to time. One individual, generally the attorney, labor relations advisor or senior industrial relations executive of the company, should act as spokesman for the committee, and later, in joint negotiating sessions, all requests to speak should be channeled through him.

Employer associations which bargain as a unit should select different employers to serve on the committee. It is necessary that they be representative of their constituents' opinions and not of just a fringe group. Individuals with differing backgrounds in production, operation, finance, and administration, should be chosen so that all aspects of the subject matter may be thoroughly covered. The paid staff, if any, of the association should also play a major role in negotiation arrangements and strategy.

When managements' committees are thus comprised, a broad view is obtained and the chief negotiator has "built-in" experts that can help him on specialized matters as they arise either in private consultations or in the actual negotiations. To accomplish this best, each individual who is selected to serve on the committee should be requested to familiarize himself with areas that his job functions cover. For example, the production man must be prepared to talk about workloads, the financial specialist about costs and so forth.

In very small businesses where there is no such detailed division of management's function, the need to prepare still cannot be overlooked. The company principal, instead of throwing up his hands, must use his head and, wearing several hats, do the thinking that separate executives would do in a larger company. Even the small, single proprietor can meet in advance of negotiations to discuss matters with his attorney or other labor negotiator, and it may prove beneficial to invite the firm's accountant to some of these sessions so that he may work up fiscal data both to clarify and support the company position.

It is important that all executives of the company who deal with the contract while it is in force be encouraged to comment on problems that arise during its term. These problems should be listed systematically as discussed in Chapter 16. They should be subjected to careful evaluation and thorough deliberation by the negotiating committee prior to contract reopening. It may be worthwhile to have special meetings with all supervisory personnel during the period of preparation to elicit their comments and suggestions. Thus assembled and primed, the management negotiating committee can start preparing for the basic substantive issues.

Most contracts have automatic renewal clauses. If neither party gives notice to the other of a desire to reopen the contract, the collective bargaining agreement is extended for another year. In the event of a decision to terminate the contract, however, the party so deciding must notify the other sixty days in advance of the expiration date. The wording of the notice usually includes an invitation to start negotiating a new contract. Notice of the reopening must be sent to the

Federal Mediation and Conciliation Service and any appropriate state agencies which have jurisdiction.

Management must make the major decision whether or not it will, on its own, demand the contract be reopened when the old agreement expires. If the union chooses to terminate the current contract, this problem is academic and management will have to negotiate. But, if the union does not, then the company must decide whether it will demand a reopening or will go for renewal. As a general rule, if the union is willing to by-pass a reopening, the industry representatives are well-advised to let well-enough alone. With rare exceptions, contracts renegotiated result in increased costs for employers. A wage cut or the elimination of a fringe benefit previously granted is rare. A wage reopening demand by management, therefore, seldom has a point. The exception is where the existing contract contains a particularly onerous clause or provision or where management is on the verge of bankruptcy and cannot survive without concessions from its employees. But a cancellation of the standing contract by the company for the purpose of improving its position can often boomerang. Responsible union leadership may often caution against a reopening to their members prior to negotiations because they recognize industry's plight, but once the contract is opened, then the leadership must go in to win and come out with gains. As a general rule the following test is suggested: if management truly believes that without relief from provisions of the present contract it will not be around to negotiate next year, then the contract should usually be reopened. If this rigorous test is not met, the company should allow an automatic renewal.

In the event the union chooses to cancel, (and chances are that it will), the company should endeavor to hold concessions to a minimum and plan so as to attain this. As a practical matter, if a business is going well and returning a profit, management should be prepared to grant increases. If it is in a poor competitive position, or otherwise unable to be liberal, it is essential that these facts be established prior to negotiations. In many firms this "setting the stage" may include only some executive complaints about how bad business is. This is a weak approach. Employees are accustomed to hearing this before negotiating sessions and are not generally inclined to believe it.

Preliminary indoctrination in the form of effective statements is worthwhile and tends to focus the employees' aims more realistically when they, in their union caucus, decide on their demands. Such a presentation to the employees often saves later disappointments. However, this is not always a persuasive technique if used alone. Prior to negotiations, certain action should be considered. Management should make an effort to keep the number of employees at the regular level and to avoid hiring additional workers. It should run a taut shop, have the work in before recalling laid-off employees and endeavor to avoid over-staffing at all costs.

Overtime should be kept to a minimum. Experience has proven that workers believe a company is doing well if its sales volume is high, and overtime means more sales. Efforts to prove that overtime work may be particularly unprofitable because it is premium time or that it is not lucrative but only necessary to service customers usually are useless. The average employee thinks the company is making money whether it is or not. They have a very simple criterion —you do not keep doing business if you are not making money.

For organized workers, unions demand a share in company profits as a practical matter. In our economy they have been doing this to a greater or lesser extent. For the individual company to endeavor to reverse this trend at the bargaining table is like tilting at windmills. It is next to impossible for a profitable company to avoid giving increases. When a company is profitable, the practical thing is to see that the increase is reasonable and sensible so that there are also shares of the profit for non-union personnel, management, stockholders, creditors, expansion and development, the replacement of machinery and the building of reserves. If a company's status is marginal, it is essential to let the workers know this so that reason and a sense of proportion prevail and the company may be helped back on the path to profit.

While this over-all climate is being set in anticipation of bargaining, the supervisory personnel, as noted earlier, should be canvassed to review their problems in relation to the union and its agreement. Counter-demands should be formulated which are at once specific and practical. Requests for wage decreases, an end to pension or welfare or a cut in other substantial benefits usually are not even taken seriously. Sensible, limited demands do serve a purpose. Example: a request for a change from weekly to bi-weekly payroll saves the company money in cutting its payroll check costs, its bookkeeping and audit costs, its paymaster's time. It means an actual dollar saving and yet is something which a union might very well consider and accede to. Counter-demands may be prepared even if the company doubts they will be accepted. Such requests can be traded against labor's demands at the bargaining table, thus mini-mizing increases and also serving to show a strong, thorough and integrated pattern of labor relations management on the part of the company. The counter-demands must be carefully considered by key management executives to weed out both the absurd and the trivial. When proposed to the union, requests should actually be in draft form ready for inclusion in a contract, since precise wording is so essential. An explanation and rational reason for each management demand should be prepared.

Policy must be determined concerning the actual mechanics of the negotiation. A definite commencement date should be planned subject to the union's agreement. Executives of the company should see that work is programmed, wherever possible, so as to anticipate all facets of negotiations. These might include intentional slow-downs, loss of worker concentration and production due to their focusing on negotiations and attendance at union meetings, and the possibility of a strike. Members of the negotiating team as well as outside counsel must arrange their schedules so as to be available for the duration of negotiations. The company officials with the power to make ultimate decisions, whether chief executives or direc-tors, must arrange to be available at the critical time during the last days of negotiations and within reach during all other phases if the negotiating team is expected to report to them.

Decisions as to the location of the negotiations and many details surrounding it should be made in accordance with the discussion in Chapter 9. While company officials are not expected to be interior designers nor stage managers, they should be sure that the talks are conducted in an atmosphere that is conducive to work and progress. It is essential that adequate time be allowed between the initial date for reopening the negotiations and the contract expiration dead-line to ensure that there will be mature and careful deliberation and so that every opportunity to reach an accord is preserved. An understanding as to the costs of the proceedings should be reached in advance with the union. If public meeting halls are used, it is customary for the union and the company or employer's association to share the expense equally.

A more delicate question arises concerning pay to the company's employees for the time which they spend in negotiations and there-fore are not producing for the company. Situations vary. Sometimes the union pays its members or expects them to donate their time, often the cost is split, and in some cases the union demands that the company pay the men for time lost in negotiations. The latter course can often mean an undue burden on the company. Moreover, since some employees prefer negotiating to working, the employer may find that sessions drag on unnecessarily when he picks up the tab. The company should be careful before committing itself to this generous course. If it does this once, precedent will be set and the company will be expected to foot the entire bill in all future negotiations. In smaller companies it is often wise to schedule sessions for late afternoon so that too much working time, for members of both employer and employee negotiating committees, will not be lost. And the company cannot reasonably be asked to pay employees for negotiating on their own time after working hours.

All pertinent data should be prepared in advance for the negotiators. If they are going to argue that competitors have lower wage rates, they should have the contract decreeing this, or if there is no contract, other documentation for their statement should be at hand. If management plans to complain about increased hospitalization costs which it must absorb, it should have the bills, cancelled checks or comparative figures available. When claiming that competitive companies have been driven out of business by the union's demands, the negotiators should have a list of the names of these companies instead of relying on generalities.

An effort should be made to anticipate union demands. This can be done by analyzing the public statements of the union's officials and scrutinizing its publications as well as by following its current demands and settlements with other companies. Able counsel must be informed about potential problems and should keep abreast of union developments. It is generally believed that labor will soon press for a thirty-five hour work week. Different locals and internationals also have policies, less well-known, but equally important to the employer with whom they deal. For example, in the metropolitan New York area some locals now have a policy to insist on (and get) a minimum hourly wage that is at least a set amount over the legal minimum rate. These particular requirements should be known to management in advance. Unlike the first negotiations, the company now knows the people it is dealing with. It must judge all of its strategy and tactics in terms of the personalities of the union leadership and the shop committee.

It is advisable to evaluate the union's probable position from the most authoritative source of all—its own negotiators. A company representative or counsel, whoever is the key company negotiator, is well advised to meet with his union counterpart. In a fair give-and-take, the union can be informed of the company's problems and the company, in turn, can learn of the union's needs as felt by both the rank-and-file and the leadership. While this is a good time for a frank discussion, it is still too early for either side to indicate the lines of final settlement which would be acceptable. This will come later.

Finally, in preparing to negotiate, the company must make a thorough and detailed appraisal of its own position and determine just what it can and cannot do consistent with a profitable future for the company, just as it did before the first contract. Thus prepared, the management negotiators are able to move with confidence and will effect a better settlement.

21

Renegotiating Know-How

When management and labor approach the bargaining table to negotiate a second or subsequent contract, the atmosphere may be somewhat more relaxed and the parties more familiar with each other than at the first contract, but the outcome of the meetings will not be of diminished importance to the continued prosperity of the company. Consequently, although the stresses may be more subtle and the strains less apparent, the low index of these superficial barometers should not be permitted to lull management into a false sense of complacency.

As the law requires, notification will have been given to appropriate governmental agencies in advance of the actual commencement of negotiations. Accordingly, mediators assigned from a state or Federal agency may contact both parties involved in the collective bargaining and offer their services. As a general proposition, third-party intervention at this point is premature. The mediator should be informed by the company's representative that he will be notified just as soon as it becomes apparent that he can make a real contribution to the conduct of the meetings, which is to say: in the absence of a settlement arrived at by the parties themselves. In certain situations it may be worthwhile for a management representative to make periodic telephone calls to the mediator assigned to the case and keep him current with developments. The advantage of doing this is that if it becomes necessary to call him in on short notice to render assistance, the mediator is not entirely unfamiliar with the situation.

The negotiation, in its early stages, will in many ways parallel the initial negotiation held between the company and the union which has freshly organized. The major significant differences will be that the union should have submitted its proposals to management well in advance of the expiration date of the contract so that the company will be more acquainted with the actual substance of the demands. Moreover, as a practical matter, the parties having lived together will be in a better position to assay the intentions and needs of each other based upon their respective knowledge of the various personalities and factors involved. After the preliminary and almost ritualistic aspects of the negotiation involving recitation of the union demands, explanation of these, keynote speech made by management, its response to the union requests, and its rejoinder, the actual bargaining will commence.

At this point, the first line of defense of management might often be that it will extend the present contract for a period of one year with no changes whatsoever. If this position is properly conveyed, the union's committee will realize that, although all of its demands are in effect being rejected, there nevertheless is an element of compromise in the proposal set forth by management. When management proposes extension of the duration of the prevailing contract, it is based not upon the fact that it is particularly happy with the present terms, but rather on the premise that it wants changes and that the union wants changes. As attorney "A," a management negotiator writes: "When I negotiate this proposal, we note that the company is not in a position economically to make the changes which the union requests. The company itself has modifications which it desires to effect. Consequently, despite the fact that we have certain proposals of our own which we have been preparing, we offer to forbear from making these requests if the union in return will refrain from insisting on improvements from its viewpoint. This is often an effective position. Its effectiveness, however, will be negated if employer representatives quickly move off of this stand. If management, to start off, requests prorogation of a contract for one year and then later, within the same bargaining session, shows that it is already prepared to make certain concessions to the union which violate this principle, it is admitting that what it has said is meaningless. As a consequence of this retreat, the union will, and rightly so, give very little credence to any company statement since management itself has demonstrated that it is quite ready, without a fight, to move off a position which it has insisted is important. The entire sincerity of management's position relative to various other aspects of its relationship with the union will consequently be questioned. The definite time period in which management should stick to this primary line cannot be set forth. But I would say that as an absolute minimum the company must remain consistent at least through the entire first negotiating session. This means that for several days between conferences its position will percolate down to the union rank-and-file and become known to them."

At the second, or subsequent negotiating session, if the company sees that this first line of defense is untenable it may then retrench at its second line of defense and re-group its forces around the concept that it will consider the union's proposals, but that the union in turn must consider counter-demands which the company is making.

The previous chapter points out the importance of the employer's preparation of a list of proposals which it may present to the union in which it describes the contract modifications the company requests. As a practical matter, these counter-proposals will actually fall into three separate categories. First, there are those proposals which management must get. As an example of this "A" recently negotiated for a factory where the rate which the company paid for unskilled labor was approximately 50 per cent above all of its competitors. "A" recognized that he could not successfully insist that any of these presently employed general helpers take a pay cut, but it was absolutely imperative that wage rates be brought into closer alignment with those of competitors. As a consequence the counter-demand was that a new and much lower hiring-in rate be established for all workers in this category who would be brought into the company after the date of the new contract. "A" told the union quite simply that if they expected to get money from any place to improve the conditions of those people already in the employ of the company they would have to give the employer some relief in some other aspects of its operation. "A's" proposal pointed out the most likely place for such respite.

Second, there is a category of counter-proposals that management makes and would actually like to get, but the denial of which will not force it to refuse a new contract. Lawyers used to request that the union agree to a "most favored shop" clause. This stated that if a union enters into contract with other companies that compete with the negotiating firm, it will not institute provisions in the contracts between it and the said competitive businesses which are more favorable to the other firms than to our company. Some unions may have resisted this, but there were others which would go along. This was the type of proposal which was sensible for management to request because it reinforced in the mind of all the committee members that management's ability to grant increases is not curtailed by its reluctance to improve the lot of its workers. Rather it is limited by its position *vis-à-vis* competitors in the industry. (A recent court case appears to ban the use of such provisions.)

Third, there is the counter-proposal which is used as a stalking horse—that management puts forward with the realization that probably at a subsequent stage in the negotiation it will have to give this up. The purpose in making this proposal is that the company will, if it must, surrender it at cost to the union. By the way of illustration: the company may insist on "management prerogatives" clause. This provides that, excepting only specific powers arrogated to the union, the right to manage is exclusively that of management. The union may resist this strenuously, and at some later date the company is in a position to trade this demand in return for labor dropping some request which it has made.

In discussing its counter-proposals and the union's proposals, the company should use every technique of persuasion to convince the leadership and the rank-and-file of the union of the sincerity and soundness of its position. In this connection the use of statistics and factual data is certainly relevant and worthwhile. However, it is important to be selective in choosing the figures which are to be presented to the union. Union negotiating committees have been drowned by a veritable torrent of statistics. The figures in thousands and millions replete with endless columns of zeros get the people so groggy that any real meaning is certainly lost well before management makes its point. The company must always remember that the men or women with whom it is negotiating are not highly skilled statisticians or accountants but working people. Consequently, when statistics are introduced to bolster the position of management, these should be particularly significant items which truly mean something to the people in the company. Moreover, comparisons with outside companies many miles away or in indirectly related enterprises which do not actually compete with the employer are not persuasive. Basically, the statistics which management chooses to present should be pithy, should be few, and should be important. For example, in a recent negotiation, it was indicated to the rank-and-file workers that the average wage which was paid in their shop was $2.18 per hour, that the fringe benefits amounted to another seventy-two cents per hour and that as a consequence the total hourly cost per man in the shop averaged $2.90 per hour. This was then compared with the average for the four competitors in that area. Counsel pointed out that his client was paying more than 10 per cent above competition. The point was driven home. Further statistics would have simply dissipated its impact.

It is extremely important that management be accurate, trustworthy and entirely truthful in the figures and statistics it presents and, in fact, in all statements which it makes. It is good company bargaining technique to announce to the union what the total cost of labor's demands, both wage and fringe, would amount to over the period of the contract. A total dollar figure should be given. Then management spokesmen should proceed to break this figure down on a dollar for dollar basis into its various component parts. For example, twenty minutes of coffee break per day at an average hourly wage of $3.00 times 500 employees cost over $125,000.00 in one contract year. This totaled cost of the union's demand can graphically demonstrate to labor the excessive nature of its own requests. But if management exaggerates its calculation of the union's demands, this will be promptly pointed out. Union delegates can add too. A false statement or grossly padded figures will undermine the company's position and leave the workers suspicious, distrustful and of the opinion that none of management's arguments can be believed or taken seriously.

The company should recognize that while the group it is talking to are not all trained negotiators, these people have a very accurate understanding of the kind of work they are performing and of the nature of the company's business. Moreover, they have a reliable picture of the company's competitive position at least insofar as wage standards are concerned. Talking down to a committee can certainly be as harmful as pitching an appeal that is too celestial and therefore totally incomprehensible to the workers. While undue theatrics will unquestionably tire all the parties, a dramatic presentation of management's position should not be avoided if it can be done effectively and cogently. For example, some time ago a labor relations attorney was renegotiating a contract for a group of employers in a certain industry. He recalled to the union committee—about 90 per cent of whom had been present at the sessions two years earlier—that he had then predicted that if the union won its demands, it would accelerate attrition in the industry, and certain shops would not be present to sit down at the next negotiation. Now he was able to show them that, in fact, what he had forecast had

proven true, and that certain firms were absent from this negotiation. He suggested they all observe a moment of silence—in memory
of the shops that had died in the interim—and read a roll-call of
the names of the companies which had closed up, moved out of the
area or gone bankrupt. "Gentlemen," he concluded, "once before
we warned you what undue pressure would do to management, and
now again we state that you can do great harm to these employers.
I have read you the names of the defunct companies to remind you
that when I spoke to you at that time my words were not idle. Time
has proven management to be correct. For our sake and yours,
bear this in mind when you consider our statements at this
conference."

Once the actual bargaining is under way, the skilled negotiator
will concentrate on narrowing the gap between the parties. Management will ask the union to come back with a set of demands revised
downward to accommodate the position that the company has set
out. In many cases the union will do just this since they are prepared
to concede. In other cases they will not do this and management must
be in a position to "barter" with the union. It is of paramount importance that when the "horse-trading" of demands for concessions or
of demands against demands begins, management get rid of the
most obnoxious union proposals first. For example, in a situation
where the union demanded severance pay if the company were to
move, management realized that it was absolutely essential it
knock this out in the opening stages of negotiations. Failure to do so
would have exalted this demand in the very minds of the union rank-
and-file themselves, who were originally not particularly enthused
about it. Allowing the proposal to be carried on would necessarily
force labor's leadership, as negotiations continued, into a position of
supporting this demand more and more strongly as one of their few
remaining proposals. Moreover, this particular negotiation was for
an employer association. Some shops in the association would not
be prepared to take a strike over the severance issue as they had no
plans to move out of the area. As a consequence, a union tactic of
pushing this clause would isolate certain shops which could not
afford to give in to this, and, on the principle of divide and conquer,
the group would be weakened. Further, several shops that were
most militantly opposed to this provision were strenuously unwilling to give any concession whatsoever until the severance pay issue
was knocked out completely. This, too, would stymie any progress
towards a settlement. First and foremost, therefore, "severance" had

to go. Only then could negotiations proceed. The most unpalatable demands should, then, be bargained away as soon as possible.

As the negotiations continue, management will most likely make concessions to the union in return for which the union will be constantly revising its demands downward. Management's compromises will consist of agreement in whole or in part to certain of the union demands. It may also entail the gradual withdrawal of its own counter-proposals insofar as these can be safely given up. But the company must be careful not to come upward in its concessions faster than the union goes downward in its demands.

During the course of negotiations, each side will withdraw to caucus rooms. After a management proposal, its committee should step out of the room so that the union may reflect on its offer. The union's committee will do the same. This is a time-consuming procedure, but it is necessary. The break gives each side time to cool down and seriously reflect on the issues. It enables responsible labor negotiators to present the facts of life to the rank-and-file. This may help management in that it makes the employee's expectations more realistic. Furthermore, caucuses demonstrate that each party takes the other's position seriously enough to withdraw and give it thought. In conjunction with this it might be noted that on specific occasions when the union's demands are outlandish, management can effectively deflate the union representatives by refusing to adjourn to discuss them, telling the union that such consideration would be pointless. This tactic is explosive, however, and must be handled with care.

Giving in too quickly or too easily can create the false impression that the company is prepared to go all-the-way. There is an almost telepathic sort of shorthand that experienced negotiators use when they evaluate the demands of the other party. For instance, a union first asks for an increase of fifty cents per hour and management at the second session says it will not budge and that labor must come down in its demands. Then the union at the third session revises its demands to forty cents per hour and management makes an offer of ten cents per hour. Next, the union comes in and says, "Now, gentlemen, our position is that we want thirty cents." It is often a sound conclusion, absent special circumstances, that the union is signaling to the company that it is prepared to settle for something like twenty cents.

It is particularly significant to observe the words with which the union surrounds its proposals or the reduction of its demands. Obviously, if a party says that "this is our final position," or "this is an ultimatum," there is reason to believe this. A bluff of this sort could be foolhardy. Management should always avoid taking the line that an offer it makes is on a "take it or leave it" basis unless this is actually the case. A falsely tough line can mean that management may have to "eat crow." A refusal to move at all from the initial point in negotiations may be considered a failure to bargain in good faith. Not only are the words of the union bargainers particularly significant in indicating just how firm they are on certain points, but in some cases even their actions will disclose their true intentions.

Some time ago, attorney "A" negotiated with a very skilled and experienced union officer who carefully expressed the position that the union decidedly wanted certain concessions. He studiously avoided giving a firm ultimatum, but he stated his demands in very strong terms. At first it was quite difficult to discern if, in fact, this actually was the required minimum that the union insisted upon, or if it was simply a proposition for bargaining purposes. After many, many sessions with the same union representative, when management's spokesmen met to discuss the entire matter and dissect the course of previous negotiations in detail, it developed that the union negotiator had a certain habit which really gave away his inner thoughts. When the request which he made—purportedly the final union position—was truly just this, he would invariably look at his wrist watch. When it was actually only a tentative offer, although pronounced in the same definite terms, he would not check the time. After the final negotiation this union leader was preparing for retirement and said his farewells to management's team for good. One of the industry's spokesmen, session over a few martinis, advised the departing union leader of his proclivity to do some clock-watching when he made a final offer. The union negotiator took note of this with interest and replied to his informant:

"You do the same thing. You light your cigar after making your true final offer. But when you make a proposal that you say is final and you don't really mean it, you don't light up that cigar."

Timing is of extreme importance, and the company must generally see to it that the new contract is closed as near to the expiration date of the previous contract as possible. Unlike the first negotiation, when no agreement exists, at subsequent negotiations there is a definite time when the collective bargaining contract between parties will expire. If sessions drag out and finalization is difficult to achieve before the deadline, management can often agree with labor to a stipulation extending the duration of the contract for a certain number of hours or days. The union generally will insist that the company agree to retro-activity back to the original expiration date in the event that an agreement does occur.

A settlement which is concluded too far in advance of the actual expiration date, a "cold settlement," is hard for the rank-and-file employees to accept and requires much "selling" by the union leadership. If the contract expires at midnight on a Friday, and it is settled on the Monday before for "X" cents an hour, the average worker in the shop will always believe that if the company had been harassed a little bit longer during Tuesday, Wednesday and Thursday, and through most of Friday, it would have settled not for "X" but for "X-plus." There is always the feeling that the union has not really done its job and that the company has "gotten off" too easily. This is a psychological fact. It is particularly significant in a democratic union where rank-and-file ratification is actually important and the leadership will not try to force a settlement down the members' throats. Although it can be extremely drawn-out and tedious, it is my feeling that negotiations should usually be concluded one or two days prior to expiration of the previous contract or, even better than that, during the very afternoon or evening of the last day. The only frequent exception to this is the case of companies where shutdowns in the event of failure to settle will require much advance notice and planning. Even here it is often more costly to have the settlement reached far in advance than to negotiate right up to the wire. Such a premature agreement may be rejected by the union membership, resulting in the same confusion which the company sought to avoid. Or it may require much greater management concession to make it acceptable well before the expiration date than would be necessary at the last minute.

This kind of crisis bargaining is not necessarily desirable; but like practices in other fields where the pragmatic applies, it continues to occur, presumably because it works. A lot of people decry the last minute haste and pressure of such eleventh hour settlements. They point out that it inconveniences the parties and the public and defies rational planning. Perhaps the most popular substitute has been the development of year-round union-management meetings. These conferences, in theory, are supposed to smooth the way for an early contract settlement. While this technique may work on some occasions, it is not universally accepted by any means. Moreover, there is often resentment on the part of union rank and file members that such inter-termination meetings weaken the union by the time of contract negotiations, and that the conferees are usurping the prerogatives of union negotiators. In at least one case, the role of these committees has been deemphasized recently. In sum, a settlement well in advance of the expiration date would, indeed, be desirable, but in many cases this goal is hard to attain.

If, in late stages of the negotiation it appears that little progress is being made, and the sides are stalemated in their positions, then it may be wise to call in the services of a Federal or state mediator. The presence of these impartial third parties often serves as a catalytic agent to precipitate a settlement. Moreover, such intermediaries can be utilized as "face-savers" for a union or a management which has taken too extreme a position and is reluctant to come back off the limb. Experienced negotiators will know when and how to utilize mediators best.

In certain circumstances when some issues cannot be resolved at the negotiation or with mediators but are not significant enough for either side to want a strike, the parties may consider another alternative. They can agree to a contract with all the settled issues incorporated and provide that open issues be resolved subsequently by an arbitrator. Under these circumstances the parties must either agree that the ruling of the arbitrator will be binding or that if the arbitrator's ruling is not binding, the no-strike clause is off and the parties are free to take whatever steps they desire. Counsel may well be reluctant to put the fate of a company into the hands of an arbitrator in this way. Many times arbitrators have an inclination to cut things down the middle. If the company actually cannot afford to make certain concessions, it should stand fast. Once it agrees to an arbitration clause it is placing the settlement of the matter out of its own control and into that of a third party. However, this is a technique that some negotiators favor and perhaps on suitable occasion it should be considered as a practical alternative to strike.

When the company deals with more than one union and each collective bargaining agreement expires at a different time, management will negotiate each contract separately. When terminations are simultaneous, however, the company may be faced with the choice of either having joint negotiations with all unions, or negotiating separately and concurrently with each. In certain instances the company may be in a position to negotiate contract duration so as to arrange for simultaneous expiration of all contracts. On the one hand, joint negotiations may be dangerous because the union with the greatest demands often becomes the pace-setter and the common denominator holding the several unions together. Distinct problems concerning employees in each separate function or operation are often blurred in over-all negotiations where little attention can be paid to details. On the other hand, separate negotiations can result in the "whipsawing" of the company. Each union feels it must do better than the other and so it regards the earlier settlement as its point of departure—a minimum base from which to begin with the definite objective of obtaining more. Few generalities as to the best approach are safely applicable. The decision has to be made depending on circumstances.

In a company with multiple facilities, a similar problem presents itself. Management may consider holding a company-wide bargaining session or negotiating a separate contract for each of its plants or stores. The former pattern permits uniformity of contract and may minimize disruptions due to labor-management problems. It condenses all problems into one major, periodic negotiation time and one contract. This takes the place of many smaller individual sessions and agreements each of which can possibly result in work stoppage, arbitrations, disagreements and the diverting of management's attention. But if there is a strike, the total operation can be stymied. The contrary arrangement allows for an emphasis being put on local conditions that require resolution, and, in case of breakdown of negotiations, localizes the difficulties and does not cripple the entire organization.

After all pertinent factors have been considered, one of the alternatives will prove the most sound, and management should press for this. The decision will depend not only on the attitudes of the respective unions at different units of the company's operation but also on the nature of the company's operations, and particularly on the degree of interrelation from unit to unit or function to function.

As discussed earlier, the final management package should be one which is tailored to the political as well as the economic demands of the union committee. In other words, the respective requirements of the actual workers in the shop, the local union leadership and the international union leadership must be considered when an offer is made so that it will be acceptable to all parties, and no one segment of the union will block it. Very often there is no definite way for management to know the minimum it can hold the union to. However, within certain boundary lines it can ascertain what the *sine qua non* for a settlement will be. Experienced management bargainers will observe with interest the reaction of the rank-and-file when it comes to a ratification vote of management's last offer. If this acceptance is overwhelming, management may have a clue to be more parsimonious in future bargaining. Conversely, when its offer is accepted by a bare majority, the management negotiator will be quite pleased to see that he cut his offer as close to the line as possible. This test is only possible where the ratification vote is a true one and in those cases where the union leadership does not automatically report "unanimity" at all times.

Unless management's negotiating committee has distinct authority to bind the company, it should be clearly stated that the agreement which has been forged in the give-and-take of negotiation is contingent upon approval by the company's higher authorities. As a practical matter, a negotiating committee without extensive power serves very little purpose. But this "hedging" may be a good protective device to counter the union's "acceptance" which is generally contingent on ratification of its rank-and-file, and therefore, also only tentative. Thus, if the union rejects a final agreement, management can save face and announce that it too has rejected the settlement so that when a strike does occur, no offers remain on the table and "all bets are off." Naturally, if the union ratifies and top management then vetoes its own company committee's final offer, the company will have a very serious problem not only immediately but also at future negotiations. Such a move is most inadvisable.

When the settlement has been reached it should be immediately reduced to writing—even in memo form—and signed by representatives of the parties. No matter how late the hour or how weary the people this is essential. In the absence of such a record, misunderstandings can grow. Since an unwritten agreement is not a bar to election, other unions may intervene and general misery can result. This brief memorandum of settlement should be copied or duplicated at once and both parties should take such a signed document away with them when they leave.

After acceptance by both sides, the representatives of the union or management will draft the new contract embodying the negotiated changes. The other party will then review it, check that it accords with the agreement reached at negotiations, and the new, integrated contract will be reproduced. To insure accuracy and speed it may be to management's advantage that it do most of the work, and its attorney should volunteer to do the drafting job.

When the time is ripe for formal signature of the new contract, some think it is well to do this with a small ceremony. Management's top representatives as well as its entire committee should be present and so should labor's negotiating team. Press releases and pictures may be appropriate. I believe it is both gracious and good business for a management spokesman to say a few words about the spirit of negotiations and the prospects for continued mutually fruitful relations between the union and the company. It sets the stage for a quick return to routine and systematic work by the employees and is generally appreciated.

Until a final agreement is reached and both sides have ratified— or at least will beyond a doubt approve the tentative settlement—the company must remain prepared for a strike. Thus, throughout the entire negotiating sessions management must actually divide its thinking into two compartments. It should, predicated on the successful outcome of negotiations, plan for continuous operations. But to do this alone is foolhardy. The company must have an alternative plan keyed to the possible occurrence of a strike arising after the contract termination date.

22

Telling
Management's Story

Successful negotiating means effective dealing with people. Management's relations with its unionized employees, its non-unionized employees, the negotiating committee, the union's leadership, its customers, competitors and suppliers, the community, and the entire public must be a concern at all times. The problem is most particularly acute during negotiations. Each segment of the company's "public" must be carefully dealt with and policies should undergo continual re-evaluation so as to ensure both sensible content and well-projected communication.

During negotiations, management's ear must be to the ground to assess the temper of the people in the shop. Accurate knowledge of these employees' expectations enables management to plan its strategy more thoroughly. Between the collective bargaining sessions, informal soundings should be taken which will indicate what these people think of the company's position, and if they feel the union is too soft or too hard towards it.

Simultaneously with its ascertainment of employees' feelings, management can communicate its views to these people. In my opinion this is most effective when it is done informally and subtly. As a general rule, a direct address by company executives to the workers, distribution of propaganda leaflets in pay envelopes or an advertisement in a commonly-read newspaper will have adverse results. Employees and the union will feel that the company is "going over the union's head," and labor's leaders will be forced into a more militant anti-company position to protect themselves. This direct technique should be reserved only for the special circumstances when management feels that its position has been distorted to the people, and that clearing up the misrepresentation is absolutely essential.

The negotiating committee is set up to represent the company's employees. Its members should never be given a sense of insecurity because they receive lower pay than management's negotiators nor should they be imbued with a feeling of inferiority if they are less articulate or polished than company executives. It is important that the committee's hopes not be built up by effusive or conciliatory remarks of management only to be later dashed. If at any time management is confused or uncertain about the correct response to a union proposal, the answer should be negative. It is easy and gracious to retract a "no" answer, make a concession and move to agreement. It is bad form and bad faith to assent and then, after detailed consideration, withdraw acceptance.

On many occasions a compliment to employees and the union, if sincere, is well-advised. Some negotiators state that management has no quarrel to pick with the men and that it appreciates their efforts and cooperation. At other times they observe that the union's effective leadership has, with the firm's progressive management, achieved standards of living for its workers that are far above those of competitive companies with different unions or no union at all.

Between professional union representatives and company officers a rapport should inevitably grow up during the term of the contract. Trained management negotiators know—and other company representatives should learn—that most of these union men are not out to "get" the company. Their histrionics at negotiations are aimed as much at labor's side of the table as at management's. The relationship between company men and union men should be intimate enough to permit off-the-record discussions. In fact, many management advisors feel it is wise to have a friendly private lunch or an informal meeting with the union's chief negotiator prior to the opening of sessions at which time each side can discuss with the other its problems and its hopes for the outcome of negotiations. As the collective bargaining process reaches a critical point, further informal discussions are often indicated. At these, the spokesmen for each side can speak frankly and to the point without the need of impressing either their own or the opposing committees. It is unfortunate that such meetings lead many to think that an unholy deal is being made between the parties. The amateur will often conclude that such an evil alliance is being plotted; but in the vast majority of cases this fear is absurd. Obviously tact and discretion are necessary. The management team should not single out a union man in front of the entire shop negotiating committee and ask him to step into a private conference with them unless they have first ascertained that he will have no objection to this and that such an invitation cannot embarrass him. This kind of conference is particularly helpful in negotiations involving smaller bargaining units or single companies rather than in major industry-wide negotiations since, when the number represented is not too great, the labor representative has a more accurate grasp of his rank-and-file's position.

Customers, creditors, suppliers, competitors and other business connections of the company will all be directly interested in the conduct and outcome of negotiations. Management should see, wherever possible, that these people are kept informed. Lack of knowledge in these quarters can have dangerous consequences. Rumors of interruption of business or work stoppage can spread causing customers to curtail orders and creditors to get jittery. Suppliers may allocate hard-to-get commodities elsewhere if they believe the company will not call on them for deliveries. The reverse situation may be true. Customers expecting schedules to be met resent hearing from a third party or reading in the papers of a strike when the company could have spared them embarrassment and inconvenience through notification of the actual situation as it transpired.

The community in which a company is situated, particularly when the business is large and the town small, will have an obvious concern over labor-management relations since a break-down can effect its entire economic health. Moreover, it may be important for the company to have the sympathy of local citizens. Particularly when the union tells its story, then, the company must make known its views.

In certain cases—for example in major basic industries such as steel, the railroads, and the airlines—both labor and management may buy space in the press and communicate their respective positions to the entire nation. This is important not only as a means of announcing the truth, but also because public opinion, either directly or channelled through a governmental agency, may be of help to one side or the other. Management sometimes must counteract labor's announcement of its views and promulgate its own interpretation of matters. In all these efforts to project its position, management may find that it will be benefited by obtaining the aid of trained public relations counsel.

During the course of bargaining, particularly if the outcome will affect the public interest, both parties are beset with inquiries from the press, radio and television as to the progress of negotiations. Popular journalism and successful labor relations may often conflict. Some newspaper headline words like "deadlock," "loggerheads" and "stalemate" apparently sell more copies than calmer, understated expressions indicating that no settlement has been reached but the parties are still negotiating. Most people in the communications profession are responsible and can be counted upon to accurately portray events. Some labor relations people insist upon excluding the press from negotiations. If this is done, management representatives must work closely with the reporters, giving them pertinent and authentic information either in the form of interviews or releases. Failure to inform these people can create a vacuum which will be filled by people on the periphery of negotiations who do not truthfully recount developments. Rumor and innuendo can triumph over fact due to the abdication of the latter's advocates.

In disseminating information, the company must be careful to recount only what has transpired, not what will occur, insofar as offers or rejections are concerned. The union representatives will resent learning of the newest management position in their newspapers over morning coffee prior to the session at which the proposal is presented. The company's statement should be made first at collective bargaining meetings and afterwards for the press. In the early stages of negotiations, statements generally should be couched in moderate terms and should not be inflammatory in nature. The urge to editorialize or pontificate should be reserved for very special occasions—and then indulged only after careful consideration.

The press can be most helpful at times to management's spokesmen. It aids especially in keeping participating companies posted in industry-wide negotiations. In the textile finishing industry, for instance, some one hundred or more firms bargain jointly with the Textile Workers Union of America concerning conditions in the Metropolitan New York area. Negotiations have occurred for many years—the most recent in October, 1966. As the tempo of bargaining heightened—sessions beginning at ten in the morning and often continuing through the evening—it was impossible to have industry-wide meetings after each negotiating session, yet it was important that all concerned be kept informed. Through the medium of the *Daily News Record* and *Women's Wear Daily,* both trade papers, which most employers read, the industry's representatives were able to communicate the latest events to members. Not only may the substantive developments of the meetings recounted, but also procedural details, including the time and place of future meetings, can be printed and available to all interested parties in less than twenty-four hours. Arrangements with trade or local papers or appropriate news services should be considered in major negotiations so that information concerning events can be quickly distributed to all interested parties.

Tactful utilization of the media of mass communication can advance management's cause. An important element in bringing about a fruitful conclusion in labor-management contract bargaining and indeed, to over-all company-union relations, is effective dissemination of management's story. Being conscious of this, the company should plan its public relations campaign to supplement its collective bargaining program.

Union Weapons:
How to Blunt Them

Strikes and Picketing

Unfair to Management:
Secondary Boycotts and Other Illegal Union Practices

Righting the Wrongs:
Help from the Labor Board and Courts

23

Strikes
and Picketing

Strikes are the ultimate weapon which unions can employ in their disputes with management. A strike is the concerted action of a group of employees who withhold their labor from an employer. In 1964, more than one million, six hundred thousand workers were involved in 3,600 work stoppages and twenty-three million man-days were lost due to strikes in the United States. The average strike lasted twenty-three days. There have been worse years. In 1945, for example, more than 12 per cent of the total persons employed were involved in 4,750 strikes and there were thirty-eight million man-days of idleness that year. To comprehend fully the nature and meaning of a strike one must first understand that there are different kinds of strikes. This analysis will discuss the varying types of strikes and deal with picketing, which is not the same as striking but usually occurs in conjunction with it.

Economic strikes are probably most familiar to the general public. An economic strike will occur when there is an impasse on a major issue or issues at negotiations between an employer and the union recognized as bargaining agent for his employees. Such a strike may take place before the company and the union have even entered into their first collective bargaining agreement. After a union has been initially recognized by an employer or certified by the N.L.R.B. it becomes the bargaining agent for the company's workers. It then will bargain collectively with the company to reach an agreement. If an agreement is not reached after a period of negotiations and the stalemate seems unbreakable, the union may call the workers out on strike. An economic strike also may occur when a company and union have had bargaining relations for many years. If the parties come to a deadlock when renegotiating the existing agreement, the union can refuse to work when the contract expires or at some time thereafter, thus initiating the work stoppage.

The term "economic strike" does not refer only to those strikes caused by disagreements over wages. An economic strike may develop when there is a failure to reach accord on any matter about which the parties must, under the law, collectively bargain. These subjects include wages, fringe benefits, seniority and other terms of employment. (In fact, from a legalistic viewpoint an economic strike is technically one in which the striker retains a right to reinstatement upon requesting it if he has not been replaced. Thus recognitional and organizational strikes are "economic" in this sense.)

When collective bargaining negotiations ensue, the employer should be aware that an impasse might develop and that a work stoppage can result. When a strike is possible, steps should be taken to prepare for it. Such preparation, as mentioned before, may include particular attention to the scheduling of work and the forewarning of customers, suppliers, creditors and the public. It may also necessitate a phasing out of operations in anticipation of the strike, but the employer should be prepared to show good business reasons for such action. Subcontracting out of work also may be considered.

The key question which every employer may sooner or later have to face is whether to stand firm and let a strike come about or make concessions to avoid it. As yet no electronic computer has been developed that can give a precise, accurate and unequivocal answer to this dilemma. A decision by the men who run the company is necessary. They must balance the danger of over-extending themselves and settling for terms detrimental to the business against the problems which can arise from a strike. To do this accurately, there must be a weighing of the relative strength of both parties. Obviously, a company with several plants, diversified holdings and extensive reserves can better afford this combat than a small, cash-poor business. The resources of the union and the employees must also be considered. This involves knowledge of many factors, including relevant state laws.

In New York, for example, employees on an economic strike may collect unemployment insurance from the state after seven weeks of striking. An executive in New York once expressed his views on this. "The benefits a worker gets in unemployment insurance and strike aid from the union come close to what he earns at work. While on strike he has no deductions for withholding tax, social security and so on and no cost of lunches and carfare to and from work. As a result, there is not a severe enough pain in the pocketbook to deter our employees from striking." This may seem an extreme statement and yet another company official who anticipated a strike said that if the company could not win the strike in the first seven weeks it would be out in the cold. "Once they get that weekly check from unemployment," he averred, "they will be able to stay out 'till hell freezes over. . . . Or at least," he amended "until the unemployment insurance runs out."

A wealthy union with reserve funds can support strikers better than an impoverished union. Similarly, a labor organization with diversified membership can better sustain a strike in one company which represents only a tiny fraction of its members than a union which has all of its members concentrated in one struck firm.

A company should also contemplate the consequences of a strike. It is generally the expectation of responsible management that operations will resume after a strike. Employers, however, must consider the attitudes of their employees who will return to work after the work stoppage. Often a feeling of bitterness develops among striking workers, and some observers opine that it takes a long time to dissolve the residue of this emotion. These commentators believe that the "hangover" of a strike can make for a sick business long after the settlement is finally reached. They point out that when the company is victorious, the workers nurse a grudge, and when the union defeats the company, it is hard to maintain shop discipline afterwards.

Management must be aware that during a strike there will be continuing expenses but little or no income. The company must defray fixed overhead costs including insurance, rent or property taxes, interest on loans, salaries of supervisory, clerical and other non-union personnel, etc. Management will have to calculate how long the company can sustain such a drain. Moreover, it must reckon what the company's financial position will be when there is such a depletion of funds.

Management must try to envisage the other effects of an operational hiatus. Non-striking competitors, whether in the same neighborhood, in distant parts of the country, or abroad, may capitalize on the struck employer's problems. Temporary interruption of business relations with customers or suppliers might become permanent and markets may be irrevocably lost. Firms which are the exclusive source for certain customers are afraid to take a shut-down for fear that the customer will thereafter diversify his business so as not to have all his eggs in one basket. After all, the strike will suggest that the basket can break. Other businesses are concerned lest a customer who once leaves them and tries a rival product will be so satisfied that he will never return.

A company's public relations are often damaged by a strike. Even after resumption of operations, many people, particularly when the product is sold to a mass of consumers, may refrain from doing business with a company which impressed them as anti-labor. Similarly, a strike often causes non-unionized employees, particularly foremen and the professional staff, to move on to other jobs, depriving the company of talented personnel.

Attention should be given to the possibility that a worse settlement will prevail after a strike than that which could have been negotiated at the bargaining table before the stoppage. After the employees have walked out, their attitudes often harden. A company offer that might be acceptable at pre-strike negotiating sessions may cease to be such once the work stoppage is on, and the union may revise upward its demands as the price of settlement.

Many employers might feel that most of these questions can only be sensibly answered if they could calculate how long the strike would last. There is, in my opinion, no way of accurately estimating the duration of a strike. So many variable factors can occur after its inception that predictions of the term of a strike generally are a fruitless exercise.

This discussion is not an exhaustive listing of the consequences of a strike. These are only some of the factors to be considered in the light of the particular details of the company's situation. Unreasonable or adamant demands by a union may leave management no choice but to incur a strike. This may be a more reasonable choice than to sign an agreement which the company cannot realistically expect to live up to or with. On this basis, taking a strike may be the only sensible course left open to management. It must be emphasized, however, that such a decision is a critical one for the company and it should be made only after rational deliberation and never for spite or in a fit of pique.

Employers need not close down during a strike. They may choose to function with replacements for their regular workers who are striking. In the event a company does this, it must ensure that it neither violates the laws regarding the importation of professional strike-breakers nor otherwise interferes with the employees' right to strike. The Federal Anti-Strikebreaking Act makes it a crime to transport persons in interstate commerce for the purpose of interfering with peaceful picketing or with employees' rights to organize or bargain. And management should assume that operating during a strike will cause deep feelings of resentment on the part of many of its workers.

The rights of economic strikers to vote in a representation election are discussed in Chapter 6. Their right to reinstatement in the company's employ at the end of the strike is a qualified one. If their jobs are open, the employer must rehire them. But if substitutes were hired while the strike was on, worked during this time, and remained after the settlement, these replacements do not have to be fired to make room for the strikers whose positions they have filled. Moreover, it is up to the strikers to come forward and claim their right to reinstatement. Where the union has not given the required sixty day notice in advance of its strike, the strikers forfeit their claim even to this limited right to reinstatement. Such notice must be given with respect to strikes over termination or modification of a contract.

Most employers will endeavor to avoid an economic strike before it starts, and after it commences they will try to settle it. Negotiations continue while a strike is going on, with the balance tipping against the side that is hurting most from the strike. Frequently Federal or state mediators assist at this stage. Most of the principles discussed in relation to other collective bargaining sessions apply here with equal validity. After a strike has been settled the employer should consider taking special measures to smooth over feelings and refocus the attention of all personnel on the work at hand.

Next in this consideration of work stoppages is the "organizational strike." This can occur at a company which does not recognize the union and is faced with a demand for recognition. In this case the workers are both demonstrating their solidarity with the union and supporting their demand that the employer recognize the union. If the employer does not choose to voluntarily accept the union he ultimately has recourse against this business interruption. When the organizational strike is accompanied by a picket line, as it usually is, the employer may apply to the N.L.R.B. for relief. He may petition that an election be held forthwith. Under the law the union cannot continue its recognitional picket line for more than a reasonable time if it does not request an election. A "reasonable time" may vary depending on the circumstances, but in no event is it allowed to extend beyond thirty days. When an organizational picket line extends past a reasonable period, the Board's regional director may seek an injunction in Federal court to prevent its continuance. In the event that a unionizing drive manifests itself in the form of an organizational strike and picket line, the employer should move swiftly and surely to help himself to the relief available.

The third category of strikes includes those which are called "unfair labor practice strikes." These are work stoppages which occur when the workers walk out in protest against an unfair labor practice committed by the employer. On the theory that management provoked the workers to do this by its unlawful behavior, unfair labor practice strikers have an unqualified right to be reinstated in the employ of the company. If substitutes have filled their jobs, these replacements must be laid off to make room for the returning strikers. An economic strike can be turned into an unfair labor practice strike, if subsequent to the commencement of the strike, the employer commits an unfair labor practice.

The fourth variety of strike is comprised of those which are unlawful. There are many kinds of unlawful strikes including "hit-and-run" strikes, slow-downs, sit-down strikes, "wildcat" or minority strikes, strikes in violation of a no-strike clause, strikes in the absence of notice, strikes arising from jurisdictional disputes, and strikes which support illegal purposes.

"Hit-and-run" strikes are short, sporadic and generally unannounced work stoppages. Because operations are suddenly disrupted, these strikes are considered by their perpetrators to have a certain shock value. A sit-down strike occurs when the workers camp on company property and refuse to leave or to work. This has the effect of stopping non-strikers from working also. In a slow-down, the employees remain on the job but purposely lower their efficiency, producing less for the company. The first two of these are easily visible to the average observer. A slow-down, however, may be harder to prove. An employer should not move against a slow-down based on a vague feeling that the workers are letting him down. A charge of "slow-down" should be bolstered with production data for factory workers, sales records for retail clerks and other appropriate documentation depending on the industry. The important item to be established is the concerted diminution of activity.

The term "wildcat strike" is applied when workers suddenly and without the authorization of their union walk off the job. In a minority strike a minority group of workers, not the recognized union representatives, incite a work stoppage. If the strikers ignore a no-strike provision in the contract or an arbitration award decreeing that they should not strike, the strike is unlawful. A strike occurring when the union has not served the mandatory notice of contract termination sixty days in advance of the strike date is also unlawful.

All strikes intended to further illegal purposes are banned. Thus, workers may not strike to achieve an end which in itself is unlawful. For example, it is unlawful in all states for a union to strike to obtain a closed shop, since closed shops are illegal. As noted in Chapter 12 several states have gone even further. They have banned the existence of a union shop with legislation called "right-to-work" laws. In these states a union cannot negotiate a contract in which all workers after a specified period of employment must join the union and maintain membership in it. The employee's right to refuse to join a union is protected by law. In states which have adopted this law, a strike for the purpose of establishing a union shop is illegal. Strikes actually backing up secondary boycotts or "hot cargo" rule violations or aimed at incorporating forbidden provisions in a contract are also banned. Strikes to force an employer to discriminate against non-union members, to pressure a self-employed person to join a union, or to coerce an individual company to join an employer's association are also unlawful as are strikes to compel illegal featherbedding.

Recognition picketing is a violation when, as noted, a petition for election is not filed with the N.L.R.B. within a reasonable time. Such organizational lines are also illegal if another union has been certified and therefore represents the workers or if an election under Board auspices has been held within the last twelve months.

An employer should move quickly to terminate an unlawful picket line. The company may protect itself in several ways. It can file unfair labor practice charges against the union with the Labor Board which, in turn, may seek injunctions interdicting the unlawful conduct. The company can itself try for a restraining order in state courts and perhaps sue for damages in Federal or state courts. These remedies are discussed in detail in Chapter 25. In addition to resorting to such relief, the company is free to discipline workers who partake in an unlawful strike. These strikers may be fired by the company. Once they leave work on an illegal strike, they have no lawful claim to reinstatement if the employer does not wish to hire them back.

Employers may in certain cases request an official statement of position from the union on an unlawful strike. The responsible international unions will be reluctant to endorse unlawful activities particularly since such approval would leave them open for damage suits. Often their failure to back up the unlawful strike enables the company to rectify the problem expeditiously.

There are cases where employers, anxious to end an unlawful strike, offer a general amnesty to all workers if they return to regular work within a certain number of hours. A failure to return, they often add, will result in discharge. This type of ultimatum sometimes makes good sense. It does not allow the situation to harden into tightly drawn battle lines and may spare the employer the difficult task of trying to discipline an entire work force or suing his employees' union for damages. In many cases the company needs its skilled workers as much as these employees need the company. Such quick action can save a rift from widening. Often after a one-day wildcat strike, for example, excess steam is "blown off" and negotiations may be fruitful. One hears of instances where these reprieves are reneged on by the employer after the workers return to their jobs. This is wrong. The company's reputation for honesty and a history of keeping its promises is important in successful labor relations. If it follows devious or dishonorable tactics the company will damage both its short- and long-term interests.

Picketing is the patrolling or congregating of people generally outside the employer's premises. Pickets usually carry signs designed to influence the public. In addition to patrolling with placards picketing may include the distribution of handbills, etc. As a general principle of law, picketing is allowed in the U.S. as a form of free speech. However, as with all freedoms in a democratic society, this freedom is not an unlimited license. It is important that the employer recognize when the permissible bounds of picketing are overstepped. Picketing may have a lawful or unlawful objective. When it occurs to further an illegal purpose, picketing is not a protected activity. If the picketing is connected with any of the strikes discussed above which fall into the classification of unlawful activity, the employer has recourse. As Chapters 24 and 25 develop, the Board may and sometimes must seek an injunction against unlawful picketing. In some jurisdictions the state courts will protect the company which itself seeks relief. For example, in some "right-to-work states," upon the employer's application, local courts may enjoin picketing where the purpose is to force the employer to grant a union shop. As a practical matter, to obtain quick help without spending money, the company is often best advised to go to the regional office of the N.L.R.B. and enlist the Government's aid.

In limiting the right to picket, the courts have gone even further than barring only picketing connected with illegal strikes. Even picketing for a lawful objective can be stopped when it is done in an improper manner. The right to strike and picket peacefully and lawfully is guaranteed, but the protection ceases when violence and intimidation are introduced. Picketing which is accompanied by coercion, threats of violence or attacks on employees who want to cross the picket lines will not be permitted. Mass picketing that blocks company entrances and exits or which denies access to the employer's premises can be banned. In these situations, the Board, state courts, and in rare circumstances, even the Federal courts will act to stop this activity. Picketing extended to the fronts of private homes of employers and others may also be blocked as undue harassment. The employer may unconditionally discharge or otherwise discipline workers who engage in serious violence or major illegal activities regardless whether the ultimate purpose of the strike is lawful or not. Management's right to fire those guilty of only minor transgressions is more qualified. Reinstatement of even unfair labor practice strikes is not unqualified if unlawful acts are committed during the strike.

When picketing is for a lawful purpose and properly conducted, wide latitude is given to the union. For example, "stranger picketing" is allowed. This term refers to the situation where people who are not employees of the company picket it. These picketers are strangers to the employer. Many employers find it particularly galling that outsiders are injected into their problems, but it is definitely permissible and objecting to stranger picketing is fruitless. Moreover, as a general rule an employer cannot punish his employees if they refuse to cross a picket line either at their place of employment or elsewhere. This demonstration by workers of their solidarity with strikers is considered a proper type of concerted activity. However, there are exceptions to this rule. For example, employers may negotiate contract clauses which specifically deny the company's workers the prerogative to observe other picket lines. A refusal to cross a line in the face of such a prevailing agreement may be grounds for disciplinary action. Companies in the transportation business should check their rights to insist that their employees ignore third-party picket lines. The type and nature of the third-party picket line may affect the employer's rights to discipline his employees who refuse to cross it. The employer does not usually have to respect the employees' right not to cross a picket line when such a line or strike is not a legitimate one.

The employer will also find that the courts are lenient toward picketing when the purpose is simply to inform the public. Even where an organizational picket line is enjoined, picketing for "publicity" purposes is sometimes allowed to continue. Judges are reluctant to strike down such activities for fear that in doing so they will be curtailing civil liberties and the right of people to express their opinions. However, if the result of such picketing is to induce a work stoppage or discourage workers from passing the line it may transgress the status of mere informational picketing and can be more strictly judged. Also, if the so-called informational line is merely a disguise for organizational picketing which could not lawfully occur, it will not be permitted. Both the actions and statements of the pickets and the words on their signs become important in determining intent. The employer should be prepared to protect his interest when a union's publicity picketing is really nothing more than an attempt to accomplish an objective that is unlawful.

24

Unfair to Management: Secondary Boycotts and Other Illegal Union Practices

Just as the law regulates activities of employers, so too does it impose standards of conduct on employees and their unions. Labor is required to adhere to a pattern of responsibility designed to add stability to the collective bargaining process, preserve certain prerogatives for management and protect the rights of the individual worker. An employer should be prepared to act when labor infringes on management's rights.

Government regulation of unions covers a wide area. It may be divided into four general categories. First, internal union affairs are monitored. These requirements are discussed in detail in Chapter 36. In brief it may be noted here that unions are required to file reports disclosing financial and administrative data. These documents must set forth union policy with regard to dues, fees and assessments, qualification for membership, eligibility for welfare benefits, calling of meetings, choosing of officers, financial activities, disciplining of members, etc. Also information concerning procedure on authorization for collective bargaining demands, acceptance of negotiated settlements and approval of strikes must be included. Required in financial reports are a balance sheet, a statement of income and expenses, a reporting of compensation paid to union officers in excess of $10,000 yearly and information having to do with loans given to union officers, employees and members or to business enterprises.

A "Bill of Rights" for union members was enacted into law in 1959. This insures equal rights in union participation, the right to vote on increases in union dues, availability of union collective bargaining contracts and financial data and protection against arbitrary union discipline. Similarly, provisions are made for democratic election of union officers and regulation of trusteeship. Second, unions are regulated in their attitudes toward employees. They may not engage in physical or economic coercion of these people nor may they discriminate against certain employees simply because they are not union members. Unions may not seek better conditions for their members than for non-members when they negotiate or administer a contract. Discriminatory or excessive union fees are also prohibited. Third, to a limited extent labor's conduct toward the employer is controlled. Fourth, union actions concerning those who are neither principal employers, employees, nor union members is supervised. In this classification are company supervisors or guards and secondary employers who are not directly involved in a labor dispute but are nevertheless affected by it.

The employer is not usually directly involved with the union's conduct towards its members or employees in general. The Government polices these areas of regulation and the employer is not charged with this responsibility. On the contrary, management interference in the internal affairs of a union may boomerang and the company may end up being accused of meddling. When an employee mentions to an employer that a union has impinged on his rights, the employer should move cautiously. If the employer is too zealous in "protecting" his employees with regard to the union's behavior, he may find himself in a morass of quicksand where inept attempts to save only doom. The soundest practice is to suggest that the employee go directly to the N.L.R.B. for help. Alternatively, employers should seek expert counsel to advise them. In the balance of this chapter we shall discuss the third and fourth categories of union initiated unfair labor practices.

The law places certain restrictions on labor's conduct in relation to the employer. Labor may use many legitimate means to organize companies and maintain union strength. It oversteps its rights when it uses threats of force, intimidation or other forms of coercion against the company. Reprisals, destroying company property or other violence is taboo.

It is also an unfair labor practice for the union to refuse to bargain with the employer when it is the recognized bargaining agent. And when it does bargain, it may not demand provisions which are unlawful. Thus a union cannot insist on obtaining a closed shop or propose wording which amounts to a "hot cargo" clause. Nor can a union bargain and create an impasse over an issue that is a non-mandatory subject of bargaining. Furthermore, the union is barred from putting pressure on a company to force it to discriminate against non-union members. In fact, pursuant to Board decisions, if the union is instrumental in getting non-union employees fired, it may be forced to pay such employees for their financial loss due to the union's action. Because the union cannot require the employer to give preference to union members, particular attention must be given to clauses in which provisions are made for job referrals by the union. The union may be entitled to receive advance notice of the vacancies and it can send applicants over to the company for employment. It may even run a hiring hall, but it must open these facilities to all people who request them, union and non-union workers alike. The employer cannot be inveigled into any arrangement in which he abets the union in an unlawful exercise of discrimination. The company may not fire a worker who is anti-union, even if it wants to cooperate with the union, if there is no valid cause for discharge.

Employers must be on their guard not to unwittingly fall into a situation where they collaborate with a union in discriminating against certain personnel. Many company executives have had this identical problem. Their firms had union shop contracts with dues check-off provisions. Particular employees balked at signing the authorization cards. "Boot them out" the companies were told. The firms' officials were in a quandary. They had nothing against the employees in question and yet they wished to maintain cordial relations with the union and to live up to the contract. The recalcitrant workers cannot be forced to sign the check-off card even if there is a union shop arrangement. This would be depriving them of their rights. Arrangements may be made for these "holdout" employees to pay dues directly to the union's shop steward, at the union offices or in some other way that is mutually satisfactory. They can be discharged if they do not tender union dues; but if they tender dues, these workers cannot be fired even if they refuse to sign the check-off card or will not join the union.

"Featherbedding" is an unfair labor practice, but employers cannot rejoice that this exasperating practice has been completely curtailed. The common concept of featherbedding is that an employer must pay for services he does not get or that he is forced to have work done in an uneconomic manner. For example, a bricklayer's delegate limits the number of bricks that can be laid in a day; a rail-roadmen's union insists that an extra man ride in the engine cab to be a fireman for a furnace long since extinguished; a painter's local will not allow rollers to be substituted for the less efficient brushes. These are instances of what the public calls featherbedding. But, the law which proscribes featherbedding is much more confined in its application. It states that a labor organization cannot make or try to make an employer pay for services which are not performed if such payment is in the nature of an exaction. Thus if *some* work, even though unnecessary or inefficient, is performed, then no viola-tion exists legally. Moreover, even if there is no work done, it must be proven that the money which the employer paid was in the nature of an "exaction" before the union can be found guilty. Extortion or racketeering, akin to this kind of legally defined featherbedding, is a violation of the Federal criminal law.

Featherbedding, in a broader sense than the technical interpre-tation, is a device some unions resort to in order to preserve jobs for their members. The concept of limiting the work an employee can perform emerged partly as a defense against sweat-shop conditions when workers were unfairly exploited. However, today this "legal" featherbedding goes beyond protecting the workers from these evils. It forces the company to pay for work it does not get. It violates the concept of "a fair day's work for a fair day's pay" on which solid labor-management relations can be built.

As the pressure of domestic and foreign competition grows, it will be necessary for businesses to modernize. Many firms will turn increasingly to automation. Unions, fearing that unemployment and displacement of their members will result, may set-up featherbed-ding-type demands.

Dramatic examples of what is commonly considered feather-bedding existed for years in the railroad industry. In 1930 railroads had 1,517,000 employees whose aggregate compensation was two billion five hundred eighty-nine million dollars. By 1963 employ-ment roles were sheared to under 700,000 persons, but their total pay was four billion six hundred ninety million. While paying higher wages, the railroads have persistently tried to institute work rule that will prune superfluous employees. Their executives have pointed out that technological shifts, (from steam to diesel, from manual to mechanized track maintenance, from outmoded to auto-mated clerical operations) and the loss of business which the roads have suffered both allow and necessitate curtailed employment.

The unions, on the other hand, believe that they must fight for their members' jobs.

The results of this controversy were frequent showdowns between the parties. Finally in an arbitration board established by Congress to ward off a strike in the railway industry made an award authorizing elimination of most firemen's jobs and set the stage for bargaining which could ultimately result in the elimination of a number of train crew jobs. The reduction in the firemen's ranks was to be accomplished by guaranteeing most firemen their present positions or comparable jobs in the industry and letting natural attrition thin out their ranks. Pursuant to this development, the New York State Legislature, as an example, in the 1966 session repealed two of the three provisions of the Railroad Full-Crew Law, thus permitting railroads to phase out 600 jobs held by brakemen, conductors and baggagemen, providing that the individuals holding the jobs were not discharged. An interesting observation about the progress finally made towards eliminating "featherbedding" on the railroads is that this was not accomplished primarily through the strength of the employers. Rather it occurred due to governmental intervention which developed when it became apparent that the public would suffer as a consequence of the labor-management strife.

In the printing industry also, types of "featherbedding" occurred for years. This has been called "bogus" or "dead horse" and involves the resetting of type in a print shop when there was a "mat" available from an outside source. Thus, a local advertising agency would produce an advertisement for one of its clients and submit a mat—the type already set in a form for printing—to a newspaper. The publisher would use this mat and then either before or usually after publication, his employees in the composing room would make up an exact duplicate and then destroy it. The publisher paid for something which he never used. The union's purpose was to preserve the jobs of the typographers.

The present labor law, standing alone, is not broad enough to protect the employer from featherbedding-type demands. No panacea for this serious problem has yet been developed on a nationwide basis. While some businesses do not have featherbedding difficulties, others are very seriously beset by efforts of unions to "make work" that is not necessary. Until the individual company or industry works out a solution to this dilemma—involving job-retraining. or some other formula—management will have to depend primarily on its economic strength or government assistance and on the self-restraint of unions to keep the ills of featherbedding, in a broad sense, from mushrooming. In industries where labor resists technological improvements, constant efforts should be made by management to overcome the foisting of uneconomic methods upon the company. On an industry-by-industry or company-by-company basis, some progress has been made. These examples should be studied. In 1960, for instance, the Longshoremen's Union on the Pacific Coast agreed that the shippers would be permitted to introduce automated machinery and modify work rules that allowed inefficiency, but the stevedores were guaranteed an annual wage regardless of how many hours they worked. From 1960 to 1966 industry paid $29,000,000 into this jointly administered modernization fund. In 1966 a new five-year agreement was signed in which management agreed to pay $6,900,000 per year into this fund. The money will be used to promote early retirement. Everyone agrees that efficiency on the docks has been advanced tremendously by this agreement.

Another situation in which progress has been made is at Kaiser Steel Corporation which agreed with its union that when a worker is displaced by automation he goes into a reserve pool, getting paid an averaged wave while he is being retrained and awaiting reassignment. Whenever possible, in the event of disputes on workloads, management should consider proposing the introduction of neutral third parties as arbitrators or mediators. A disinterested and objective view is often beneficial. Professional industrial relations arbitrators or specialists are often reluctant to condone blatant featherbedding-type arrangements.

The labor law declares that strikes, picketing, threats or coercion which further the union's ends in certain jurisdictional disputes are unfair. These fights between two unions for the right to represent an employer's workers have proven to be extremely perturbing and unfair to management. In addition, jurisdictional disputes have discredited unions in the eyes of the public and lost labor much sympathy. It is often the innocent employer or third party that gets hurt in the squeeze of internecine warfare. Generally, unions cannot picket an establishment to organize its workers when another union is already certified as the agent for these employees.

The law is also concerned with jurisdictional disputes arising when unions clash over which organization's members will get particular job assignments or kinds of work. It is forbidden for union agents to foment or threaten a work stoppage to further their demands for reassignment of work. For example, in a factory which makes trailer bodies, eight general helpers, all members of an industrial union, who are temporarily unassigned, are told by the manager to paint the interior of the factory premises. A painter's union, hearing of this, may feel that its members have a superior right to paint and should be called in for the job. The painter's business agent is allowed to demand the reallocation of work and the manager can, if he wishes, accede. But, the painter's union may not picket or otherwise employ coercion to achieve its end. Disputes over work assignments have been particularly rife in the construction trades where modern methods have broken old, established craft lines. Conflicts also occur between industrial unions that seek to enlist all workers in an enterprise and craft unions which assert jurisdiction over certain kinds of skilled work wherever it is being performed.

On some occasions, as in the air transport industry, the very life of the union may be at stake. Two men in a jet cockpit must be pilots. The Air Line Pilots Association insisted that the third man also be a pilot. The Flight Engineers International Association claimed that this slot should go to an engineer. For a time, some airlines, in order to avert a head-on collision, had four men in the flying cabin, one of whom was an engineer. Costs pressed the industry to economize. Neither safety considerations nor either union demanded four men. The companies were trying to cut back to three. The question posed was whether one of the three be a flight engineer, or if all three would be pilots. If the pilots got that "third chair" for their members and froze out the flight engineers, then the Flight Engineers International Association might cease to exist as a union. In actual practice after years of attempts at arbitration, work interruptions and government intervention, the pilots emerged as the dominant union. (As in the railroad industry, airline labor relations are governed not by the Labor Management Relations Act, but by the Railway Labor Act.)

The employer, who may be quite willing to have a union, is caught in the middle of jurisdictional disputes. Frequently the public suffers. When work assignment disputes occur, the employer can file an unfair labor practice charge under the Labor Management Relations Act. The N.L.R.B. often seeks an injunction in these cases to end the disruption.

Pursuant to Section 10(K) of the Act, the Board is empowered to decide which union should get the work. In *Columbia Broadcasting System,* a landmark case decided in 1961 by the U. S. Supreme Court, a hesitant Board was told to make the work assignments. In formulating its determination in many cases decided since then, the Board has relied heavily on the original assignment made by the employer. It has indicated that it will also be guided by past practices in the locale, industry or company, by the individuals' own skills, by the language in the collective bargaining agreement, by agreements between unions and by awards of arbitrators in parallel cases. The employer who has been damaged may sue. It has been Board policy to encourage private settlements of these disputes whenever possible and, to this end, many unions have entered into "no-raiding" agreements with each other. Within the AFL-CIO itself there is machinery for settlement of inter-union disputes.

When the company sees a jurisdictional dispute over work assignments brewing, it should first endeavor to arrange a tri-partite meeting between representatives of management and agents of the two conflicting unions. If such informal discussions do not resolve the problem or if a work stoppage and picketing erupts, then the company should proceed swiftly to the Board and seek its intercession.

It is an unfair labor practice for the union to coerce employers in the choice of their bargaining representative. The union cannot pressure employers into an association, nor, under certain circumstances, may it by-pass an association and deal with individual employers in an effort to break the association if the individual company elects to be represented by the group. A union cannot force a self-employed person to join a union or employer association. As with all other unfair practices, the employer is advised to go to the Labor Board when these violations occur. This recourse is also advised whenever there is an actual or threatened strike or picket line if such activity is or would be for an unlawful purpose. Another major type of unlawful activity is the coercion of a secondary employer by a union. This term "secondary employer" applies to a business whose employees the union neither represents nor seeks to represent. The union in taking "secondary" action, moves not against the company with which it has a dispute, but against an employer who merely deals with the primary antagonist.

The term, "secondary boycott" refers to a union's use of pressure, by striking, picketing, restraint, coercion or threats of such actions, on a "neutral" party in an effort to force that third party to refuse to deal or to stop dealing with an employer with whom the union is in conflict. For example, a union is in the midst of an economic strike with the "C" Company which manufactures clocks. The strikers do, of course, have a right to lawfully picket C's premises and call attention on their signs to their dispute with C. However, unsuccessful in weakening C, pickets are sent to march in front of "D" Department Store which sells C's stock. The patrolling picketers urge truckers not to deliver to D because it trades with C. This is a secondary boycott. Another aspect of secondary boycott would be the use of coercion by the union representing D's salesclerks to convince the jewelry department buyer at D to stop doing business with the C company. Action designed to encourage the employees of the secondary employer, in this case D, not to deal with the struck employer, C, nor to sell C's products, could similarly be considered a secondary boycott.

A union which has a dispute with an automobile engine manufacturer also represents the employees of corporation "Q" which makes sparkplugs. If it tries to stop Q from selling sparkplugs to the auto engine company by causing a work stoppage at Q, it will be charged with committing a secondary boycott. Union "R," is the bargaining agent for employees of heating contractors. Its call to all workers to quit working on a building where heating devices made by non-union workers are being installed may similarly be deemed a secondary boycott.

In the event that a business finds it is a victim of secondary boycotting, it can seek immediate help from the N.L.R.B. and institute the appropriate action. However, the prohibition of secondary boycott has certain major exceptions of which a firm must be cognizant. Special provision is made to exempt manufacturers, jobbers, contractors and sub-contractors in the garment industry. Hence, apparel unions may take certain action when the prime manufacturer contracts work out to a non-union subcontractor.

A union which has a conflict with a primary employer may picket him even though the site of the picketing may be in front of another's premises. Thus, if an electrical union has a dispute with a lighting contractor, and the contracting firm has workers installing fluorescent fixtures in a restaurant, the electricians' union may picket in front of the restaurant. Similarly, the plasterers who are striking against a plastering contractor may picket at a building construction site, even though the workers of electrical, plumbing, masonry, glazing and other contractors are not on strike and are working at the same location. In both these examples, the primary picket line may prompt other employees not to cross it and adversely affect unstruck employers. This is deemed a lawful incident of primary picketing and will not be sufficient to void the patrolling. In these cases, however, the picketing is legal only if employees of the struck employer are actively at or about the site and the picket signs clearly state the object of the dispute and do not mislead the public or other workers.

A union may publicize the fact than an employer is unfair to it. However, when this type of listing or picketing, which often requests consumers not to patronize the primary employer, has the effect of causing a secondary work stoppage or strike, it may be curtailed. The burden, as a practical matter, is actually on the complaining employer to show that a secondary boycott develops from such union action.

The protection for innocent employers who are caught up in such struggles does not apply if the employer who suffers the secondary boycott is in fact a close economic ally of the primary employer. The law prohibiting secondary boycotts does not expressly differentiate between "neutrals" and "allies," but some courts and the N.L.R.B. do so distinguish. The status of "allies" does not necessarily exist between manufacturers and distributors of a product, or suppliers and consumers, ordinarily. However, if one employer helps another who is the union's primary antagonist, then he is deemed to have lost his neutral status and to have become a partisan of the company in combat.

For example, Company "A" is struck. It farms out the work which it ordinarily does to Company "B." Company A continues to sell the product. It solicits orders and turns them over to Company B. Company B produces the items and ships them. Company B may then be considered to have thrown in its lot with Company A and cannot claim that it is the victim of a secondary boycott if the striking workers of Company A move against it. An employer, recognizing that his cloak of protection will be taken away if he loses his neutrality, should be careful to consider the consequences before engaging in such transactions with companies which are embroiled in a labor dispute.

A once popular device used in conjunction with secondary boycott techniques was a contract requirement between an employer and his union restricting the primary employer's rights to deal with a company involved in a labor dispute. These provisions also allowed the primary employees not to work on goods produced by a company having a struggle with a union and ensured that employees would not be required to cross any picket lines. Such agreements, called "hot cargo" clauses, forced the employer to cease or refrain from doing business with certain other employers. Today, a union is prohibited from demanding or trying to enforce such terms, and the company and union are not permitted to enter into such agreements. This rule does not usually curtail the employees' right to refuse to cross the primary and lawful picket line of another employer however. Specific and qualified exemptions to hot cargo rulings exist for the construction and garment trades.

These legal provisos are highly technical and their application to specific situations must be carefully judged by proficient specialists.

Company guards may join labor but cannot be in the same unions as other employees. And unions that take in guards may not be affiliated with other unions that accept general workers as members. Supervisors are not protected as "employees" under the labor laws and do not have clearly defined rights to organize. However, union coercive activity directed against supervisors that will influence other workers may be barred.

Congress and the Board have provided the means whereby management may be protected from unfair activity. It is up to the company which is plagued to grasp its opportunity for relief.

25

Righting the Wrongs: Help from the Labor Board and Courts

When a company is the victim of an unfair labor practice committed by a union, the National Labor Relations Board and the courts will aid it. If the employer believes that certain union action is unlawful, he can file a charge with the regional office of the Labor Board. Depending on the situation, a company that suffers from illegal union behavior may endeavor to reach an understanding with the union before official channels are pursued. If this fails, or if it is tactically unwise to try, then the claim should be pressed with the Board. The employer must realize that the Government has no way of policing the entire area of day-to-day relations between particular companies and unions. The filing of the charge serves to bring the matter to official attention. It poses the problem in such a way that the Government can intervene to ensure justice.

The technical procedure for such filing is relatively simple. All charges, whether leveled by an employer, a union or an individual employee, are, generally speaking, processed in the same manner. If an employer is confused by the details and does not have professional counsel, he may seek aid from the Board itself as to the mechanics of instituting such action. The employer cannot, however, get legal advice from the Government people in the regional office since they are not permitted to give it.

The filing of an unfair labor practice charge is initiated when the party making the charge submits a written statement of the relevant facts to the Board. There are forms available for this purpose. On these the employer sets forth the section of the Labor Act which he feels is being violated, and describes the activities of the union which he believes give rise to this violation. The form is then signed and sworn to and the original, with four copies, is given the Board. The so-called "charging party" must also serve copies on the parties against whom the charge is filed.

The first step taken by the Board, upon its receipt of this statement, is to determine if the minimal requirements for a valid charge exist and if Board requirements for jurisdiction are met. It checks the charge briefly to see if there appears to be a violation of the act. Finally, it ensures that the charge is not stale. As a general rule allegations of unfair labor practice must be filed within six months of the occurrence. If, after this survey, the Board finds the charge stands up, it will invite the charging party to "back-up" the allegations.

At this point the employer should submit corroboration of his statements, as well as leads to other evidence. This will include sworn affidavits, names and addresses of witnesses and any other information which would help the Board validate the charge. The employer should have as much of this data assembled as is possible when the charge is filed. The Board expects to receive this supporting evidence almost immediately after the initial filing. Barring a worthy excuse for delay, it may refuse to entertain the charge if supporting material is not submitted in time.

Now the Board's machinery has been activated. A field examiner or attorney is assigned to investigate the charge. This official will go into the plant or shop if that technique of inquiry appears merited. He will talk to witnesses, often interview the parties in detail, and generally reduce what he is told to writing. He will then ask witnesses to read over their written statements, and if their words are accurately summarized, to sign the statements under oath. The employer who levels the charge will, of course, collaborate with the Board to the fullest extent in an effort to have the accusation upheld. If the charge is filed against the employer, he is also expected to cooperate with the Board. In this case, particularly, the employer is well-advised to seek counsel.

If there is supporting evidence of a secondary boycott, hot cargo violation or an organizational picket line, the regional director will assign the highest priority to processing the case. In the event of some alleged violations, the Board will go to court at an early stage in the investigation to ask for an injunction against the activity. In most cases, however, the regional director will not seek an injunction before he issues a formal complaint.

At this stage of the investigation several courses of action may develop. First, the charging party may withdraw the charge. This may be done if the party decides, upon more careful evaluation of the situation, that the charge is not worthy. More likely, it will happen when the employer and the union have, themselves, arrived at any amicable adjustment of the matter. Then no further Government intervention is deemed necessary. In effect this is a private, non-Board adjustment of the matter.

Second, there may be a settlement of the charge. Such an agreement, called an "informal settlement," must be approved by the regional director. This is accomplished when both parties agree to the settlement and the guilty party promises not to repeat the contested behavior. Moreover, the Board, as part of this informal settlement, can direct that a notice be posted for sixty days confirming that one party has done wrong and reaffirming the rights of the aggrieved party. These notices will be posted where appropriate on the employer's or the union's premises.

Third, the regional director may determine that the party making the charge had no case. In this event he will dismiss the charge. Should a company find that its charge against the union is thus discounted it may appeal the decision. Within ten days after dismissal a request for review of the regional director's finding may be filed with the Board's General Counsel in Washington. This high official may reverse the holding of the regional office, or he may uphold it, in which event the charge dies.

Fourth, the regional director may find that the charge has merit. In this event a complaint is issued against the accused party. Within ten days after receiving a complaint the recipient may file an answer which denies the charges and, like legal pleadings in a court of law, frames the issues. Failure to file an answer is tantamount to an admission of guilt.

The regional director may still try to effect a settlement. However, a solution after the complaint has been issued is generally a "formal settlement" and its provisions are enforceable in court. Even after a complaint, however, the parties may reach an accommodation, and this type of resolution is always encouraged. If the parties cannot agree to a settlement the charges go to a hearing. It is now no longer a case of one party against the other but rather that of the Government, on behalf of the injured party, against the malefactor.

The hearing is a formal event. Those involved include the trial examiner, who acts as the judge; the Board's trial attorney who is, in effect, the prosecutor; and the attorney for the party charged, acting as defense counsel. Additionally, the charging party may be represented by counsel who supports the Government's attorney and aids him in developing the case. Witnesses are called to testify under oath. Written exhibits and stipulations may be brought in, and subpoenas compelling attendance or ordering that relevant documents be produced may be issued.

At the end of the hearing the trial examiner issues his opinion in the form of an "intermediate report." He may uphold the regional director's issuance of the complaint, or he may find that it was unjustified and dismiss it. This report is purposely called "intermediate" because it may be appealed. Based on objections at the hearing and displeasure with the report, a party may file exceptions to the opinion of the trial examiner. This must be done within twenty days after the report is issued. If no such appeal is taken, the report moves from the status of "intermediate" to "final." This occurs when, in the absence of an application for review by the full Board, the report is automatically adopted by the Board. If an appeal is filed, the Board in Washington will make a determination of the issue and render its decision. The entire Board may decide a matter or it can be delegated to a panel of three members.

After the final report has been issued, the regional director's office will see to it that there is compliance with its terms. If it is necessary to work out additional details in order to implement the directions, this office will do so. For instance, if an award of backpay is given an employee who is found to have been discriminatorily discharged, this office will direct the employee to submit data to substantiate his claim. Then officials will sift through this information and will apply the regular formula: total earnings which the employee would have received had he stayed in the company's employ plus the expenses of obtaining a substitute job, if any, less any earnings during the period. This computation will be made in dollars-and-cents and the bill will then be rendered to the company. If a party fails to comply with the Board's orders, the regional director will proceed in the Federal courts to force compliance.

In the Board's report for the fiscal year 1965 it disclosed that of more than 15,000 unfair labor practice cases closed, approximately two-thirds were withdrawn or dismissed before issuance of a complaint. Another quarter of the cases were settled or adjusted before a trial examiner's opinion was rendered. Only about six per cent of the cases initiated actually went to the Board in Washington for decision.

This book has discussed the bases for charges against a union and against an employer. Knowing these and also being cognizant of Board procedure in processing unfair labor practice charges, the employer is in a position to weigh his acts and those of the union intelligently. If a charge is made against the employer and he believes himself innocent, he should contest the charge at every level possible. Particular attention should be given to both deadlines for filing and to appeals procedure. Carelessly overlooking either may prevent an employer from obtaining a full review. Time requirements may change and the company or its counsel should always triple-check when involved in Board proceedings.

Suppose, on the other hand, that the employer has evaluated the allegations against him and feels that the charges are valid. Then it is often to his advantage to settle at the earliest possible stage. An accord between the company and the union resulting in withdrawal of the complaint is better than an informal settlement. An informal settlement is preferable to a formal settlement. And a formal settlement is often more desirable than a hearing resulting in a Board order. Involved proceedings are costly and serve little point if it is a foregone conclusion that they will be resolved against an employer. Moreover, the more drawn-out the fight, the more publicity the union can give to its ultimate victory. Most important, Board-ordered settlements are automatically enforceable in court, whereas informal agreements are not. If the employer is in error it is better not to have a court order hanging over his head. Some employers see a virtue in fighting a case that cannot be won just for the sake of harassing the union, but they might consider that there is frequently scant point in proceeding when there are no chances of winning and the fight does not involve principle. Most unions are fully capable of waging their fight and may retaliate by filing charges or engaging in activity which will be very costly to the company in the long run.

When the employer feels that the union has committed an unfair act, he should contemplate how he can best turn this to his advantage. One course is to file and press charges against the union. This will result in Government action against the union which can be publicized to the workers and may be to the employer's advantage where there is a labor-management struggle. Another and sometimes equally fruitful course is to use the unfiled charge as a wedge to reach an over-all accord. In talks with the union, the employer can agree to drop the charges in return for a cessation of such unfair conduct plus other concessions. All this may lead to a major accommodation. The company should think carefully about trying to work out a friendly settlement before initiating formal charges, particularly when the employer and union have a long-established and satisfactory relationship.

If a party is dissatisfied with the Board's ruling on an unfair labor practice, it may appeal the decision to the United States Court of Appeals. This is the intermediate Federal court. It hears cases appealed from the first rung of U. S. courts known as District Courts and certain administrative agencies like the N.L.R.B. Decisions are subject, in turn, to review by the U. S. Supreme Court, the highest court in the land.

The Court of Appeals will review only final orders of the Board on unfair labor practice charges so there is no appeal to the courts on many of the activities that fall within the Board's authority. Intermediate reports, and activities of N.L.R.B. personnel below the level of the actual five-man Board itself generally will not be questioned in the courts. For example, the refusal of the General Counsel to issue a complaint in an unfair labor practice charge is not reviewable nor is the dismissal of such an allegation by the regional director. Moreover, there is generally no direct review of that other major sector of Board activities—representation proceedings. Issues that arise from the Board's determination of an appropriate bargaining unit, or concerning union certification are, therefore, not routinely appealable to the courts. However, there is a "back door" through which these matters can be brought to court. This door is opened when the representation issue—which cannot be reviewed—is converted into an unfair labor practice charge— which can be reviewed. To illustrate, if the employer disagrees with the Board on its action in a certification matter he generally cannot seek relief from the courts. But if he subsequently refuses to bargain with the certified union then the issue will be joined. An unfair labor practice charge will be leveled against the company for failing to bargain collectively, and the company can then demand and obtain review of the Board's final determination of this charge. Its appeal to the court will, in effect, bring into question the propriety of the Board's ruling on the certification.

The court will examine the findings of the Board to see if the evidence supports that decision. The judge may study the record of the hearing and also consider the trial examiner's intermediate report. In weighing evidence, the test of the court is not whether it would reach the same decision as the Board but rather if there were enough evidence to allow the Board to reach the conclusion it did. Even though the court may disagree with the Board's logic it will still uphold the result if it finds that the Board had sufficient substantial evidence before it to warrant its determination. Moreover, the court will usually give particular weight to the Board's expert knowledge as an agency specializing in labor relations.

If the court does not approve the Board's remedy, it will not generally substitute itself as the agent to find a solution. The judge, under these circumstances, will either deny the order, modify it or remand it to the Board for further proceedings.

In some unfair labor practice review cases the court will be asked to rule not on whether there were sufficient facts to support a Board decision, but if the Board applied the correct rules of law. In these situations the court will render a decision based on its interpretation of the law, and it will be influenced by previous court decisions.

The N.L.R.B. has no police with which to enforce its own orders. And yet, obviously, if there were no sanctions behind the directives of the Board, many parties could simply ignore this agency and consider its findings to be so much prattling. Accordingly, the law empowers the Board to move in the Federal courts to enforce its orders. For instance, an employer receives a direction from the Board to cease interrogating his employees before a representation election. He fails to do so. The Board will seek an order from the court bolstering its own rulings. Only the Board itself can apply for such orders. The party that was hurt—as in this example, the union—cannot so move. Moreover, it is left to the Board's discretion whether to seek such court action or not. When its orders are being violated there is, naturally, good cause for the Board to move. But even before a violation, if the Board anticipates that it will have difficulty in enforcing an order, or is dealing with a union or employer that it knows to be particularly recalcitrant, it may obtain a court order. Where there is prompt compliance with its directions it ordinarily will not seek court enforcement.

Once the court has issued such an order, the party which ignores it may be cited for contempt of court. This puts the "teeth" behind the Board's rulings. If it is demonstrated that a party has gone on its own way, disregarding the Board's direction and the court order supporting it, then findings of contempt will be returned. If the accused party is a corporation, contempt findings may be made against individuals provided that they are corporate officers responsible for its affairs. Defendants in contempt proceedings do not have trial by jury. Costs and other penalties may be adjudged against a guilty party.

An analysis of these judicial consequences following the processing of unfair labor practice charges should lead the employer to pursue either of two alternatives. If, after consultation with counsel, the company remains convinced that its conduct was proper, despite the Board's ruling, it may seek court review recognizing that regardless of the outcome it will sustain additional expenses. However, if it is decided that neither the facts nor the law support the company's position, then the company should comply with the Board's order. Failure to do so means involvement in the courts, expenditure of time and money and ultimately the risk of being found in contempt of court. There is no point in pushing to this brink when heeding the admonition of the N.L.R.B. will spare the company. Furthermore such behavior may be subsequently taken into consideration if and when other aspects of the company's conduct come under investigation and can be deemed part of an overall anti-union attitude.

In the event of a breach of the collective bargaining agreement by the union, the employer may sue to seek damages or other appropriate redress. The Taft-Hartley Act distinctly widens this avenue for an aggrieved party to a labor-management contract. A suit for damages would be appropriate, for instance, if the employer were the victim of an unlawful strike. In this case the company would sue in Federal district court to collect the actual amount of money which it lost as a consequence of the illegal action. However, a court will only award a judgment to rehabilitate the injured employer. It will not add so-called "punitive damages" as it can in other types of litigation. Moreover, if a money judgment is returned against a union, it can only be collected from the financial assets of the union itself. No levy can be made against the individual workers or union members.

On other occasions lawsuits may be commenced seeking a remedy other than a damage award. For instance, if the union were to refuse to abide by an arbitration award, the employer might request the court to specifically direct that the union comply with the arbitrator's decision.

Suits for damages in the Federal courts are not limited to employers who have signed a labor contract. Other parties, such as a company that is caught in the middle of a struggle between an employer and his union and suffers from a secondary boycott, may bring a lawsuit against the offending union.

In addition to recourse to the Federal courts, the company may often also have the right to sue the union in state courts. The most practical course to adopt would depend on the specific situation.

Before passage of the Norris-LaGuardia "Anti-Injunction Act" many employers were able to obtain court orders enjoining the collective action of their workers. This proved an effective method of thwarting union activities. The law was enacted in 1932 to protect, specifically, the rights of workers to strike, join a union, assemble, organize, picket, patrol and combine with others in joint endeavors to achieve these goals. Now when there is peaceful union action directed to a lawful goal the company cannot obtain an injunction against it.

In certain special circumstances a private party can still seek—and win—an injunction. These situations are rare, however. When a labor dispute exists, specific requirements of the Norris-LaGuardia Act must be met before an injunction will issue from the court. Section 7 of the Act requires that a hearing in open court be held, and that prior to issuance of an injunction, the evidence must show an entire set of circumstances. These include requirements that the employer must prove that unlawful acts have been threatened and will occur unless the potential perpetrators are restrained, that substantial and irreparable harm can follow, that there is no other legal remedy and that local authorities are unable or unwilling to cope with the situation. Additionally, the employer seeking an injunction has to show that he will suffer greater harm if it is not issued than the union will sustain if it is. Only after a judge is convinced of this, and in the face of a truly explosive situation, will he enjoin the activity protested. Even when such an injunction is decreed it will be written in the narrowest terms necessary to meet the danger. It will not be sweeping in scope.

State courts are not deprived of their authority to issue injunctions. They may do so under the police power of a state to prevent unlawful conduct. Many states have laws paralleling the Federal anti-injunction act which restrict state courts much as Federal courts are restricted. Nevertheless, injunctions may be sought by private parties aiming to head off any injury before it occurs. In some states injunctions can be obtained in state courts much more readily than they may be in Federal courts.

The Norris-LaGuardia requirements do not apply to injunctions sought by the N.L.R.B. as distinguished from those a private party asks for. Unlike a company or union, the Board can move for injunctions where unfair labor practices are being committed. It is likely to do this if there are proceedings before the Court of Appeals for enforcement or review of a Board order, and the unfair practice continues despite the order. The Board also may ask for an injunction after the regional director has issued a complaint if there is reasonable ground to indicate a need for immediate prevention of the unfair practice. The principle behind allowing the Board discretion in these matters is the recognition that the mills of justice may grind slowly and that in an emergency, first-aid may be necessary. The Board can go into district court to seek injunctions. In effect it is then asking the court to order a temporary halt until other courts have made a final ruling. In certain cases the law requires the N.L.R.B. to seek an injunction. Then it is not that the Board *may* ask for an injunction but that it *must* do so. For example, this duty is imposed on the Board when it finds, after preliminary investigation, that secondary boycotts, hot cargo infractions or recognition picketing are occurring in violation of the law.

When a court issues an injunction against a party it is prohibiting that party from engaging in certain specified actions. Ignoring an injunction can result in contempt proceedings. The Board may obtain injunctions against unions which strike in violation of a no-strike clause, or without having given the sixty-day notice when required. Similar legal action against employers can result, for example, if the employer discriminates between union and non-union employees.

Perhaps the most well-known type of injunction in labor relations is that which is requested by the U. S. Attorney General to force a "cooling-off" period. When a strike or lockout threatens national health or safety, the President of the United States will appoint a board of inquiry. This board will report the facts only and make no recommendations. The President considers the report, makes it public and files it with the Federal Mediation and Conciliation Service. Then, if he deems the situation grave, the President may direct his Attorney General to move in Federal district court for an injunction. If it is obtained, the court order requires that the strike or lockout be postponed for eighty days. After this, no further Government action can abridge the rights of union or employer to take lawful action as they see fit.

Criminal prosecution will result for violation of certain laws. U. S. Government employees cannot strike at any time, and, after entering such service, they must sign an affidavit pledging this. Violation of this oath is punishable as a felony.

Certain other unlawful acts related to the labor-management relationship may result in punitive action in Federal or state courts. As discussed, a payoff to union officials or to a union is a crime and offenders may be prosecuted. Falsely swearing to certain disclosure reports can lead to indictment for perjury. Extortionate picketing, and an ostensible "labor leader's" attempt to extort money from an employer for calling off the picket line, may result in criminal proceedings. If convicted, the culprit may be fined up to ten thousand dollars and can receive a twenty-year prison sentence. The same maximum penalty can be meted out to those who violate the "Hobbs Anti-Racketeering Act" and engage in robbery or extortion in interstate commerce.

This chapter shows that all three branches of our Federal governmental system are concerned with labor relations. The legislative branch makes the laws, the executive branch administers them and the judicial branch enforces them.

26

Interfering
with the Union

It is essential that the employer know what his rights are and what he may do. But, it is equally important that he be aware of what he cannot do. In its most sweeping sense the mandate to the company is "don't interfere with the employees' rights to organize into unions and their right to engage in collective action." The opportunities of workers to select their own representatives, form into unions, strike, bargain collectively or do none of these things are all protected by the Government. The employer who interferes with these safeguarded activities does so at his peril.

Use of certain power-plays and pressure by a company to thwart a union either while it is trying to organize employees or when it bargains for them is banned. Acts which are deemed coercive by the Board fall into this category. A company may not engage in espionage against a union or hire spies to infiltrate union ranks and report back to management or to act as *agent provacateurs*. It is illegal for management to physically attack or threaten organizers with bodily harm or to employ henchmen to do this. Blacklisting of employees known to be pro-union may not occur. Different employers cannot join together and, by circulating lists of men they consider to be trouble-makers, freeze these individuals out of chances for employment in the industry. Employers are barred from promoting anti-union petitions among their workers in most cases.

Strike breaking is another activity forbidden to the employer. When regular employees are on strike, the company may hire replacements and continue to operate. This is a lawful test of economic strength in which the employer may try to outlast the union. But management cannot curtail the workers' right to strike and to this end may not import professional strike-breakers from across state lines, discredit the union, sponsor public rallies against the union or inspire "back to work" movements. Moreover, the ruling is that if employer groups, citizens committees or the local police engage in such harassing tactics because of the company's influence, their activities will be attributed to the company, and it will be held responsible for these events.

Interrogation of employees by management is deemed coercion in many cases. Workers should not be called into the boss' office and threatened or cross-examined on their union affiliations or sympathies. Even if the employer does not intend to intimidate, if this results and the worker feels that he is being subject to pressure, the Board may consider the Act violated. However, in some specific cases, discussions with an employee regarding unionization may be allowed as when, for example, the employer must prepare his own defenses to unfair labor practice charges and information from an employee is necessary.

The company will be held to be restraining its employees in their right of free choice if it awards or withholds benefits for the purpose of influencing them in this direction. The very same kinds of threats and promises discussed in Chapters 7 and 8 which can result in setting aside an election may, at the same time, be unfair labor practices. Generally speaking, when the company offers an increase hinged upon the workers rejecting the union in an election or threatens a mass discharge if they accept the union, an unfair labor practice will be committed. The Board goes even further and is suspicious of any increases or additional benefits voluntarily granted by the employer just before an election.

However, these prohibitions on employer actions are by no means absolute. The employer is entitled to free speech and the right to express his opinion. Often this freedom of expression involves an employer's prophesy or prediction that the establishment of a union will be injurious to his workers. Taken in a context free of interference or coercion, this type of remark is permissible.

A company may continue to operate the business in the manner it did prior to an organizing drive. The general manager of a company consulted attorney "A" in late December about a problem. For many years this non-unionized corporation had traditionally announced raises on December 24th for all its employees, to be effective as of the first of the next year. But this year a union organizing campaign had started just after Thanksgiving and it was in high gear. In fact, a meeting to see if a consent election could be arranged was already tentatively scheduled for the week after New Year's Day. The troubled executive put this question to "A:" "Could the company follow its usual practice and announce the increases?" They agreed quickly that the union might file a charge against the company, but the crux of the situation was whether such a charge would be successful. "A" advised that the company proceed with its long-established and traditional policy. It was following a routine and sensible business practice and saving itself from the possibility of losing employees who might quit if these regular raises were not given. The company had no obligation to sacrifice its interests by delivering the votes of displeased employees to the union. Moreover, the key to the defense of the company's action was that the raises were not being used as a tool to influence the employees' thinking or manipulate the outcome of the election. Counsel would probably have given the same advice if the company had traditionally given merit raises at this time to less than one hundred per cent of its employees and wanted to do so again, provided that its criteria in selecting those persons to be rewarded were based on the quality of their service, not their attitude toward the union.

A company may not refuse to bargain collectively with a union that represents a majority of its employees. As discussed earlier, it is mandatory that the company bargain on certain issues such as wages, working conditions and terms of employment. The duty to bargain does not impose any obligation to agree. The company may not evade union delegates or avoid sitting with them to discuss these issues. When there is a conference it must be in good faith, and a company must not announce in advance that its position is inflexible and that the ears and minds of its negotiators are closed. As a practical matter, however, it is my opinion that the obligation to bargain really only amounts to a direction that the parties must spend time trying to reach an accord. If the company cannot accept the union's proposals, then its "no" should be uttered after listening to the union representatives' arguments. As with the proverbial horse, the Board only seeks to lead the parties to the water, it cannot make them drink. The Board cannot force a company to improve its offers nor can it insist that it accept the union's proposals. But it must be noted that recent decisions indicate that if the company makes one offer at negotiations and thereafter refuses to deviate or budge in the slightest, and most significantly, will not bargain further, it may well be considered evidence of an unfair labor practice, the Board holding that it did not bargain in good faith.

Management is prevented from encouraging or discouraging membership in any union by discriminating amongst its employees in regard to their hiring or terms of employment. A company cannot retaliate against pro-union people. This prohibition extends to all aspects of company personnel policies. Workers cannot be fired for engaging in union activity, nor can they be suspended or laid off, demoted or disciplined for this. And an employer cannot refuse to hire someone because he is a union member.

But, the employer must be aware that his rights to manage his company are not suspended. "A" received a telephone call from a works superintendent who wanted to know if he could discipline an employee who came to work drunk and started a fist-fight in the plant. The man was the chairman of the union shop committee. "A's" answer was an unequivocal "yes." The company's rules clearly forbade such behavior. The man had a previous record of alcoholism, and the company has taken the same measures against other employees for similar infractions. If there had been no union in the plant and if this man had been known as the chief advocate of unionization, the advice would have been the same. There is no reason to favor a man because he is a union steward, or to hesitate to impose sanctions because of his affiliations. In a case like this it would be clear to all interested persons that there was no anti-union bias behind the company's move. Management can exercise its rights to discipline for any just cause.

A company which has a decline in work is generally entitled to lay workers off. The fact that the individuals furloughed are union men does not affect this management prerogative provided the company can demonstrate that they were not laid-off for this reason. The company can most effectively negate any complaints of anti-union discrimination if it lays off in accordance with rules of seniority. Transfer of an employee from one job to another that is harder or less pleasant is also justifiable if necessary for business reasons and not done to hurt the union or as a form of retaliation.

In the event that a union contests the rights of management to make any of these moves it will have to show that the employer had an anti-union motivation. The Labor Board's investigators are not psychiatrists and do not give the employer's representatives lie-detector tests or have any other special way to see into their minds. Accordingly, Board agents will weigh all the evidence and consider the employer's particular act in the light of his past behavior and attitudes. Naturally, the union must establish that the employer knew that a certain worker, against whom he allegedly discriminated, was a union man. The employer is deemed to comprehend the foreseeable consequences of his act. He cannot defend his conduct by professing, for example, that he did not know that by unjustifiably firing the shop steward he was discouraging unionization. Employers should be prepared at all times to document their reasons for disciplining, transferring or laying off workers. Mere excuses or trumped-up charges of employee misconduct will be ignored by the Board. That is why it is essential that every company follow its own rules and enforce them uniformly and keep appropriate records to support its actions.

A company may not fire a worker by indirection either. If the employer makes working conditions so intolerable as to force a man to quit, he cannot then smile smugly and say: "He left on his own. We didn't discharge him." Forcing a man to resign is the same as discharging him, and even the employer who takes the precaution of having the employee sign a paper saying that he quit of his own accord will not be excused.

A company will be held responsible for the acts of its management personnel. If a foreman threatens the pro-union workers, this unfair labor practice will be charged to the company. Even if the company can prove it did not authorize the foreman to say what he did, it will not be excused. Only a prompt and complete disavowal of such words or activities by the company may save it from trouble with the Board. The general rule is that statements or actions by any supervisory personnel, whether prompted by top management or, indeed, spontaneous and independent, will be attributed to the company.

The other side of the coin which bars management from discouraging a union also blocks it from encouraging union activities. A company generally may not insist that it will only hire union members. This amounts to a closed shop and is illegal in almost all industries. An employer may not give preference to union men in promotions or lay offs, nor may he pay them higher rates than non-union personnel for the same work. An employer cannot force a man or woman whom he employs to join a union nor can he act in collusion with the union to fire people who are anti-union. However, there is one significant exception: in a company which has a valid union security clause, workers can be discharged for failure to tender union dues. This does not mean that they must sign a check-off authorization card where provision for that exists. It does require that they make some arrangements to tender to the union the money for dues and other fees.

The employer may express a preference for a union but he cannot show favoritism to it or to its members. He shall not actively solicit membership for a union or permit one organizer on the premises when an agent of another union is barred. The employer cannot recognize a union before it has gained the approval of a majority of the employees. He cannot grant bargaining rights to a union in a new enterprise (except in certain construction trades) before employees are hired in. However, a company may negotiate with its existing union to extend the prevailing contract to cover employees in new operations or a new plant or facility under certain circumstances.

Top management is free to take whatever position it wishes with regard to its own supervisors. A corporation president may discharge a foreman who has just been promoted from the ranks for refusing to quit the union. Employers are allowed this freedom of action towards their own management staff because the labor laws which guard employee rights exclude supervisory personnel from coverage. The right, therefore, of foremen, store branch managers, and other administrative or executive personnel to organize is not a protected activity. The only qualification on senior management's rights in this connection is that it may not take action with regard to foreman, etc., which will have the effect of influencing rank-and-file employees in exercising their own rights.

A company is forbidden to act against an employee because he files charges against it with governmental authorities or testifies against the employer. Such retaliation is considered to inhibit the employee from exercising his Government-given rights.

Employers cannot make individual deals with their employees if the effect of these "private arrangements" is to frustrate the purposes of collective bargaining. Thus a non-unionized company, which considers itself farsighted, cannot hire employees and make them promise they will never join a union or bargain collectively. Such provisos are termed "yellow dog" contracts and are specifically invalidated by the law. The U.S. courts have voided some subtle variations of the yellow dog contract, too. Artistically worded agreements of employment that ostensibly leave an employee his prerogatives but which, due to technicalities and fine print, are found to negate these rights, have been thrown out as illegal. The employer may, under most circumstances, make a *bona fide* individual contract with an employee provided that this does not, by its terms, contravene the collective bargaining agreement in force or restrict the right of the employee to organize, join or remain in a union. If management wants to hire a particularly skilled and valuable artisan or specialist, even though he may be included in the bargaining unit, it can usually contract to give him certain benefits or job security over and above what is provided for in the labor-management agreement. In the absence of a union, management can enter into separate and specific arrangements with its employees as to their wages, working conditions and terms of employment provided no infringement of their right to ultimately organize, if they so desire, is included.

Throwing employees out of work or shutting down some company operations if motivated by anti-union objectives is considered an unlawful "lockout" of workers which is an unfair labor practice. Such a temporary cessation of operations designed to force workers to accept terms or reject an organizing union is improper. Recent decisions indicate that, indeed, even the subcontracting out of operations previously performed by the employer may be deemed a partial lockout and called unfair if it is shown that the employer did this to hurt the union. The Supreme Court has held that when a large industrial combine closed the operation of one of its companies, this was unlawful in view of the fact that it had been found that this action was designed to strike fear into and curtail unionizing among the employees of affiliated companies.

Nevertheless, the employer may lay off his employees for good business reasons. In the face of an impending strike which is expected to occur at the time of contract termination, a company, to protect itself, is generally entitled to commence curtailing its operations. To this end it may lawfully lay off workers even before the contract deadline. If an employer sees, two weeks in advance of a contract termination date, that an impasse appears likely, he may hesitate to maintain full production up to the last minute and then be left with a warehouse full of his inventory (or customers' goods in the case of a service industry) that cannot be shipped. Accordingly, workers may be furloughed, and the company can consequently prepare sensibly for the strike with an orderly wind-up of its activities and the staged shutdown of its heavy machinery and assembly lines.

Other company activities such as domination of a union or the unlawful relocation of a plant—actual or attempted—are also illegal practices. These are discussed in other chapters of this section.

It must be obvious to the reader that when the Board is called upon to decide if management's behavior was permissible or unfair, it must consider many subjective factors. Whether or not it will hold against the company depends on its judgment of the employer's motive in taking the action in question. If the company is intimidating workers or meddling with their rights, it is transgressing the laws.

When the Board finds that the company has erred, it will fashion the punishment to fit the crime. When there is an isolated but serious act of misconduct, the Board can order the employer to cease and desist from engaging in such unfair tactics. If the employer's conduct has demonstrated an integrated pattern of violation of the laws, the Board has the power to issue a broad, blanket order that the company stop all interference. When there are specific problems, the N.L.R.B. may right the injustices it discovers by precise directions. It can order that a company reinstate an employee who was discriminatorily discharged or laid off, and it can award him back pay at the company's expense for time lost from the job. This can be done even if a newly hired employee has to be discharged to make room for the returning worker. The Board may direct that a company must lay off and recall workers in accordance with seniority, and it can even force a company to modify its work rules if it believes that these are designed to discriminate against union activities. The techniques of prosecuting an unfair labor practice charge and the procedure for enforcement or appeals of Board directions is substantially the same whether the charge is leveled against management or the union. This is discussed in Chapter 25.

27

The Company Union

"Do-it-Yourself" has lately become a popular trend with many Americans. But the idea was adopted even earlier by certain companies as a device to avoid being unionized by an outside union. Instead of waiting for strange organizers to enlist employees in a regular labor organization, these companies "did it themselves." They organized their own unions, financed them and ran them and this way blocked honest bargaining and outside interference. In short, many employers found that the most effective method of union busting was union building.

The term "company union" refers to such a union organized or run by the company. It is important that all employers recognize the pitfalls and problems of attempting such action. It is even more essential that management refrain from certain actions whereby, although inadvertently, it may be doing things which can result in a charge of helping a "company union" and consequent unfavorable developments.

Company unions are banned and any employer action which is deemed to be domination of a union is an unfair labor practice and will subject the company to remedial action by the Board or courts. The Government moves firmly against company unions because of its belief that such organizations contravene the employees' right to freely select or reject their own bargaining agent. Moreover, it is felt that when a company dominates the union, management dictates policies and programs for the company's advantage rather than for the workers' benefit. As a consequence, there is no true arm's-length collective bargaining, and the workers are considered deprived of their due.

There are many actions an employer may think he can take innocently which he actually should not and which may trap him and be considered unlawful conduct. Conversely, there are some things which companies may often be afraid to do because of the erroneous impression that this would be considered union domination.

Any direct financial aid to a union is forbidden. Paying salaries of union officers, contributing dues for the workers (unless there is a *bona fide* check-off system), providing the union with office space—all are barred. Less direct devices such as paying a fee for the union's attorney or picking up its bills on other occasions or putting supervisory personnel in the union are similarly taboo. Even more subtle company pressures for the union are taken as evidence of company domination. For example, the company cannot solicit membership for the union, it cannot grant any benefits to union members only, or base employee participation in health, welfare or pension plans on union membership. It cannot allow organizing by the union on company time when outside unions are denied this right—or otherwise discriminate in favor of one union. It should not even pay union officers for time spent on union business except for that time when they actually meet with management.

Doing anything unlawful "by proxy" is no way out. Top management of a company should always bear in mind that the activities of foremen or any other level of supervisory personnel are usually attributed to the company itself. The company's supervisory people are considered agents of the company. Even a showing by the company that it did not instruct its foremen to take certain action will not necessarily convince officials investigating company union charges of the company's innocence. For example, if the foremen get together to organize a "Senior Worker's Council" which will aim to act in place of a union, or to replace the union in the shop, the company will be blamed. In cases where one or two supervisors take such improper action, the company may be able to pull its "chestnuts out of the fire" and be excused from charges of unlawful conduct if it promptly, publicly and clearly announces to the workers that it disavows this type of action. Senior management must, for the safety of the company, ensure that absolutely no management representatives play any role in labor relations without first obtaining approval from the proper authority in the company.

Many people think that a company union charge can only be leveled where the union is an independent group consisting solely of the employees of one company. This is incorrect. A company union can exist this way, but even a local which is part of a large international union, independent and unaffiliated as are the Teamsters or affiliated with the AFL-CIO can be so charged. Under the present laws the tests for a company union are the same, regardless whether the union exists company-wide, plant-wide, or industry-wide and is independent or affiliated.

Some businesses have endeavored to organize company unions to forestall outside and truly independent unions from coming in. Other companies try to set up such unions while they have another union in the hope of spear-heading a drive to oust the union in this way. The action of these companies is intentional, but there is a third category of companies which, by sheer mistake and to their ultimate misfortune, bring upon themselves the hazards of a company union situation.

Example: The "X" Corporation has a contract with a union local which is part of an international union associated with the AFL-CIO. This contract covers 700 production employees in one plant in New England. The union-employer relationship is truly at arm's-length. No union officials have ever been bribed to obtain concessions and all dealings are entirely clean. The union is reasonable and sympathetic to the employer. It recognizes that too much pressure against management may push the company over the brink and force it to close up or move south to a non-union zone. The employer appreciates that he has a responsible union. So far no problem exists. Then a new production vice-president comes into the company. He, too, understands the situation, but he decides to take steps to keep the union happy and the workers satisfied with the union. First, he announces that the company will install, at its own expense, automatic vending machines for cigarettes, coffee and soft drinks. A company employee will service these, but the profit will go to the union's welfare fund. Second, he suggests that the union's three shop officers may have every Friday off so that they can prepare for their weekly executive board meeting, and the company will pay them for the eight hours of lost time. Third, he sends the company maintenance men to the union's office to give it a fresh coat of paint. Fourth, he tells the union president that the company will take care of mimeographing the union's monthly news letter and mail it out for them. Each of these four separate acts would not strike the average person as particularly immoral, illegal or corrupt, but taken together, they may indicate that this vice-president has pushed the company into the posture of "dominating" the union. Considering these and other surrounding facts, an investigator might well decide that the union is a captive company union. If he should, the company has lost a lot. It may, at worst, lose the union which has understood and worked with it. At best such an investigation, and possible conclusion that there is a company union, will be followed by an order to the company to discontinue these subsidizing practices, and will force the union to be more militant and anti-company just to keep its now-sullied name clean and its now-suspicious members happy.

The reader may wonder who would even raise the charge of company union in such a situation. The answer is simple—it could be any of the company's 700 employees who thinks the union is too soft and the company too rich or who has ambitions to run for office against the incumbent union president. Or it could be an outside union seeking to break into the plant and "rustle" 700 members from the established union. A contract with a "company union" may not be a bar to an election.

In brief, an employer should scrupulously keep his hands off his union. First, not to do so may result in an unfair labor practice charge and an allegation of company union. Second, on the practical rather than legal level, if the rank-and-file employees sense too close, too friendly and too intimate a relationship between their union and their employer they will soon decide something is rotten. If the employer helps the union, the workers will reason the union must be helping the employer. And if the union is helping the employer, they will further conclude it is not helping the employees as much as it should be. This may not always be a logical conclusion, but it is a frequent one.

The rule against company unions does not prevent the employer from helping groups of his workers provided such employee groups do not operate as a union. For example, the company may buy athletic uniforms for the plant basketball team or instruments for the shop band. It may aid social clubs and lend assistance to a credit union of employees. It may even, on isolated occasions, aid a union function—as by contribution beer for the Annual Picnic provided it is open to all employees regardless of union affiliation.

The dividing line between permitted and prohibited conduct is blurred. Actual litigation has taken place on practically all of the examples given. Any actions that will benefit groups of company employees or the union and which are not required by the collective bargaining agreement, the law, or otherwise, may be suspect. The best policy for the company to adopt is to check with its labor-relations advisor to be certain such steps will not lead to trouble.

The National Labor Relations Board, recognizing the difficulty of applying any simple test to determine if company domination of the union exists, has adopted the so-called "totality of conduct" rule. That is, it will examine all the acts of the employer, not as isolated incidents, but as part of an over-all pattern. In effect, it will put the pieces together like a jig-saw puzzle, and if it then sees a picture of company domination emerging from the evidence, viewed as a whole, it will act. Naturally, when the employer's alleged acts of domination are coupled with substandard conditions, or wages and benefits lower than competitors, or if the union has been weak, inactive and practically unrepresented at the bargaining table, the likelihood of a decision against the company will be heightened.

In defending itself against company union charges, the employer cannot argue that the workers wanted this. Employees under the law as now written have the right to accept or reject a bargaining agent, but they do not have free choice to select a bargaining agent controlled by the employer. If they trust the employer that much, the reasoning is, they can vote to have no union. But to have what is in name, but not in substance, an uncontrolled union, is forbidden.

When the Board concludes that a company dominates a union it can order the company to cease and desist from all practices which aid the union and are instrumental in rendering it a company union. If it considers the situation too far gone for this and finds the company is entrenched in its control of the union, it will order the disestablishment of the union. And then it is as if the company had no union at all so that the employer becomes susceptible to approach by other unions.

Where a company union is ordered dissolved, a new union will be legally recognized only if it is completely divorced from the tainted union. The mere withdrawal of financial aid to a company union will not whitewash it if the Board has ordered it dissolved.

In addition to the practical and legal reasons to eschew company unions there are other persuasive reasons. The same financial support to a union which may lead to the conclusion that it is a company union can be a violation of the Federal criminal law. Moreover, the company must report such expenditures, under the Labor Management Reporting and Disclosure Act of 1959, to the U. S. Government. So the employer who is making improper payments will be confronted with the unhappy choice of filing a perjurious report or admitting violations of a Federal penal law—neither very appetizing alternatives.

If the employer, having read this chapter, still feels he would like to try to set up a company union, one can only conclude that he is not very sensible. And for this kind of childishness there is an appropriate fairy-tale: Once upon a time there was a shepherd with a big herd of sheep who was afraid of wolves attacking and stealing his sheep. He decided that if he had his own wolves raised with the herd, strange wolves would leave him alone seeing that he already had his quota of wolves. So he went to market and bought four little wolf cubs. He told everyone but the wolves that they were his wolves, but he told the cubs that they were really little lambs. The shepherd fed them, and they grew and they grew and they grew, and if the cubs snapped at the shepherd, he took away their supper until they were good again. Then one day the shepherd's wolves met other wolves at the local bar and grill and they found out they were really wolves and not sheep after all. They also decided that they liked meat better than grass, so the shepherd's wolves joined the big wolf-pack and, through it, the International Wolves' Association. They were made very honored wolves and appointed to several committees, and they took all the sheep with them when they left to join the other wolves. The shepherd lived unhappily ever after.

The moral is Don't create a Frankenstein; it may grow strong and affiliate with an International Union and you will have only yourself to blame.

28

The Sweetheart
Contract

A sweetheart should bring delight, but there is one kind that can mean disaster. "Sweetheart contract," a term which has been widely used in the press over the past few years, means a collective bargaining arrangement in which the employer receives favored treatment for which he pays a union official. All sweetheart contracts are illegal.

There can, however, exist situations where the union gives a better break to one employer than to others or where it gets less for its people than it has the economic strength to force. Provided there is no payoff to a union official or third party, this type of arrangement is legal and, in fact, quite proper. Good negotiators will always look for such a situation.

There are several reasons why such circumstances can exist. A union seeking to break into a hitherto-unorganized industry or area will often make inducements to a "bellwether" employer in the form of a "good" contract. Similarly, a union which is anxious to pick up additional membership in a hurry may offer relatively "good" contracts to prospective employers. In this fashion the union endeavors to turn the employer into an ally in an organizing drive. It may be good business in such a case for the company, provided it has evidence of worker support, to sign with the "easier" union rather than to wait like the proverbial sitting-duck for a more militant union to pick off its employees.

Often unions which are beset with their own internal troubles will sign up for less than they know they can achieve through pressure. This has happened in cases when unions are under pressure from Government agencies investigating racketeering or Communism, when unions anticipate a raid from a competing organization, when inside political troubles and election dates require the leadership be free to mend their own fences and concentrate on their survival, or when other union endeavors require the organizers to spend time in more fertile fields. In all of these cases there is one factor in common: the union leadership is eager to complete an acceptable contract—not necessarily the best it can obtain—and wrap up the negotiation in a hurry or with minimum effort.

An employer's negotiators not only can but should take advantage of such circumstances to get for their company the most beneficial contract. These may appear to be "windfall" situations, but experienced labor negotiators will agree that they can and do occur with some frequency owing to the fluid economic and political factors affecting unions today and the constant jockeying of some for membership outside of their specific areas of jurisdiction.

Finally, it should be noted that unions often will not push the employer to the limit when to do so is to imperil his entire enterprise. This is particularly true of smaller shops engaged in very sharply competitive fields.

"A" negotiated for just such an employer. "A" said, "The plant hired between 70 and 200 men depending on the season. We made no false claims about our ability to withstand a strike. In fact, it was actually admitted at the bargaining table that this company was hardly a match for the economically powerful and large local representing its workers, in a contest of strength. A strike or shutdown would mean no reopening. We successfully convinced this union's responsible leadership that if they forced us to accede to their demands, which presumably they could do, the very future of the plant, all employees' jobs and the union's members would be placed in jeopardy. After careful presentation of this quite factual position, the union scaled down their demands to realistic proportions and a contract was made. This company is still in business today. Its workers receive better-than-average pay. A less responsible union might well have won its increase and lost its plant."

Negotiators for the company should always be alert to the kind of situations discussed in this chapter. They must be familiar with internal union politics as well as the company's position and be prepared and able to indicate the mutual advantage of a "softer" contract to the union's leadership. Such accords are neither illegal nor improper.

In the "sweetheart" situation, the employer gets a "better deal" at the expense of his men and to the profit of their union leaders. Sweetheart arrangements can manifest themselves in several ways. In individual store, shop or plant negotiations, the employer may pay for an "easy" contract which includes substandard wage rates and minimum benefits. Where this cannot be done, either because of a militant rank-and-file, a vigilant international union, or an industry-wide uniform contract, the money is paid so that the union will by-pass contract provisions and give favors to the company over and above management rights under the contract. These include winking at "private arrangements" on fringe benefits between the employer and an individual or permitting pay that is lower than contract rates, countenancing "kick-backs," or allowing an undue increase in work loads or a speed-up, agreeing to harsh and unfair discipline against an employee, not processing grievances or purposely losing arbitrations, or any other action which is a service to the company and a disservice to the employees.

The sweetheart deal is consummated between the employer and whomever he thinks can deliver for him, including the shop chairman, the business agent, the local business manager or president, a union international representative, or a complete outsider who promises results. In nature, the sweetheart payoff can range from a one-time deal to a continuing transaction.

Some dishonest union officers or "paper-local" officials may commence an organizing campaign solely to receive money for withdrawing the organizational picket line and calling off the organizers. Once paid off, they may disappear forever or until they decide to return. The "insurance" which the employer has bought against unionization is as good as a dishonest man's word—something a wise person would not count on. On the other extreme, a union delegate may actually be on retainer like any other company man who performs services for it. These relationships can conceivably continue for long periods of time. Also there are situations where money changes hands in a single transaction to "buy" a good contract or ensure that the firing of an employee is not contested or for some other reason.

Newspaper articles and magazine stories indicate that the "take" can be accomplished in literally dozens of ways. Outsiders may be used as conduits, goods may be sold to the union official at less than cost, bets may be placed in his name or loans may be made or cash actually handed to him or his emissary. The employer who is paying for a sweetheart deal is committing an act which is illegal and which also, in the long run, will prove unwise for other reasons, even if undetected.

Some payments to unions or their officers may be for lawful purposes. In this category are payments made to legally qualified welfare or pension funds, payments of checked-off dues, payments pursuant to a court or arbitration award, payments for union labels, sales in the regular course of business, or payments as a compensation for work actually performed. Other payment, gift or giving of merchandise runs afoul of Section 302 of the Taft-Hartley Act and thus violates Federal law. Employers may sit up nights scheming how to make the payoffs under the guise of legality. But the law is sweeping in scope and quite clear in spirit. Even the most ingenious man who thinks he has discovered a new way to by-pass the law may find himself facing a Federal judge in the United States courthouse. The penalties for each infraction go as high as a $10,000 fine, a year of imprisonment or both.

The employer who is paying for sweetheart deals must be constantly concerned that a full-scale investigation will be touched off and that he will be "on the griddle." Governmental scrutiny is here to stay with Congressional committees spotlighting and the Justice Department focusing on these areas of corruption. Daily papers and other publications also do the community a valid service in periodic investigations and exposés, and the honest international unions police their own organizations. The individuals who make the payoffs and those who countenance and direct it, whether managers, stockholders, principals, officers or directors, must be constantly aware that detection can mean arrest and prison. With such a threat hanging over their heads, executive personnel can hardly be expected to achieve full and clear-minded capacity. Unlike cheating on taxes, this Federal violation involves at least two parties—the fixer and the fixed. The chances of being caught, therefore, are easily doubled.

In many states, also, such activities are declared illegal. In New York, for example, this is the case. Moreover, in that state all employers must file a sworn statement and acknowledge or deny that they have engaged in such illegal arrangements. The guilty employer is between the devil and the deep blue sea, and must admit to a crime or may face eventual perjury charges.

Since illegal payments and illicit methods of getting cash to a unionist are not tax deductible, the employer faces the additional dilemma of either making such payoffs out of personal "after-tax" dollars, or taking it out of the business and claiming an illegal deduction as part of his operating expense. Receipts are not given for bribes, and with the intensive audit of expense deductions by the Internal Revenue Service, more difficulties face such an employer.

If the rank-and-file union members get wind of illicit arrangements existing to their detriment, the consequences can be bitter. An angry group of employees will often throw out their own corrupt leaders and turn on management, seeking to right the wrong it has done and punish it by greater demands, stringent contract enforcement and militant anti-company behavior.

The character of the union official who will take tainted money creates yet another problem. They know they are engaging in forbidden activity. Often they may behave like blackmailers. The price for the illegal favors can go up at any time. The employer may buy a union official and discover that his purchase doesn't stay bought. He may wake up to find that there is a new, silent partner in the business. As in other illegal arrangements, when the law cannot be invoked between the parties, there may be recourse to non-legal sanctions such as violence.

Some businessmen may think that to hand out money every so often in return for a special favor is a clever thing to do. A few have learned, to their sorrow, that they are soon "hooked" and are riding a fast moving merry-go-round where the tame sweetheart union turns into a tough tiger held by the tail and the racketeers get increasingly greedy for their share.

There is no need to learn this the hard way. Management should make it a basic principle that no gifts, money or favors are given to union officials or any others to influence labor relations. As a practical matter this means giving nothing to union officials who do not work for the company, and paying no more than fair compensation for the work actually done by union leaders who are regularly employed by the firm. The vast majority of union officers have no desire for this graft. They do not wish to break the law, and will respect the honest employer. A sound, sensible business-man will scrupulously endeavor to comply with the law. He will not look for sweetheart deals, and if they are offered, he will reject them unswervingly.

29

Disengagement
from the Union

"Unionization," a fat man once told me, "is worse than overweight. It's even harder to avoid, and tougher still to get rid of once you've got it." And another observer, speaking of unions, once said, "It isn't fair. They move in and even if you beat 'em they're back in a year like locusts. But if they win you've had it. They're with you forever." The analogies to both afflictions—medical and entomological—are not entirely accurate. The slogan, "Once unionized, always unionized," while in some circumstances valid, has somewhat limited application. This chapter discusses the three primary ways that a company and union may be divorced after they have been married through employee action, employer action or union inaction.

As has been stated, the guiding tenet of the Federal labor law is that employees be given the opportunity to exercise their free choice in selecting a bargaining representative. A corollary of the freedom to select is the right to reject. Consequently, there are now provisions for an election to dislodge a union. This is called decertification procedure and is in many ways similar to certification elections.

The Labor Board will arrange to hold a decertification election if certain requirements are met. There must be a showing of interest on the part of at least thirty per cent of the employees in the unit having an election. This is the same proportion of interest as required in certification elections. No decertification election will be held within twelve months after a union has been certified, or if there is a valid contract in force. When the election comes, the workers in the collective bargaining unit will vote to indicate whether they wish to keep the incumbent union as their certified bargaining agent or reject it. Whatever their decision, the employer will then know, as a result of the election, if he continues to have a legal duty to bargain or not.

The petition for a decertification election should come from the employees themselves. Unlike a certification election petition, it cannot be filed by the employer. In fact, it is essential that the company have no hand in any aspect of the decertification proceedings. The company is forbidden to inspire such a move by its workers, and must be quite careful in advising them regarding this. The N.L.R.B. scrutinizes the filing of decertification petitions carefully. If there is any hint that certain workers are being used as a catspaw by the company, the regional director may order that a detailed investigation be held. Indications that the company did, in fact, influence the workers' petition may void the petition and knock out the decertification proceedings and may also result in unfair labor practice charges being brought against the company. On other occasions, if the Board believes that the decertification move is bona fide but that the employer has been involved, it may hold the election, but, nevertheless charge the company with an unfair labor practice.

Employer interference will be barred whether it is direct or indirect. Consequently, the employer should not send employees to his own lawyer, or even pick up their bill for legal fees, printing, meeting halls, mimeographing, etc. Whether the company instigates and manages the movement for decertification from start to finish or if it merely lends assistance at certain points, it is engaging in dangerous action.

If the vote is less than a majority for the union (or even a tie), the Board will consider the union ousted. In this event the employer is free to treat the decertification as evidence that the company's workers have selected no union to represent them. Furthermore, the Board will not hold another election in the same unit for one year. Even an outside "third party" union cannot, consequently, petition for an election during this period. In rare cases, the Board may cancel a decertification as a bar to another election if the complexion of the unit changes appreciably. If the union wins the decertification election, the Board's announcement of the result is tantamount to certification of the incumbent union. Again, another election for at least one year is barred, and the union has a new lease on life.

The outcome of decertification elections will, of course, depend on the circumstances in the particular situation. In representation elections held, unions won 60 per cent of the individual votes; in decertification elections, 36 per cent. This is according to N.L.R.B. figures promulgated in 1966, covering the fiscal year 1965. Moreover, these figures indicate that 200 decertification elections were held under Board auspices. Unions lost 128 of these elections covering 4,718 workers and won 72 contests allowing them to continue to bargain for 7,847 employees. The trend is the same as in fiscal 1964 where the unions won decertification elections in the larger units and lost in the smaller ones.

Less known and less employed than a decertification election is a deauthorization election. A deauthorization vote does not oust the union. But it weakens it so materially in a financial sense and affects its prestige so adversely, that it amounts to a significant step in undermining a union.

A union representing employees may properly bargain for and obtain the right to have a union shop with dues check-off provisions in most states. No specific consent by the union membership to these particular clauses is required. The union's collective action and negotiated agreement with the company will, of course, result in the employees all being bound to the terms of the contract. Under the law, the employees in a bargaining unit now may curtail labor's right to maintain union security clauses. The union's right to so act cannot be blocked before the agreement is concluded, but it can be repudiated after the contract is signed and clauses requiring maintenance of membership and the union shop can be vitiated.

At least 30 per cent of the employees in the unit must sign a petition which is filed with the N.L.R.B.'s regional office. The employer should not prod his employees to take this action, but even if another union is found to be at the root of the "revolution" the petition is not disqualified. Assuming that the Board finds that a valid union shop clause is in the prevailing contract and if there has been no deauthorization election held within the last twelve months, an election will be scheduled. At this time, by secret ballot, the employees indicate if they wish to allow these clauses to remain. The outcome of the election will be based upon a majority of the possible votes in the bargaining unit, not a simple majority of the votes cast, as in representation elections. As a consequence of this technicality, and unlike certification or decertification elections, the failure of an employee to cast a vote is equivalent to a vote against deauthorizing the union. In other words, no vote is a pro-union vote.

Even if a decertification contest, coded by the N.L.R.B. as an "R.D." election, is precluded, a deauthorization vote (called a "U.D.") may occur. Consequently, in cases where disgruntled employees wish to take a slap at the union but cannot have a decertification election, they select a deauthorization balloting as the next best move.

Unions which are deemed "Communist-infiltrated" are even easier to deauthorize according to the provisions of the Subversive Activities Control Act. For example, where a union is so labeled the petition for a U.D. need be signed by only 20 per cent of the eligible voters rather than 30 per cent. In these cases, even the employer may file the petition. The purpose of the Act is primarily to weaken unions considered to be red-led.

In deauthorization elections when the union is triumphant the *status quo* continues. Where the deauthorization petitioners have won, the collective bargaining agreement between the union and company remains in effect except that the union security provisions no longer prevail. It is as though, with a scissors, these clauses were simply snipped out of the contract.

Although some labor relations students may predict growing utilization of U.D. procedures by dissatisfied union members, the actual holding of such balloting is still comparatively infrequent. In 1961, fifteen deauthorization elections affecting nearly 2,000 workers in the whole United States were actually held. In 1964 there occurred 34 deauthorization elections, and in fiscal 1965 there were 48 such elections involving 3,975 employees. In 27% of the elections, the union retained its right to make union shop agreements. These units covered 1,216 employees. In 35 elections, or 73% of the total, the union lost. These elections covered 2,759 workers. Although deauthorization contests are more frequent than five years ago, they still are a rarity. The 48 U.D. elections of 1965 are a small part of the total of 7,824 elections held in that year.

In certain instances union action or inaction may presage the end of its relations with a company. Theoretically, if a union, at the termination of a collective bargaining contract, does not serve

notice of an intent to renegotiate, or if management so signifies and
the union does not respond, then the contractual relations between
the parties will cease. Thus after the expiration date, barring contract provision for automatic renewal, the employees will no longer
be represented by the union. Moreover, prior to contract termination management may refuse to bargain with the incumbent union
on the theory that it no longer speaks for a majority of the workers in the unit. If it can support these charges, the Labor Board
may require the union to prove its majority status and thus its
right to be bargaining agent. Even while a contract is in force,
total union inactivity might be deemed to vitiate the agreement
and the Labor Board may entertain petitions for certification or
decertification elections. In cases where disorganization and schism
in the union are rampant, the Board will also hold such elections
during the term of a contract which might otherwise have been a
bar to election. The N.L.R.B. may act in this manner when there
is disaffiliation of a shop from a local, a local from an international
union, or the latter from the parent federation and confusion on
the part of the workers and doubt by the employers as to which
entity they have a contract with.

Finally, certain management actions can result in ousting the
union. The termination of an entire business by management, assuming it is for a cause other than simply to shake off the union,
will effectively result in cessation of relations with the union. In
the opinion of some observers, the trend of cases indicates that
eventually even a complete closedown of the business, if motivated
by a desire to thwart the union, will be deemed an unfair labor
practice. At this time, however, a total shutdown, regardless of
motive is allowed. This is a rapidly developing area of the law.
There does emerge with increasing clarity the proposition that a
shutdown, even if not motivated by anti-union animus, is a matter
company officials should discuss with union representatives with
regard to why as well as how it is being done. Management should
bargain with labor on the impact of the closing. Going even
further, it appears that management may have to bargain on
whether or not it should shut down.

Between a total and permanent close-down and the routine maintenance of operations is an entire realm of possible company
changes. Many of these can affect the relationship with the union
representing the firm's employees or seeking to organize them. A
partnership can throw its assets into a corporation and operate

under a new name. A corporation listed on the New York Stock Exchange may sell one of its operating plants to another such company. One of two 50 per cent stockholders in a closely held corporation may sell out to the other. A small over-the-counter concern can dispose of all of its fixtures in one store to an individual. A receiver in bankruptcy may continue to operate a small motion picture company under court auspices. The possible variations are virtually as wide in scope as the imagination of modern enterpreneurs.

Intelligent businessmen contemplating a sale, acquisition, trade, merger, spin-off, or reorganization will determine the labor relations effects in advance of such a move just as they would weigh the tax consequences or corporate law ramifications. The actual terms of the transaction may be influenced and shaped by the existing labor situation.

The point of departure for the investigation is that a collective bargaining contract is a legal agreement between two separate parties—the union and the company. As noted, under circumstances where the union's status is materially altered, the contract may be affected. Similarly, when the business entity is changed such results can occur. The basic principle is: if the business continues to operate in the same manner and with continuity then the contract probably remains in force. For example, when a new corporation is formed to succeed an old one and the stockholders are substantially the same, the new corporation is bound to continue with the union. This is true even though the new corporation may not yet have been incorporated when the agreement was signed between its predecessor and the union. Corporation "Y" is a stevedoring concern. Mr. A who owns 100 per cent of the stock sells out to Mr. B who continues the business as before. The union had a contract with corporation Y, not Mr. A. nor Mr. B., and the contract remains unaltered since Y is functioning as it did before. The same result may occur when the ownership of Daily Newspaper "T" is transferred from its local owner to a large publishing chain. The latter is a separate and new corporation. It had no part in negotiating the existing contract. However, it takes over the business intact, including plant, property, equipment, distributors, franchises and circulation lists, advertising contracts, accounts receivable and payable, and it retains the same workers. It may be deemed a successor firm.

Thus when the buyer of a business takes over its obligations and

assets or, particularly, its shares of stock, and plans to operate it
without substantial change, he may be under a legal duty to live
up to any existing union contract. Recent decisions have been giving the union greater security. At one time, if S sold the assets of
his business to P, P could refuse to honor the union contract.
Assuming that it was an arm's length sale and there was no relationship between S and P, P was entitled to assert that S's employees were not his employees, and that S's obligations were not
his obligations. S would have been liable for contractual commitments up to the time of sale, such as accrued vacation, pension
rights or sick pay, and P would take over with a clean slate. This
concept is being eroded, and it appears clearer that employees'
rights are not completely terminated merely because of a change
of ownership. In a recent case, company R was merged into corporation W. The employees of R, who were unionized, went to
work for W. They complained that W was not affording them
some of their rights and demanded an arbitration. W claimed it
was not bound by any contract between R and the union. The
U.S. Supreme Court held that the successor corporation, here W,
had a duty to arbitrate under the predecessor's contract. In another
case, where assets of a business were sold to another company and
most of the employees continued to work for the new firm, it was
ruled that the entire labor contract applied to the new employer.

It is now becoming evident that a purchaser of a business may
take over certain obligations regarding the seller's personnel. The
new employer may find that the entire contract is deemed to prevail in full force and effect. Alternatively, if the Board or courts
do not go this far, they may declare that the new employer is
obligated to recognize the incumbent union as his employees' representative and bargain on a new collective bargaining agreement
with them. Still a third possibility is that these Federal authorities
can direct the new employer and the union to submit unresolved
particular questions, or, in fact, the entire issue of representation
to an arbitrator in accordance with the provisions of the existing
contract. Precisely because the law on this point is fluid, it is essential that the potential acquirer of a business have his attorney review this entire question in advance of formal commitments being
made. As a general rule, the prospective purchaser of a business
should be aware that he probably will, in some way, become involved with the seller's union. The possibility of accommodations
in advance should be considered. It may be more practical and

less expensive in the long run for a purchaser to agree to honor the seller's union contract than to face the prospect of extended litigation.

Certain unions in their collective bargaining agreements set forth in legal terminology that the assignees and successors of the employer will be party to the contract. This further minimizes the possibility of avoiding the union.

The seller of a business who has agreed with the buyer that the latter will take over his labor contract should be careful to see that he is released from liability under it when the new owner accepts responsibility. To this end, an assignment of the contract from the seller to the buyer should be executed with the union joining in.

When a new business entity buys the plant and equipment of another company but does not take over all other assets and liabilities nor keep the same employees, it may successfully assert that it need not observe the existing contract. This position will be strengthened if there is a cessation of operations, if new principals replace the old, if the working force is substantially cut down or added to, and if major aspects of the operations are changed. When such a change takes place, the union may acknowledge that is has no right to remain the bargaining agent, or it may insist that it does. Then, based upon a careful and expert assessment of the facts, the new operators can make an informed judgment whether to go along with the union's claim or fight to support their own position.

Several years ago, "Z," a 50 per cent partner in a concern, formed a new corporation for purposes of buying out some assets of the old business. It was counsel's opinion, after examining all the facts, that Z was truly operating a new enterprise and would be entitled to disregard the collective bargaining contract between the old firm and the union.

"What's the point," Z's assistant said. "The union has the entire industry organized. They will undoubtedly get the company in no time. We might as well take the old contract." This commentator was overlooking several important factors. Concede that the firm would be organized immediately and sign an industry-wide form contract. Assume that the wage and fringe benefits would be the same. Nevertheless, important cost savings and improvements in operation could be effected if the new employer took a strong stand. Several advantages come to mind. First, the new firm would not be bound by the old seniority list. It could hire in employees as it saw fit. It could either hire completely new workers, or rehire and retain some of the old firm's employees with regard to their efficiency, not their longevity. Second, for purposes of computing entitlement to some benefits based on years of service with the company, the slate would be clean. Vacation-time, severance pay, etc., had all been based on the number of months in the company's employ. With the old contract in force, the date of original employment with the old firm would be the determining factor. In the event of a new contract, Z could date longevity from the present. Third, employees would be hired in at the contract minimum rates for new employees; super-standard and "red-circle" rates would be eliminated. After this discussion it was soon apparent to all that the new firm would be wise to take advantage of its full opportunities under the law.

It may seem callous to deprive old workers of these accumulated benefits due to what may be called legal technicalities. But unions will often go along without a fight for good reason. The purchasing partner would only have bought the business if he was assured, in advance, of this "new deal." For the workers, it was either a choice of losing their jobs which paid good money or of forfeiting accrued seniority rights while retaining their employment. Union-management cooperation saved the jobs.

Although the same ownership continues, a drastic change in company operations may warrant a search by the firm's counsel into the possibility that the sweeping realignment of business activities serves to vitiate the existing contracts. These situations are rare. Even in bankruptcy reorganization proceedings the debtor-in-possession must continue to bargain with the incumbent union.

Corporate or business reorganizations that are purposely designed to achieve disengagement from a union will usually fail for that very reason. If the new firm refuses to recognize the union and the case is taken to the Board, that agency will carefully examine the entire situation. Should it find that an anti-union aim predominated in the employer's motivation to change, it will reassert the employer's obligation to bargain with the union.

Subterfuges such as transferring stock to relatives, leasing corporation assets to a "friendly" former employee, setting up "dummy" holding companies, etc., will all be seen through quickly by the investigators and doomed by the Board. The N.L.R.B., in formulating its decisions, will not permit even the fanciest structure of corporate pyramids to eclipse business realities. The goal of the

Government agency is to preserve the bargaining relationship whenever it can, consistent with the law.

This policy of following substance rather than form will prevail when related questions arise. If the management, direction and objectives are the same for separate corporations with similar ownership of stock or for two or more firms with a common holding company acting as parent coporation, the Board may consider them as one entity for labor relations purposes. The test of central control will be applied whenever the operations of two or more businesses are so integrated that they can be deemed to constitute a single enterprise. However, when the businesses are carried on as separate endeavors, although there may be an interrelation of owners, or even a common owner, the businesses will be considered distinct for labor relations purposes.

In all of these situations it is necessary for management to ascertain the applicable law. But this is not enough. The effects of reorganization and transfer of businesses on labor relations cannot be assessed in an ivory-tower resting on a foundation of theory alone. This will create an unbalanced and leaning tower. The decision of management must be formulated in the light of the consequences surrounding its relationship or the cancelling of its relationship with a union. What a company could do to get rid of the union may be legally permissible and yet totally unworkable in practice. Once the company's rights are clear, then an intelligent appraisal of the proper course of action can follow.

30

Subcontracting, Plant Relocation and the Runaway Shop

It is safe to predict that nearly every company's management at one time or another in its relations with a union has wished that it had no union at all. There is neither a magic wand to be waved nor a pre-packaged formula that can be applied to make a union disappear. It is not necessarily true that, once installed, a union can never be disestablished, but in certain industries and geographical areas this often is the case for all practical purposes. In some localities and in particular kinds of businesses there are companies which previously were organized and today are not. This book has discussed different ways to sever relations with a trade-union. Some are legal, expedient and desirable. Others are not.

For certain kinds of businesses, the most direct way to get away from a union is to physically relocate operations. Obviously, this can only be done by companies with produce products or services in plants that can be moved and which are not locally dependent for customers or supplies. Employers in retail trade or communication and transportation, state, county or municipal governments, companies engaged in road-building and general construction or maintenance, operators of hotels and restaurants, management in real estate or entertainment enterprises, certain personal service and distribution industries and many other businesses cannot move the site of their operations. To exist as employers they must remain where they are. Even the companies which could realistically consider moving must take into account a wide variety of factors that would also have a substantial effect on the success or failure of the venture in a new location. These considerations include cost of plant relocation, rents, capital outlay required in a new plant, proximity to sources of supply and markets, freight differentials and costs, psychological adjustment to new areas and a host of other factors.

The actual merits of a decision to move must be carefully weighed. A move to another location is not always the panacea that it appears to be. All the factors noted above must be considered. The prospect of "no union" is, of course, frequently attractive. But management must realize that labor in new areas may not be as productive, or might be unfamiliar with the operation and that a pool of skilled replacements, often channeled via the union, may not be available. Moreover, the new workers may, after a time, themselves become organized and select a union which, from the employer's viewpoint, can be better or worse than the incumbent union. On the other hand, the expected lower wage rates, diminished fringe benefits and greater work loads and productivity may more than counteract any disadvantages. Along with advice from relocation specialists, the company should consider the effect of a move on all facets of its operation including its labor relations. Over and above purely economic factors, it should evaluate the decision to move in the light of the effect it will have on the personal lives of the individuals concerned from highest echelon managers or owners to long-term employees.

Assume that all these aspects of the problem have been considered, and it is decided that relocation is indicated. The method of effecting such a move becomes crucial from a labor relations viewpoint. As the law is presently constituted, a company is permitted to move its plant for certain reasons but will be barred from doing so to accomplish other purposes. A firm which removes its operation from one geographical location to another for the expressed goal of getting away from a union is today termed a "runaway shop," and is precluded from such conduct by the labor law. However, a company which relocates for good business reasons is usually free to do so. In the event of an unfair labor practice charge accusing the employer of runaway shop tactics, the National Labor Relations Board will investigate and render a decision. If it determines that no such allegation can properly be maintained, the company is in the clear insofar as the Government is concerned. But if it finds that, in fact, the company was motivated by a primary desire to evade the union and had no other legitimate or valid purpose for moving, the Board will order remedial action. Compliance by companies with such orders can be extremely costly. The Board can direct a company which has moved to hire the employees who have been left behind, paying their transportation and relocation costs. It can direct the employer to recognize the union from the old site as bargaining representative for employees at the new location. In extreme cases the Board may even order the company to abandon its new plant and actually move back to its original site! It is essential that strenuous efforts must be made by a company envisaging a move to minimize the possibilities of successful assertion that a runaway shop situation exists. A program of precautions can be adopted and the ground work laid to avoid such troubles. The company must be prepared to show sufficient reasons to move which, taken together, would convince an impartial observer that such a step was practical for business reasons without regard to labor relations. For example, comparisons of rent are significant if the company can show it will effect a material saving in the new location. Lower costs of electricity or gas and less local tax liability are persuasive. Demonstrating greater convenience to both customer and supplier will strengthen management's case. In some cases it is proper to point out that there would be economies effected in labor costs. A particular concern may decide to state that other businesses in the same industry have moved first. This tends to prove that economies are truly obtainable. Furthermore, it indicates that the particular firm in question needs to relocate to remain competitive. This technique of showing an industry pattern has been used to the employer's advantage.

In summary, if the company demonstrates that because of the relocation its business is on a sounder economic basis, it improves its opportunity to refute the accusations. Recent N.L.R.B. decisions suggest that an employer's right to relocate may be more qualified in the future. It would now appear that the safest course for a company contemplating a move is to bargain with its union on this subject. The company should discuss its need to move and allow the union the chance to convince it to the contrary. If this fails, it should bargain with the union about the consequences of the move to the workers. The company may have to offer employment at the new site to its workers. It may agree to pay moving expense or severance pay or to help employees get new jobs. It can even assent to continue to bargain with the union at the new location or to consider the old contract still in force there.

The technical aspects of the employer's defense to runaway shop charges can be managed in three ways. First, in advance of the move it may be worthwhile for the company to institute a program of informing its workers and the community that such action is being contemplated for economic reasons. This should not be done as a bluff. Obviously it will adversely affect morale, employee relations and often community relations. There is no point running this gauntlet for nothing. The actual technique of advising the community and employees and particularly the decision as to the timing of such announcements, require consummate judgment. Generalities about the correct approach do not apply since the program must be custom-tailored to meet actual circumstances.

Second, the company should desist from making any threats that it will move because of unionization or the union's activity. If the threats alone, unaccompanied by action, are brought to the Board, it may well find an unfair labor practice, announce that the company's conduct has been unlawful, and order it to desist from further uttering such threats. Moreover, if the plant later is moved, the threats coupled with subsequent action will weaken the company's ability to successfully deny the indictment of a runaway shop.

Third, before planning a move and after the move has taken place the company should prepare and retain the necessary documentary evidence that will enable it to establish the economic benefits of the relocation in the event of an investigation. This should be done systematically by the company's comptroller or accountants.

This discussion of plant relocation has been predicated on the assumption that there are no applicable provisions in the collective bargaining agreement between the union and the company. If such clauses exist, however, they will be controlling. Many contracts now contain a "no moving" clause which prevents the employer from operating his plant outside of a certain radius from a named central point (for example, "twenty-five miles from Times Square, New York City") or from moving outside of city or county lines. If an employer contemplates even the slighted possibility of an ultimate relocation he should resist these clauses vigorously. Once such a provision is incorporated into a contract, violation of it by an employer may produce ruinous consequences. Generally the union has several lines of recourse when such a breach of contract occurs. It may, if there is an arbitration clause, appeal to the arbitrator for redress.

An arbitrator can direct that a plant be moved back to its original site. Moreover, there is little reluctance to award damages. On the contrary, the employer is often ordered to pay large sums in compensation. An equally fruitful alternative for the union is to sue for damages. Recently a court awarded a union the equivalent of twenty years of union dues. It ordered the company to pay this when the union pointed out that the company, in breaking its "no moving" agreement, terminated workers' jobs and thus their ability to pay dues, resulting in loss to the union. One arbitration decision held, with court approval, that labor-management contract clauses requiring consultation with the union on subcontracting of work and certain aspects of seniority rights are sufficient to prevent the unilateral action of a company in moving its plant. This theory may be adopted as a precedent and influence future arbitrations.

Certain unions are particularly sensitive because of previous loss of large numbers of members due to plant relocation and will apply increasing pressure to penalize companies which make such moves. It is my opinion, based on recent court decisions and arbitrator's awards, that the trend is against management. As evidence of this direction, a word should be added about a relatively recent Supreme Court decision involving the obligations of a company to its unionized employees where the company moved its plant after its contract with the union expired. The high Court stated that the seniority rights of the workers survived even the expiration of the contract and that the company could not simply move away free of commitments to these employees. At an earlier time, lawyers could advise a company that it could move with impunity once a contract terminated. Today there is some doubt. Prudent counsel is not inclined to categorically state that mere termination of the prevailing agreement allows the company full freedom of movement.

There appears to be emerging a theory endorsed by some courts that a collective bargaining contract is unlike other contracts. The rationale is that most contracts deal with property, whereas labor agreements concern the well being of many human lives. Therefore, while the courts may hold other contracting parties to the written words of their contract, they may go further in labor litigation matters and consider the intentions of the parties more closely and, in fact, the effect that their judicial decisions would have on the future of the employees and their families. How great an acceptance this theory will gain remains to be seen in the future.

Still other management prerogatives in this area are being more tightly circumscribed. When an employer terminates even a segment of his business because of his workers' union activities and not for economic reasons, he is deemed to be violating the law. If the Board finds that one of a company's facilities or operations was closed down because of management's animus towards a union it may, if reasonable, direct reinstatement of the terminated activity. Or, if the shut-down is only partial, it may direct that the laid-off employees be reinstated in other capacities. A manufacturing company was accused of trying to avoid a collective bargaining contract for its drivers by selling its trucking operations and contracting this work out. The government held that the employer had unfairly discontinued this operation and directed him to resume trucking with his own employees, ordering him to rehire the employees he had let go and give them back pay as well. Arbitrators, in the absence of clauses prohibiting subcontracting, will probably hit the employer if anti-union motivation is suspected.

Obviously there is no black and white, no simple test to be applied to determine if motivation was good—that is, for economic betterment—or bad—namely, to dump the union. Any judgment of this nature must necessarily be subjective, and the entire flavor of the company's attitude will be weighed. Any one of many small, apparently unrelated actions or utterances could tip these delicate scales.

Now let us consider the matter of subcontracting when there is no anit-union bias involved, and no contract clause prohibiting subcontracting. An employer's right to subcontract work was for many years unconditional. Over the past several years, government rulings and arbitrators' decisions clearly indicate that this management freedom is being limited. Only when a firm's labor-management agreement specifically says subcontracting is within management's prerogative will problems be definitely precluded.

In a 1962 decision, the N.L.R.B. held that an employer must give his union notice and the opportunity to bargain on subcontracting, transfer, leasing or termination of operations in the unit. The employer was held to a duty to explain to the union the reasons for his actions and bargain with the union about his planned changes. By the same token, it was determined that a company could not unilaterally change work loads, absent provisions expressly permitting this; and that it must bargain with a union on such topics.

In effect, the Board said that when jobs within the bargaining unit are to be permanently eliminated, it is the obligation of the employer to bargain with the union. Moreover, the bargaining should be meaningful and not merely announcement of an immovable position. Even if a union requested wording restricting subcontracting at negotiating time and was unable to win such a clause, the employer is not relieved of the duty to bargain.

This Board view was affirmed by the United States Supreme Court in 1964 in the *Fibreboard* case. This court held that management had a duty to bargain with the exclusive collective bargaining representative of its employees concerning its decision to subcontract. If the work subcontracted was never in the control of the union's members, this decision probably would not apply, i.e. if the employer transferred his plumbing maintenance work from one concern to another. Similarly, if the subcontracting of a type of work was a well established past practice or if the work given to outsiders was of no significant amount, this requirement to bargain would be waived. But, it would now seem that where the subcontracting will produce effects of significant detriment to the employees in the unit, the employer must bargain on this. The Supreme Court, in its decision, weighed the employer's freedom to manage his business and protect his capital against the duty to bargain and the worker's right to his job. This probably will be the test applied in other situations besides subcontracting such as mergers or sales of businesses. Many decisions will most likely be made on a case by case basis with the fact situation in each individual instance controlling.

In view of these developments, it is apparent that arbitrators, too, will abridge the company's right to farm out work previously done by its own employees. If a company used to do maintenance and cleaning work around the plant with its own plumbers, electricians, painters, masons, carpenters and porters and decided to subcontract all of this to outside contractors, it would then permanently layoff all of the employees it had who did this work. The union, instead of filing an unfair labor practice charging refusal to bargain on this issue, may, if the contract has a general grievance arbitration clause, appeal this matter to an impartial arbitrator. Such arbitrator almost undoubtedly would rule that the company had an obligation to bargain with the union on its decision in view of the Federal case law. Indeed, the arbitrator conceivably might go further and hold that the company had no right to eradicate the jobs in the unit, and might direct that the company cease subcontracting and rehire the workers. The wording of the recognition clause, that defines what classes of workers were in the bargaining unit which the union represents, might be particularly significant here. The company should evaluate contract wording, particularly as regards the scope and function of the bargaining unit, in the light of this trend of current rulings on subcontracting problems.

Extreme caution must be taken by management and its advisors to be current on court decisions, Board holdings and arbitrators' awards. This area of labor law is developing quite swiftly, and accurate knowledge will be essential to assess the situation intelligently and thus protect management from being hurt.

SECTION VIII

Practical Handling of Key Problems

Cooperation with Other Employers

Wage and Hour Regulations

Keeping Informed:
Sources of Information and Legal Requirements

Choosing a Labor Relations Advisor

31

Cooperation
with Other Employers

Companies with common problems often combine into associations for purposes of pooling their resources more effectively and dealing with challenges more efficiently. The association may include firms in one industry which operate in a certain geographic area, or it may seek to enlist all competitive firms within the boundaries of the United States. Often business groups open membership to all firms in a given city, county or state regardless of the nature of their enterprises. Some associations of the former type exist specifically to deal with the labor problems of their members, while others engage in a full line of trade association activity and have only partial concern with labor matters. Local employer councils generally take positions on many matters affecting business, including labor relations issues.

The typical trade association, active in the labor relations field, consists of a group of firms engaged in the same kind of business, organized on a local or national basis. The association is supported most often by dues levied on its members. It may have a paid staff ranging from a single employee serving as an executive secretary and general manager to a full complement of specialists working under division chiefs responsible to its executive vice president or other administrator. Smaller associations may operate without any full-time employees. The association may provide a variety of services for its members including technical advice, promotion assistance, research, public relations, the collection, correlation and dissemination of credit information, newsletter or book publication, liaison with Government agencies and advice on labor relations.

When a collective bargaining agreement is being negotiated, the union negotiates with the association which, as a "union" of employers, acts as management's agent, just as the labor union acts for its members. The individual member firms select certain of their executives to form the steering committee that works with the association's employed labor relations counselor or attorney. The employers' committee fulfills the same function as the individual firm's negotiating team in single-company bargaining. In smaller associations, a top executive from each member company may serve on the committee and participate in dealings with the union.

The association can negotiate in either of two major ways. First, it may bargain for a uniform contract to which all member employers agree in advance to be bound. Thus the association itself can actually execute the agreement and list the member firms which are included therein. Firms agreeing in advance to be bound by the contract agreed upon may often be requested to submit a power of attorney before negotiations commence or to make other promises that they will abide by the settlement adopted by the group. In this type of association bargaining, the union will almost always seek to know, before negotiating, which companies will be party to the agreement.

Second, the association may negotiate a contract which is, in effect, a form agreement, without previously committing its members. It then recommends to its constituent firms that they individually sign their copy of this master contract. Under this system the individual company retains greater autonomy and independence of action.

An association is only as strong as its members are united. To ensure that a weak link will not damage the entire chain, employer associations often try to forge a covenant among all enrolled firms that they will only sign a labor contract which the majority accepts, and that they will take a strike if the associations' bargainers choose that course of action. The legal enforceability of such compacts will depend on the wording selected and the law of the state in which it is constructed or contested. As a practical matter, employer groups are often reluctant to sue one of their members who drops by the wayside.

Association leaders and counsel should consider hybrid variations of the typical employers' pact in the light of the needs of their membership and the prevailing law. For example, in one association where an active minority of employers wished to take a tougher stand than they felt the majority was prepared to accept, a particularly suitable form of pledge was adopted. All firms agreed to give the union no more favorable terms than were negotiated in the master contract. But any company which felt the association gave too much away had the right reserved to hold out and press for a less costly settlement. With the adoption of this wording, the association's leaders avoided splinter-group action.

In the event of an impasse in bargaining, the employers' association will continue to direct strategy for the combined companies. Stalemated companies which have collaborated for bargaining purposes are permitted to take concerted action for their own protection, particularly when the union tries to pick off the companies one by one. The union technique of chipping away at the softest companies can often have devastating effects on all the associated businesses. When the dead-end at negotiations occurs, the union may decide to strike only one company while its members continue to work for the other firms. This tactic, called "whipsawing," obviously puts the firm which is singled out to be struck at a distinct disadvantage. Competitors continue to operate, but it does not. As a frequent consequence, the company is unable to stand the pressure and will buckle and sign with the union. The union is then free to move on to the next lamb it selects for the slaughter—and so on until it defeats all its opponents. The law allows companies in this situation to band together for their self-preservation. In the face of selective striking, all the companies may close down and cease operations until the labor-management conflict is resolved. Shutdowns for the purpose of breaking the union are deemed to be illegal. But when the lockout action is taken for defensive purposes, it is allowed. Thus, all members of the employers' federation may pledge to close in the event that any one of them is struck.

However, the Labor Board patrols carefully in this territory of concerted employer action. Five food-market companies, members of a multi-employer bargaining association, found one of their members struck by a local of the Retail Clerks International Association. The unstruck quartet, which also employed members of this local, locked out their employees, but instead of shutting down, they continued to operate with temporary replacements. The National Labor Relations Board ruled that such action was retaliatory, not defensive, and as such, exceeded the permitted boundaries. The struck company could have operated with substitutes for the strikers and still be within its rights in disputing its workers' claims. Or all companies could have closed down and laid off their workers, which would be deemed a proper defensive measure to protect the integrity of the multi-employer unit. The Board decision was three-to-two with the minority dissenters upholding the action of the employers. Subsequent to this ruling of the Board, the U.S. Supreme Court held in 1965 that operation was temporary replacements and lockout of regular employees *was* a proper defensive measure and was not unlawful. The Labor Board has followed this ruling. This closely split board decision and the opposite conclusion reached by the court, also not unanimously, demonstrates the delicate balance of labor-management rights and suggests how impermanent are some areas of labor law.

There are other methods whereby members of an employer's league collaborate to support each other in the face of union attack. For example, several large companies in the airline industry have organized a "strike insurance" pool. The struck firm is subsidized by its competitors which keep running so that any profit the operating companies may make at the expense of their deactivated competitor is, in effect, shared with that afflicted concern. Moreover, this pool shores up the struck outfit so that it can more strongly resist the union's pressure. Sometimes an employer who has not been struck will permit a struck company to use his facilities.

When there is no strike or impasse and no negotiating, the employer association's labor specialists can still render substantial services to its members. They can advise the employers' association on policy and labor relations techniques. The association acts as a clearing house for information on arbitrators' awards and grievance settlements. As spokesman for the group, it may prosecute arbitration of disputes which concern all members. It will apprise associated firms of events in the field of labor law which effect their prerogatives as employers and appraise these developments.

The advantages of a multi-employer association are several. First, an opportunity is provided for small companies to band together and obtain talented professional guidance. Individual firms which could not alone afford to retain specialized attorneys and employ researchers, public relations consultants, arbitrators, labor relations advisors, statisticians and other staff personnel necessary to do an effective job can, by joint contributions, enjoy these services. Second, the weaker companies are often shored up by an association's unifying influence. Without an association, they might capitulate to union demands, leaving isolated companies to fight alone while competitors are working. In unity there is strength. A union can afford to support a strike at one plant while the majority of its membership is working. But if all of the local members or a significant segment of them are faced with the prospect of a strike, the union may be more inclined to accept a reasonable settlement. Thus the association bolsters the bargaining strength of its members. The combined financial resources of the companies can approach the economic strength of the union whereas the individual firms may be dwarfed by it. Third, industry conditions are uniform as to manpower expenses when there is a master contract. This stabilization of wage costs and elimination of favored treatment for some firms is frequently helpful in keeping the competitive situation sound. Fourth, if there is a strike, all firms act in unison and one cannot derive advantage and strength from the misery of another. Whipsawing can be prevented. Fifth, the individual firms may turn to a central point for advice and guidance in administering their contract and will probably be assured of fair and equal treatment by the union during the contract.

There are, of course, certain disadvantages when employers associate for the purpose of joint bargaining. Individual business entities must necessarily relinquish some of the control over their own destiny. Strong and weak firms are thrown together, and a common denominator must be found. Often, in this area of compromise, the stronger firms find that they are pushed into more liberal contract settlements due to pressure from weak firms which cannot afford to resist the union. An individual company which alone could exert economic strength to force its workers to settle on its terms may be precluded from doing so in multi-employer negotiations. A solid front of all member firms may be hard to achieve, and broken ranks can easily result in a route in which the companies which stand fast are left alone and exposed.

Still another drawback of these employers' common fronts is that in the negotiations many individual company problems get lost. Although important to a particular company, such items may be comparatively insignificant in the over-all picture. And there is always the problem of the independent, unaffiliated company. This maverick often hangs back, letting the association bargain, and then signs the same contract. This way it gets a "free ride," trading on group efforts without contributing to them. Moreover, if the independents work when the association members strike, they can effectively vitiate the concerted action. An association generally cannot long survive when there are many potential members remaining outside its ranks.

Unions frequently do not resist the functioning of employer associations. Labor often realizes that such combinations of competing firms can bring a pattern of stability to what may otherwise be a chaotic industry. Moreover, associations generally ensure that union leaders will deal with professional and seasoned counterparts and they will be spared the vagaries and day-to-day difficulties of negotiating with amateurs. An association can save labor leaders much time and trouble both at the negotiation and after it. There is one expiration date, one agreement to hammer out and one final contract to administer instead of dozens, scores or hundreds of documents with divergent provisions and scattered termination dates. Often union organizers figure that the weak or pro-union companies will be a moderating force on the strong or anti-union firms which, independently, would be impregnable. Some unions, moreover, may cherish the idea that in the event of a stalemate they can always try to sign up some companies and thereby fragment the association and fracture its effectiveness for a time, if not permanently.

An employers' association is only as capable as its staff. The considerations discussed in Chapter 34, *Choosing a Labor Relations Advisor,* are completely pertinent here. The leaders of the association must be diplomatic too, ensuring that the right of expression is granted to all firms. It falls to these spokesmen to reconcile the various segments of an industry, and knit together the employers who seek peace at any price and those who want a fight for its own sake. Pre-negotiation conferences must serve as a crucible, and association officers and counselors as catalysts to achieve a common ground on which all member firms can be rallied.

While applicable circumstances must control each particular case, it is a safe generalization to say that affiliation with an employer association should usually be considered favorably provided that the leadership, staff, advisors and attorneys of the association are men of ability, competence and integrity. The ultimate criterion for a unionized company, faced with the choice of joining an association, is a simple one: unless there is reason to believe that it can do better outside the association than in it, the company should almost always sign up.

This conclusion is based, in part, on the structure of our economy. Unions are large organizations, usually straddling state lines, transcending individual companies and even particular industries or trades. They are generally unaffected by anti-monopoly laws. Often the only antidote to this massive power is countervailing strength which can achieve a balance. Excepting a few dozen industrial giants, individual companies are not capable of generating this strength. A combination of companies, therefore, may be an alternative to living on borrowed time, or dying.

Companies which are already unionized may seek to join the association in their field if one exists. If there is none, several companies should carefully consider forming such a trade association. Where a particular company has a union different from the union representing most competitors who are or will be in the association, particular problems arise which must be assessed.

When a company has not yet been organized by a union, there are some additional points for it to consider in connection with association affiliation. If most of the industry is already unionized and in an association, the company has two alternatives. It can join the association and plan not to resist the advent of unionization when and if it comes, taking solace in the fact that it will at least ultimately have the same contract and conditions as its competitors. Or it may conclude that unionization is contagious and shun the association like the plague in the belief that this isolation will improve its chances of avoiding a union.

Even when most companies in an industry are not unionized, there are still benefits to be derived from joining an employer organization or cooperating in the formation of one. Standing together, the firms may be better able to hold off the advent of unionism. Moreover, if they act in concert for labor purposes before being unionized, they may, under certain circumstances, engender a situation where the entire group of firms in the area or industry will be eventually considered by the Board as one appropriate bargaining unit. This can be advantageous.

Once in an employer association for bargaining purposes, the individual company is not free to withdraw at will if its so doing can be deemed an evasion of the duty of bargain. If a firm agrees in January to be part of a multi-employer bargaining unit, takes part in negotiations, and then on March 28th, 72 hours before contract expiration, repudiates the negotiations and says it will not be bound by the agreement reached, it may be found to have breached its obligation to bargain in good faith. And the Labor Board did not allow an employer to withdraw from a multi-company bargaining unit when this attempted disassociation took place after filing of an election petition by a union. The Board did not wish to encourage fragmenting of the unit which was an appropriate one when the petition was filed.

The withdrawal from an association must occur at an appropriate time. It is indicated that such a time may be in the course of a contract, provided the employer remains bound for its term. Thus, he is only saying he will not partake as a party in the next joint negotiations. Similarly, if a contract has expired and no negotiations for a new one are in progress, the withdrawal may be timely. The company's obligation to bargain is not lightly dispensed with. The right to withdraw and the timeliness of such action will depend on the history of joint bargaining in the industry and other factors. Care must be taken to ensure that withdrawal is at the right time, and consequently, lawful.

There is much room for cooperation among employers short of a formal association. Before and after unionization, one company's executives may have much to gain if they consult with their opposite numbers in another company. Often when a firm is in the midst of a union organizing drive executives or counsel will talk to employers who already have recognized the union and obtain much valuable information. At negotiating time it is frequently important to know what provisions competitors have in their contracts and what their wage rates are. During the term of the contract, an exchange of views and information on work rules, arbitration decisions and common problems is beneficial.

Naturally such collaboration is a two-way street. The employer who wants to get information should be prepared to give it. This is sometimes a hard concept for a businessman to accept. He may ask, "Why help a competitor?" Obviously, if he feels the competitor is a greater threat to him—both long- and short-term—than the union, no argument can be persuasively advanced that he cooperate. But if the company itself will some day want reciprocating favors from another concern, it should hesitate before turning down requests to confer with other employers. In brief, each company must decide just how far it will go in supplying information, sympathy and succor to kindred companies. Disclosing confidential matters, engaging in illegal collusion, or aiding a vicious or unscrupulous competitor is obviously wrong. On the other hand, refusing to cooperate at all often reaps only ill-will. A sensible middle-course should be followed.

Insofar as cooperation among employers on labor relations problems can promote management's attainment of its goals, this should be always considered and often pursued.

32

Wage and

Hour Regulations

"Wage and Hour" legislation is the government-imposed regulation of the arrangements between the employer and his employees. The law rejects the concept that even mature, healthy persons engaged in non-hazardous pursuits may set their own terms of hire independent of some supervision. Far less does it accept the proposition that children, women, or those engaged in dangerous or health-menacing work may so contract. The parties can agree between themselves on working conditions provided that the terms are at least as favorable to the employee as certain prescribed minimum standards.

This doctrine of governmental supervision pre-dates the New Deal, the Welfare State, and even the Christian era. It has its foundation in the precepts of the early Hebrews who declared that their religion required that the toiler must rest on the Seventh Day. The limitation of work hours came to be accepted by the Christian world in the reign of the Emperor Constantine. Early in the development of English Common Law, from which American jurisprudence developed, when the parties were still called "master" and "servant," a body of law grew up defining their respective rights. Through the court's application of precedent, the protection of the laborer slowly grew. Royal decrees pre-dating the reign of Queen Elizabeth I in England set forth prescribed hours of labor for all workers. In the United States, the Federal Government, during the Presidency of Martin Van Buren, directed a ten-hour day for its employees, and twenty-eight years later this was reduced by two hours to eight. In laws regulating private employment, however, the National Government only recently overtook the individual states. In 1875, Massachusetts legislated a ten-hour working day for women; and Illinois, in 1895, trimmed this to eight. Before the start of the First World War, child labor, particularly north of the Mason-Dixon line, was limited to eight or nine hours daily. And for many years both in this country and abroad other aspects of the employment relationship were subject to government regulations.

Wage and Hour legislation, enacted both by the Federal Government and individual states has gradually raised the minimum guarantees which the employer must afford his employee. Moreover, the entire trend of history in this nation indicates that there will be increasing regulation and that these provisions will continue to enlarge the employee's legal rights and protection.

Supplementing government doctrines, organized labor seeks, through its economic power, to broaden worker's benefits by shortening the work week, raising pay rates and ensuring other advantages. In fact, government action often consolidates the gains which labor has already made for large segments of its membership. It compels legal recognition of what may already be the bargained-for rights of many groups of employees. Legal requirements are only the "floor" and never the "ceiling" of union demands in collective bargaining negotiations. Nevertheless, it behooves management's negotiators to be particularly conversant with statutory requirements. This is important for bargaining purposes and also to ensure compliance with laws and regulations, thus precluding the consequences attending violation.

One of the two most important provisions of that body of regulations known collectively as the "Wage and Hour Laws," is the forty-hour work week. It is provided that any employee who works in excess of forty hours in any given week will be compensated at one and one-half times his regular pay. This "time-and-a-half for overtime" means that a worker who is paid $2.00 per hour for the first forty hours in a week must get $3.00 for each hour worked over forty hours. Consequently, for forty hours he will get $80.00 weekly, for forty-five hours, $95.00 per week, and $110.00 for a fifty-hour week. Many labor-management contracts are more liberal in their premium pay provisions. Some agreements, after an exercise in simple arithmetic that involves dividing forty hours by five days, provide for time-and-a half pay after eight hours in any one given day. Thus the employee may only work a forty-hour week but still receive premium pay. Such clauses are negotiated and are not imposed by law. The law regards the week as a complete unit for computation purposes. While it does not require "daily" overtime, the law prohibits the employer from averaging weeks. If an employee works thirty hours the first week and fifty the next, the employer cannot deny him overtime and must, in the latter week, pay for ten hours at 150 per cent of the hourly rate.

Employers often ask if the overtime provisions do not mean that an employee can be required—if properly compensated—to work more than forty hours in a week. Particularly in union shops, if arrangements are not made in advance of employment whereby the employer explains that certain long hours will be a condition of employment, it may prove difficult to consistently compel an employee to work more than forty hours a week. However, there have been decisions permitting employers to discipline employees for refusing to work overtime, particularly in emergency circumstances or where refusal to work overtime amounts to insubordination or flagrantly disloyal conduct.

Employers can and should arrange to insert in their collective bargaining contract a clause providing that the union will not unreasonably withhold its consent to the employer's request for overtime. Thus, although individual workers may occasionally refuse such work, the possibility of the union's utilization of a denial of overtime as an economic weapon is minimized.

The second major section of the Federal laws affecting wages and hours is the minimum hourly pay requirement. Such enactments are based on the theory that it is the Government's responsibility to ensure a minimum standard of living for its citizens. It aims to see that they are reasonably contented and able to obtain and maintain certain physical standards of health and well-being. Moreover, the minimum wage assures a necessary volume of purchasing power in that it directly endeavors to balance consumption ability with production ability; and indirectly creates sufficient leisure time to encourage that consumption. The Federal minimum wage, applicable to certain persons employed in interstate commerce, was first enacted in 1938 and was twenty-five cents per hour. It remained at seventy-five cents per hour for many years, and more recently $1.00 an hour. In 1961, new legislation was enacted Congress and signed into law by the President. For those persons covered by previous minimum wage legislation the minimum was raised to $1.15 per hour in September, 1961, and effective September 3, 1963, it was put at $1.25 per hour. Additionally, coverage of the provisions of the Act was extended to workers in interstate commerce not heretofore included. As it affected those people not previously covered, the increases were more gradual and the $1.25 figure was achieved at a later time. A $1.00 minimum for these newly-covered individuals was established to prevail until September 3, 1964, when a step increase of fifteen cents per hour was mandatory. One year later, on September 3, 1965, the minimum rate was raised to $1.25 for these workers also. Legislation boosting the minimum from $1.25 per hour was proposed during the last session of Congress. On September 23, 1966 President Johnson signed into law a two step raise in the minimum wage. Effective February 1, 1967 it is $1.40 per hour and on February 1, 1968 will be increased to $1.60 per hour. Moreover, eight million workers who were not covered by any minimum wage before will be included for the first time. For these employees of some stores, farms, hospitals, hotels, restaurants and laundries, the minimum wage will be $1.00 per hour on February 1, 1967 rising eventually to the $1.60 figure by 1971.

States have parallel laws covering their residents. In 1962, four states—Hawaii, Massachusetts, New York and Rhode Island—increased their minimum to $1.15 per hour with provisions for increases to $1.25 by 1963 or 1964. Today, these states plus Connecticut and the State of Washington all have at least a $1.25 minimum wage. In Massachusetts, the minimum wage for those in certain covered categories was raised to $1.35 on September 5, 1966. And, in New York State the minimum is $1.50 per hour effective January 1, 1967, and will be further increased to $1.60 per hour when the U.S. rate is raised to that figure. Alaska legislated a minimum wage law pegged at "50c an hour greater than the prevailing Federal minimum wage law." Altogether, twenty-five states have minimum wage legislation. These laws supplement the Federal acts and include those workers within the state borders who are not covered by the Federal law. Moreover, where a state minimum is higher than a Federal minimum, the former will prevail even for those individuals covered by Federal law.

In the fall of 1962, New York City, as an example of municipal action in this field, passed a $1.25 minimum hourly wage with provision for an increase to $1.50 in one year. By a four to three decision rendered in early 1963, New York State's highest court voided this law. However, the future may bring further municipal action, and such laws may well be valid if state legislatures grant the cities permission to enact them.

In labor negotiations, unions will almost always attempt to lift contract rates above legal minimums. Partially this is because they believe the statutory rates are enough only for the bare necessities of existence and do not provide an adequate living. But they also make this endeavor because a contract settlement at minimum rates is hard to sell to the rank-and-file. "Who needs a union for that?" it is asked. And a minimum settlement smacks of an illicit sweetheart contract arrangement.

While minimum wage legislation certainly influences the cost of doing business, its consequences may be particularly significant to a company in a certain state or region. The chairman of an employer's industry-wide negotiating committee in New York was recently discussing certain so-called "welfare state" legislation with a fellow employer in the mid 1960's. The chairman stated that in his view he and all of their member employers should vigorously support such Congressional action.

"As a humanitarian, or a liberal, or an altruist, maybe I should," was the rejoinder, "but as a businessman, never."

"On the contrary," the chairman explained. "I am making my suggestion purely on the basis of our economic self-interest, yours and mine. We have a contract minimum rate with the union well above the legal floor. Our Southern competition does not. A nationwide increase in minimums can only narrow the gap and diminish their competitive advantage based on present lower labor rates."

"I certainly hope," he continued, "that at the next session, Congress will pass the Medicare bill providing medical care for the aged, based on mandatory employer contributions." He noted that the Northern employers in the industry presently paid for hospital and medical insurance while Southern competitors did not.

"We can't get away from these obligations," he concluded. "Let's see that our Southern friends have to carry an equal load."

This is an interesting approach to the question of Government regulation and should be considered in connection with the last chapter of this book.

Equally essential as the employer's comprehension of the minimum wage and hour requirements is his knowledge of the exceptions to these rules. There is a vast and intricate body of law and regulation aimed at exempting certain industries and specific kinds of workers from coverage. Familiarity with these exemptions can save the company money. Employees of federal, state and local governments are completely excluded from coverage. Of key significance are the tables of partial exemptions. Minimum wage requirements do not apply to learners, apprentices, messengers, the handicapped, students and residents of certain island territories not part of the continental United States. Employers may legally pay "subminimum" wages to such persons. Moreover, there are exceptions in the coverage of the law that may be applicable to certain specific industries such as small farms. In order to pay a subminimum wage to certain classes of employees, industries must have public hearings and receive certificates of exemption. The proceedings are before Federal examiners and very often are like a trial, with unions, public groups, and employer associations expressing their opinions on the exemption.

Managerial, supervisory and professional employees are all exempted from the provisions of the law requiring overtime after forty hours per week. But the actual definitions of "executive," "administrative" or "professional" employees are highly technical. Both the salary they earn and the nature of their duties figure in such determinations. Aid in these decisions can often be obtained from local offices of the Wage and Hour Administration or by communicating with the Washington office of the Administration which has published some clearly-written guides. If these employees in question are deemed exempt, the company will not have to comply with wage and hour rules. Retention of such key employees is obviously a major management problem, but it is relevant here only insofar as high-calibre, well-satisfied and stable executive personnel can favorably affect a company's labor relations. The employer may seek advice about senior personnel management, salary evaluation and executive compensation. He should consult with his attorney concerning employment contracts, stock options, profit-sharing or pension plans for executives and allied programs designed to attract and retain executive personnel.

There are particularly detailed government regulations covering child labor. Child labor laws set minimum employable ages depending on the type of work involved. If conditions are deemed oppressive, the products so made will be labeled "hot goods" and may be banned from shipment in interstate commerce for thirty days.

Child labor is stringently regulated by various states, and these laws should be reviewed in detail by the employer engaging in or contemplating the hiring of minors.

In summary, the entire body of laws embracing minimum wage and hour regulation, child labor, fair employment practices, rules concerning homework, convict labor, and health and safety matters, must be familiar to the employers that are affected. The major statute called the Fair Labor Standards Act, is of general importance. Other laws may also apply.

Violations of the Federal wage and hour laws can result in a private suit for wages by the employee who is sometimes compensated with double pay and reimbursement of costs. Violators may incur injunctions prohibiting continued violation, governmental administrative action and, in aggravated cases, criminal penalties. Companies doing business with the Government that violate the law may be placed on a blacklist which will bar them from further Government contracts.

Breaking the law, even though through ignorance rather than intent, can be costly. For example, the Federal Government has ruled that overtime rates are based on total compensation. If a bonus is paid as a result of a collective bargaining agreement or a promise made in advance by the company, it may be considered compensation. The amount of the bonus will be divided into the hours worked and result in upping the base hourly rate accordingly. When overtime is computed, it must be figured on this "swollen" hourly rate. The company which fails to do this is violating the law and can be penalized. A well-meaning but unlearned employer announces in April that business is good. He posts a notice committing the company to give $200 bonuses the following March 30th to all workers. He exhorts them to maintain high production in the forthcoming year to "earn" the bonus. Assuming 2,000 annual working hours, he may be, in effect, increasing the hourly base rate by ten cents per hour. Overtime pay then becomes 150 per cent of the straight hourly pay *plus* the fifteen cents which represents one and a half times the bonus pay, pro-rated to hours. The company may, as a result, be directed to add fifteen cents per hour to the overtime pay which has been paid to all the workers. This sanction will be retroactive. Clearly such a consequence was not anticipated by this generous but uninformed employer when he promised bonuses.

An error like this can be avoided with knowledge. To preclude this kind of retroactive assessment, commitment to a bonus should be avoided in a collective bargaining contract or elsewhere. If the employer grants a bonus which is strictly discretionary (a gift), or if the bonus is computed as a percentage of wages, both straight time and overtime, the company will not run afoul of the Fair Labor Standards Act. Certain welfare or profit-sharing plans can similarly endanger the employer, and care must be taken to avoid this.

To enable enforcement of its provisions, the Act requires certain other conduct by companies which it covers. Employers subject to the F.L.S.A. must maintain and preserve certain records. In most cases it is safe to regard three years as the required period, although in certain instances it may be different. Moreover, the company must post, in a conspicuous place, a document informing the workers of their rights.

A new enterprise should seek clarification of Federal and state laws which may be applicable. And an established business must be sure that it is always current and in full compliance with the laws.

33

Keeping Informed:
Sources of Information
and Legal Requirements

The successful practice of labor relations requires skill and practical experience in dealing with people, both rank-and-file employees and leaders of the labor movement. It is also absolutely necessary that those directing labor relations for the employer be fully conversant with existing laws. Lack of this knowledge and resultant flouting of the law can precipitate successful charges of unfair labor practices against the employer and may result in very serious consequences for the company itself and for its individual officers personally. Many of the laws in the field of labor relations actually have teeth (some say fangs), so that violation may result in penalties of a criminal nature being imposed against individuals. Every single employer who employs one or more people is directly affected by sets of laws made by our three major levels of government.

First, there are the Federal laws made by the Congress of the United States that will affect those firms—the majority in terms of employees, capital and influence—which are subject to Federal jurisdiction because they engage in interstate commerce. Second, there are statutes made by the separate states which affect the status of various companies. Third, are municipal, county or other local requirements or ordinances which can be of extreme significance in shaping the conduct of a business.

Federal labor law can best be discussed in terms of three sub-
divisions. There are those laws enacted by Congress which form
the main stream of labor legislation in the U. S., and are the key-
stones on which labor-management relationships are based. Among
these are the Norris-LaGuardia Act, known as "The Anti-Injunction Act;" the anti-trust laws, both the Sherman Act and the
Clayton Act which exempt almost all union activity from their anti-
monopoly provisions, the National Labor Relations Act known as
the Wagner Act, the Labor Management Relations Act, called the
Taft-Hartley Law, the Labor Management Reporting and Disclosure Act of 1959 popularly described as the Landrum-Griffin
Act, and finally the Welfare and Pension Plan Disclosure Act and
the amendments thereto. It is from some of these acts that the
National Labor Relations Board derives its authority to administer
the prevailing labor relations law. The Federal courts of the United
States render their decisions interpreting these laws, and other
governmental authorities, such as the U. S. Department of Labor,
derive some of their authority from such statutes.

Next, there are what may be termed the "ancillary" Federal
laws. These are laws that may not be of prime importance to the
entire collective bargaining process, but which nevertheless, in one
respect or another, can materially bear on some aspects of an employer's conduct of his business. For example, in this category
there is the Hobbs Act, known as the Anti-Racketeering Act, which
was designed to curb extortionist activities in the field of labor
relations. There are the Veterans' Re-Employment Acts. These are
significant since they may relate to contract negotiations and because the employer must follow their provisions. There is the
Byrnes Act which relates to the interstate transportation of strike-
breakers. There are laws concerning the jurisdiction of the Federal
District Courts, the administrative procedure of certain agencies,
and the United States Arbitration Act. Of extreme significance in
this group of "ancillary" Federal laws are the revenue provisions
affecting collection of withholding tax and social security. There
are statutes governing the control of subversive activities which at
certain points relate to labor relations. And there are the important Wage and Hour provisions and child labor laws which are
discussed in Chapter 32 of this book. A recent addition to these
laws is the Equal Employment Opportunity Act, which is treated
in Chapter 35.

Finally, there are those Federal laws which can best be characterized as specialized. These laws relate not to all industries or commerce uniformly, but to certain specific businesses in our economy. Insofar as labor-management relations in these particular industries are involved, these acts are of central importance. In the category of these so-called "specialized" laws are those statutes relating to firms which do business with the Federal Government. Employers in the field of broadcasting are particularly concerned with the Lea Act also known as the "Anti-Petrillo Law," which proscribes certain activities in the communications industry. Similarly, both railroads and the airlines are particularly affected by the Railway Labor Act which parallels the National Labor Relations Act in jurisdiction over these fields of transportation.

In studying the laws of the individual states dealing with labor, it is first important to ascertain if the state is one of the seventeen which has a specific law pertaining to labor relations. If it does, it is necessary to determine the area of jurisdiction of the state labor relations act as opposed to that of the prevailing Federal laws. In this regard the "no man's land" between the Federal and state authority has been materially diminished in recent years, and it is now easier to calculate which jurisdiction prevails. In certain states such as New York, a very extensive body of labor law has been built up, including court decisions and New York State Labor Board rulings stemming from a comprehensive enactment known as the Labor Law of New York State. In other states where a labor relations act as such does not exist, many of the principles of the common law can and must be applied to the conduct of labor relations.

Also in the category of applicable state laws are provisions relating to factory management and the conduct of employers toward employees. Many states have such laws affecting employment. Twenty states have right-to-work laws, including Louisiana where its application is limited to agricultural workers. Even more have fair employment practice acts. Five states have laws regulating welfare funds. Twenty-five have a statutory minimum wage law. While these do not entirely regulate collective bargaining as such, they are nevertheless compellingly important since provisions of these laws require certain conduct on the part of the employer and, moreover, some of these legal requirements, such as insurance coverage for disabled or unemployed workers, may even be incorporated into collective bargaining agreements. State sanitary and safety codes are all material as are laws regulating and prescribing fair employment practices and barring discriminations in hiring.

Not only state laws, but also the directions of state regulatory bodies are pertinent. For example, in California the Industrial Welfare Commission has promulgated rules which prescribe that women who work an eight-hour day, in most industries, must be given two ten-minute rest periods daily. These are paid for by the employer. Other states have requirements laid down not only by their legislatures, but by executive or administrative action as well. There are requirements in various states governing minimum wages, minimum ages and certain minimum insurance benefits which the employer must provide for the employees, such as Workman's Compensation, disability protection and so on.

There are other statutes which, while not incorporated into the labor law and seldom even considered primarily relevant to the field of labor, are of extreme importance and must be known to the employer in order to insure the safe conduct of his affairs. In New York State, for example, there is a little known but (from an employer's point of view) lethal provision of the Penal Code, 962A. This provides a prison sentence of up to one year or a fine of $500 or both for any employer who fails to pay, within thirty days, money for fringe benefits for his workers which he has committed himself to provide in accordance with a collective bargaining agreement. And if the employer is a corporation, rather than an individual or partnership, then the principal officers personally are deemed guilty of the misdemeanor. Thus to neglect or fail in what was generally assumed to be only a civil liability became a criminal violation in 1958 with passage of this law. An employer may find, to his great chagrin, that even a bankruptcy proceeding will not stay his legal responsibility to provide both wages and fringe benefits for his employees. Unions have become sophisticated in adopting the most convenient methods of effecting collections. Many an employer who never had a more serious brush with the law than a traffic infraction will be very shocked to find that if he fails in his contributions to welfare or pension funds he may be served with a summons to report to court on a charge of violation of Section 962A. In New Jersey the employer who defaults in such payments is, pursuant to a 1966 law, deemed a "disorderly person" and similarly subject to criminal penalties. In the other state jurisdictions there are laws which similarly are of great import to the businessman and of which he must be aware so as to protect his interests.

The entrepreneur who opens any establishment which employs people must be aware of the requirements of the locality in which he operates. These may be in the form of county regulations or municipal ordinances. Such regulations run the gamut from involved sanitation rules about ventilation and toilet facilities to substantial laws which can directly govern the labor relations of the employer in a very material manner. To illustrate this latter point, in the City of New York in 1963, any contractor who dealt with the City had to pay minimum wages of $1.50 per hour. As of 1063 this was well above the national hourly minimum wage and also above the current state minimum wage. Still another case in point is a law passed in New York City in 1962 which bars the importation of strike breakers.

Information can be harvested not only from the laws themselves, but from books, articles and notes which have been written about these laws. It may be garnered from the legislative history of these acts and related committee hearings, from administrative interpretations and most significantly from judicial precedents, that is, opinions in cases involving tests or application of these laws which have been decided by the courts. Moreover, there is an extensive backlog of decisions by the N.L.R.B. that constitute recognized guides and also clarify and refine provisions of the Federal labor relations acts. In the absence of court decisions to the contrary, and barring more detailed instructions by Congress, these agency rulings are often accepted as the prevailing law.

It is perfectly obvious that the men directing the sales, operations, production, or finances of an enterprise cannot reasonably be expected to know all these laws, but they can employ people who do know them. Even the smallest businessman is entitled to rely on one or more persons to see that the conduct of his business is such that it conforms to the requirements of the local, state and Federal governments. Failure to insure this compliance can result in dire consequences.

Pursuant to certain provisions of the laws discussed above, there are different forms which must be filed by employers. Care should be taken that timely filing is made. The U. S. Welfare and Pension Plan Disclosure Act requires that some employers who are contributing to certain types of welfare and pension plans or providing certain benefits must file information with the Government relating to these plans. Moreover, if a company is taking a deduction for income tax purposes on the money it contributes to a qualified pension plan, it must see that a Form 990P is filed with the Internal Revenue Service in order to substantiate this deduction.

Under the Landrum-Griffin Act, provision is made that certain labor relations counselors who work at influencing the selection or rejection of a union or who in certain ways advise a company concerning its labor relation policies must submit reports. Furthermore, employers who pay labor relations advisors for certain services must also report the payment of these funds under some circumstances. Attorneys are specifically exempted from this reporting requirement. The Act does not require that they report fees paid to them for labor relations matters, nor does it rule that their clients must disclose such payments.

Under certain state laws, there are requirements for still other reporting. In New York State, for instance, an employer must file the form LP #1 in which he sets forth whether or not he has paid money to a representative of a union which either bargains with him collectively or which seeks to represent his employees. Such payments are generally illegal. Thus, in effect, the New York businessmen must abide by the law, eschewing such payments, or be faced with the unfortunate alternatives of filing a perjurious report denying payoffs to union officials or, in a sworn statement, admitting that he has made such illegal payments. Associations of employers must also file certain information. In addition, there is a requirement in New York State that all pension plans publicize certain facts and report to certain departments of the New York State government. It is incumbent upon the business executive to acquaint himself with all these requirements and ascertain that the obligations which they impose are being fulfilled.

The Federal law requires that trustees of trust funds in which money is accumulated to pay for welfare and pension benefits must be bonded. Any company which is participating in such plans should insure that the trustees are abiding by the law, and if any individual is himself a fiduciary of such a plan, he must ascertain that his behavior is in full compliance with the law and that the necessary surety bond coverage has been obtained.

In the field of labor relations there are a mass of laws which are constantly changing as new statutes are enacted on various levels of governmental jurisdiction, as courts hand down innumerable decisions and opinions, and as various state and Federal labor boards and administrative agencies set forth their own authoritative interpretations of these laws. However, despite the mushrooming growth of new rulings and the augmentations of existing ones, there are ways to keep informed of relevant developments in this field.

First, there are loose-leaf services that may be subscribed to with supplements that are mailed out weekly or bi-weekly. These do an excellent job in keeping the reader current. The most prominent are put out by the Bureau of National Affairs, Commerce Clearing House and Prentice-Hall. Second, there are numerous books and magazines which provide good background material, some on labor law in general, others concerning specific aspects or specialized problems. Third, a wealth of knowledge can be garnered from many government publications, particularly those of the U.S. Bureau of Labor Statistics. Information is available relating to contemporary settlements of negotiations, area or industry wage and fringe benefit studies, etc. Much of this data is invaluable as an aid for research prior to negotiations with a union. The N.L.R.B., from time to time, puts out certain publications. The N.L.R.B. layman's guide is recommended reading as a good primer for a company with matters pending before the Board. Various states have excellent publications. New York State has periodicals which report intra-state collective bargaining settlements and other labor relations developments.

These sources indicate relatively detailed methods of keeping current or acquainting one's self with the field of labor relations, and will involve the expenditure of considerable time. A simple alternative, which is generally more appealing to the layman, is careful scrutiny of the daily newspapers and certain news magazines. As any reader will find, the labor relations sector is an integral element of our over-all economy. It affects both our domestic state and our international relations in this phase of our history, so that there is detailed, thorough, and informative reporting of these events by the press. While a lawyer or other labor relations professional obviously cannot rely exclusively upon newspapers or magazines to remain informed, a non-professional, particularly a person with some practical familiarity with labor relations, will find that he can stay abreast of events by checking these sources.

The attorney desiring to maintain constant communication with the changing law in this field will find it absolutely essential to subscribe to one of the principal services. He may choose either the expanded or the limited sets, but he will find it necessary to scan the advance sheets which arrive at his office periodically. The professional student of labor law will also be quite interested in reading the annual reports of the American Bar Association Section on Labor Relations Law which are extremely illuminating. The yearly summary of activity of the N.L.R.B. is also required reading. Finally, there are various treatises, case books and law review articles which the attorney can refer to for both general and specialized research work.

The purpose of this chapter is not to engulf the average employer with a feeling of futility about his attempts to keep up to date in the labor relations field, nor to impress him with the difficulty of his abiding by all of the myriad laws which restrict or affect his conduct. The goal is simply to underline that this is a great field of law, constantly developing and changing, and that it is essential that every company, large or small, abide by and be cognizant of these regulations. If employers realize this, they are then able to determine the best manner in which to maintain awareness of, and compliance with, these rules.

In larger enterprises, the creation and maintenance of an industrial relations department and the assignment to it of these responsibilities is most effective. If necessary, outside counsel can be retained to support and, if necessary, double-check the activities of such a staff. In many instances, trade associations are of assistance in the dissemination of pertinent labor relations information. For smaller firms, a labor relations advisor or attorney and, with respect to some items, an accountant should prove adequate to relieve the businessman of the strain of keeping up with these laws. Accordingly, selection of personnel to man an industrial relations department or trade association, and choice of an attorney or labor relations specialist becomes extremely significant. It will effect not only the general labor relations policy of the company, but also is of signal importance in protecting the employer from violating the law.

34

Choosing a
Labor Relations Advisor

Some call labor relations a science, others choose to term it an art, but whatever the name selected, it is a field that requires special knowledge. Many elements combine to make an individual successful as a negotiator or management representative. Certain of these are essential, such as comprehension of the law of labor relations and experience in dealing with unions. Other factors can materially aid in obtaining a successful outcome, including familiarity with the actual union involved, understanding of collective bargaining patterns in the industry and the geographical area, a background of labor-management relations in the specific company, an awareness of the type of work performed and of the skills required, and an insight into the attitudes and make-up of the employees of the company.

We live today in an age of specialization. Labor relations is a specialized area within the field of management. Broadly speaking it requires knowledge of law, economics, psychology, sociology, public relations and engineering.

Men are now populating this field who are trained and equipped to deal with labor relations problems. Among lawyers it has become a specialty just as has real estate law, tax law or corporate law, and well equipped non-lawyer labor relations counselors are also available to aid management.

Often employers—particularly smaller ones—will question if they can afford to hire labor relations counsel. The question they might better put to themselves is if they can afford not to. An amateur advocate competing with professionals may teach a costly lesson to penny-pinching management.

The cents-per-hour differentials which may be the point of conflict in a negotiating session loom large when multiplied by forty hours per week, fifty-two weeks per year and ten, a hundred, a thousand, or ten thousand employees of the company. That seemingly small increment grows larger still when certain fringe benefits which are computed on the basis of straight hourly rate, such as overtime, paid holidays and vacations are added to it. The trained negotiator knows that offering a penny at bargaining time usually means a concession of thousands or hundreds of thousands of dollars. The amateur often does not realize the ultimate dollar consequences of what may seem at first to him to be an inexpensive but grand gesture. It is equally true that when questions of recognizing a union or dealing with it during grievances or arbitrations arise, skilled and expert counsel can save management money.

The question of how to select these experts merits consideration. Often the general attorney or house counsel of the employer will either feel qualified to handle labor relations himself or else may refer it to an attorney or suggest a labor relations counselor in whom he has confidence. Sometimes management selects its own labor relations counsel directly. In choosing such people, certain requirements beyond the obvious should be satisfied.

A labor negotiator should be experienced. No matter how knowledgeable of the written law itself, management representatives can often make mistakes if they have not dealt frequently and directly with labor relations problems in the past. In organizing situations the inexperienced tend to make either of two mistakes. Some are bluffed by a hearty and confident professional union organizer. The end result is that they may counsel capitulation when it is not necessary. Others lean towards underestimating the union's strength and often pass up a judicious and fair chance at settlement only to be ignominiously beaten at the polls and driven to unconditional surrender at the bargaining table.

When the problem of negotiating collective bargaining contracts comes up, the unversed negotiator can make equally grave errors. An attorney recently told me the story of just such a management negotiator who represented a firm in a joint negotiation in which another company was represented by experienced counsel. At caucus both companies agreed as to what maximum increase they could sensibly grant. Then the joint session with the union began.

After the preliminaries, the inexperienced management representative promptly took the floor and made his first offer. It was also what would be his final offer. This resulted in havoc. The union obviously had to show some results of its negotiating and was preparing for a slow build-up so as to progress in several sessions to an offer like the one that had just been made. The very fact that the final offer was thus made prematurely rendered it unacceptable to the union. Moreover, the union rank-and-file committee quickly assumed, based on their previous experience, that an offer of twenty cents per hour in the opening minutes of the initial session could only mean that management ultimately planned at least to triple this offer.

The word "bargaining" in the phrase "collective bargaining" means just what it says. If it carries with it overtones of the give-and-take and haggling of an oriental bazaar, the point is well taken. Perhaps some day total frankness and revelation at the first session of negotiations will be the rule. It is not the case now, with the exception of some notably large employers. Few but the most powerful companies can afford to put a package offer on the table and stand pat on it permanently. Indeed, recent case law holds that to do so may indicate a failure to bargain in good faith and could substitute an unfair practice. Initial offers are usually like a bet in a poker game: everyone expects them to be raised. Whether this approach is desirable is not at issue here. That it prevails is indisputable, and unless a company decides to pioneer in relatively uncharted paths of collective bargaining methods at what may be great danger to it, it had better be represented by someone who knows the rules of the game.

To many the minuet of negotiating session, caucus, offer, consideration, rejection, reconsideration, recaucus, adjournment and so on into the night—taking up as it does many hours, many cigarettes and several adjoining conference rooms—seems pointless. But to those who understand the true nature of collective bargaining, there is a logic to this.

Workers must be convinced that they are extracting the maximum a company can offer. Union leaders must show their dues-paying members that a tough and bitter fight is being waged for them. Smart and thrifty management must be represented by counsel that comprehends the intricacies of this ritual fire-dance.

A management negotiator should have the time and the energy to properly conduct a management campaign during or preceding a representation election or to undertake a contract negotiation. Both matters are time consuming but, particularly in negotiations, "instant collective bargaining" does not work. Responsible labor relations counselors will not take on a matter unless they know that they and their staffs or associates will have sufficient time to handle the situation. Particularly where there is professional depth and support, management may be assured it will not be let down because the clock has run out and its representative is harassed with other matters.

Similarly, physical strength, stamina and vigor are necessary. Concessions have been made to unions, not out of logic or desire, but simply through sheer attrition. Management's team can be worn-down to the point where it is physically necessary to adjourn and emotionally easier to grant increases than to argue any further. Obviously, fatigue is not a rational basis for collective bargaining settlements. Experienced counsel either have the training to weather these bouts or the ability to avoid them.

In its endeavor to choose competent aides, management should beware of the labor relations advisor who promises the world. Cautious and responsible experts may make a conservative estimate of how they hope to settle. They seldom suggest that the employer will have everything his way—that is, they should not and do not promise what they cannot deliver. It is easy for irresponsible people, new to a situation, to fire-up the enthusiasm of long-suffering employers with visions of a "hard-as-nails" approach. This is often more appealing than the conservative and rational attitude. It is, however, frequently unrealistic and, indeed, can result in more harm than good. When someone promises a company a "new deal" he should be asked how he will do it.

It is not essential that counsel representing a company personally know the union officials with whom he will deal. Most labor relations specialists in any given community either know their counterparts in the unions or know someone who can give them an introduction. This can be helpful, but if it is not the case, a feeling of mutual respect can soon be developed. However, it is essential that management's advisors in a situation have impeccable standing. A man known for double-dealing or considered untrustworthy or less than entirely ethical can do irreparable damage to the company which he represents. Labor relations circles have good communications. Bad reputations, like good ones, get around quickly. Management representatives often set the tone of the entire relationship between the parties and since the attorney or labor relations advisor is the agent of management his behavior and words will, quite properly, be attributed to management.

A word should be said here to allay a fear which sometimes besets management. Facing a serious contest with a union, a company picks the best man it can to be its advocate. It is often a shock to management when their labor relations counsel meets with the union organizer for what they expect to be a confrontation as dramatic as a TV gunfight, only to see the two men exchange pleasantries and discuss mutual friends. This is no indication of divided loyalty on the part of management's negotiator. Such a person deals with union representatives constantly and therefore knows many of them. To effectively do his job he must have their respect. In return, he will respect those who are honest and capable. Abuse or rudeness to a union organizer is pointless, and the management counsel who treats his adversaries with dignity will in turn be afforded the respect and credibility that can aid in attaining a fair settlement.

In general the same qualities required of a labor relations counselor in representation proceedings and collective bargaining sessions are appropriate for the advisor in arbitration or grievance-settlement situations. In arbitrations, particularly, management should be represented by a man who is well versed in presenting a case and in cross-examination. The representative in an arbitration must be an advocate, not a judge. An arbitration is a proceeding between adversaries. Management's spokesman must concern himself with putting forth his viewpoint and in such capacity he should stand vigorously on his client's side. Final judgment is reserved for the arbitrator. For this reason management should select a representative trained in the techniques of litigation since arbitration is a trial of issues.

For negotiation, election campaigns, grievance processing and arbitration, research is necessary. The information which the company's experts must have falls into two categories—economic and technical. Effective employer representation is predicated on collecting and marshalling economic and statistical facts about an industry, area or company. This includes research into comparative wage rates, the ratio of labor costs to over-all expense and volume, a background knowledge of the nature and number of firms in the industry and an awareness of their rate of growth or decline, figures pertaining to membership in the union, and many other matters. Technical know-how requires an understanding of the company's operations and the working of the plant or store. The negotiator must know how many men are needed on a job, how the operation is best performed, how machinery functions, what customer's requirements are, what prevailing work hours and performance standards exist, and so on.

Aid and advice on negotiations, representation matters and contract administration are rendered either by an attorney or by a non-lawyer labor relations counselor. There is still another aspect of labor relations where only qualified and licensed members of the bar may be used. This is in the area where legal proceedings occur or may develop. Non-lawyers cannot lawfully nor practically represent a client when it comes to court proceedings, the seeking of injunctions, the commencement or prosecution of legal action, etc. Moreover, in relying on an opinion concerning the law of labor relations, whether Federal or state, the company must insure that qualified legal counsel render such advice. Finally, in proceedings before the National Labor Relations Board or other governmental agencies, lawyers are necessary to fully insure protection of management's rights.

Thus while lawyers can properly perform all the services that a labor relations non-lawyer advisor can, the reverse is not true. The employer may choose to utilize a combination of both legal and non-legal advisors, he may use an attorney exclusively, or he may utilize industrial relations advisors alone until such time as legal counsel is required. Many prudent executives who rely on non-lawyers insist, however, on opinion of qualified counsel so as to fully protect themselves on issues where the law is involved.

Companies which have full-time labor relations men, who are not attorneys, within their own organizations are, of course, required to seek legal counsel when necessary. Even the company that has regular staff attorneys is well advised to maintain relations with outside counsel. This gives the advantage of having specialists with general and broad experience available to back-stop the company's executives. Furthermore, it provides for an objective and independent evaluation of company positions and policies and union attitudes. Outside counsel is less inclined to "yes" a boss when it feels he is wrong than a job-holding subordinate. And being at arm's length from the picture and removed from some of the intricacies of personalities often yields a refreshing and sobering viewpoint. Finally, in time of crisis it makes available a staff with "depth." This may be necessary if several minds must be simultaneously thrown into the breach. It allows for diligent and thorough work when time is very short. And if a management spokesman must unexpectedly be absent, then his colleague, already a well-trained alternate and familiar with the circumstances, may step into his shoes.

In summary, successful labor relations cannot be handled on a do-it-yourself basis. Just as one calls an orthopedist for a broken leg or a surgeon for an appendectomy, so too a specialist must be called for a labor problem. Care should be taken in the choice. Management's representatives will be pitted against union organizers and leaders who devote all day every day to organizing, processing grievances, arbitrating and negotiating. These men are usually competent professionals. Management owes it to itself to have men of equal status and training to represent its interests.

35

Equal Opportunity Laws

and Personnel Policies

Early in 1964 as part of the Civil Rights Act, Federal laws were enacted which prohibited discrimination based on race, color, religion, sex or national origin. The provisions of the 1964 law, which covers employers, unions and employment agencies are gradually being extended so that they will affect more and more firms. Consequently, it is imperative that management be cognizant of these laws and ensure compliance with them. Even those companies not now covered may find that due to the provisions of the law or because of a growing work crew, they will become subject to the Act. Effective July 2, 1965, and for the year that followed, only companies with a hundred or more employees were affected. As of July 2, 1966, the operative figure was dropped to seventy-five employees. On July 2, 1967, any person or firm having fifty workers or more will be included, and after July 1, 1968, the law will apply to those with twenty-five or more employees. Under the terms of the present law employers with fewer than twenty-five workers are not involved. And, as usual, Federal legislation only affects those firms considered to be in interstate commerce. Certain states and cities have parallel laws and these may include even the employers with less than twenty-five workers. New York State, for example, was the first to pass its own legislation in 1945 protecting job opportunity for its inhabitants. Its law covering employees within the State will include some companies not under the Federal jurisdiction. There is deemed to be no conflict between the laws and the Federal act does not cancel State or local anti-discrimination statutes. Moreover, pursuant to Presidential Executive Orders, discrimination has been prohibited in government agencies and by contractors or sub-contractors with government contracts or contracts covering projects which are financed with Federal funds.

Unions may not discriminate. The provisions of the law affect increasing numbers of unions in a manner similar to the annual expansion of coverage affecting employers. Hiring halls are covered as are joint labor-management committees which govern training programs and apprenticeship plans.

The 1964 legislation set up an Equal Employment Opportunity Commission with five commissioners. The primary purpose of this Commission is to implement the Act and eliminate unlawful practices. There are four major types of unlawful discriminatory practices which may be committed. The first is a failure or refusal to hire based on discrimination. The second concerns discharge of an employee for this reason. Thirdly, discrimination in terms of compensation, working conditions or privileges is unlawful. Fourthly, a limitation on the opportunities of minorities, including their right to promotion or forcing them to be segregated, is unlawful.

When a charge of unlawful conduct is filed with the Commission, it can investigate. If it finds substance to the charge, it may, through conferences and attempts at conciliation, endeavor to have the offending party change its practices. The Commission is specifically empowered to cooperate with State agencies engaged in the same work. In fact, the law requires the Federal Commission to accept complaints only if no State or local agency can or will handle the matter. And, there is a required waiting period after local proceedings are finished before Federal action can commence. The Commission may study the problem areas and publish its findings, and it may refer matters to the U.S. Attorney General for appropriate action. It can institute court proceedings to compel compliance with orders that have been obtained in private actions.

After complaints are made to the Commission it has the authority to investigate and to compel testimony under oath. If no compromise can be worked out, the individual aggrieved may sue the offending company. Such suits may be started without payment of fees, costs or security and the court may award attorneys' fees to the party that initiates the litigation.

With respect to individual relief, there are basically two types of actions provided for. The first, is the private suit described. And, the Commission itself can move in court to support or have enforced a ruling obtained by a private individual. The second involves direct action by the Attorney General which is appropriate when an entire pattern of discrimination exists and the problem involves more than an isolated issue or incident. The U.S. Department of Labor deals with discrimination by government contractors.

The Commission is charged with promulgating regulations concerning record keeping. It appears that this will require maintenance of employment records, notes of job interviews, results of tests, filled out application forms, recording of reasons for disposition of an application and so on. Companies which are subject to this law must post notices so stating.

Government contractors and sub-contractors have specific duties that exceed the requirements for other employers. In essence, an affirmative responsibility to eliminate discrimination is imposed on this class of employers. For example, such contractors must include language indicating that they are equal opportunity employers in their advertisements for personnel. They must inform the unions with which they deal of the special status, file certain reports, etc. Their books and records must also be open to government inspection.

The equal opportunity law prohibits job notices or advertisements which indicate a preference or limitation based on race, color, religion, sex or national origin. There is an exception that is significant. Such advertisements may indicate a limitation or preference when the race or color or religion or ethnic origin or sex of an individual is a bona fide occupational qualification. A producer of a musical comedy looking for candidates for his chorus line would not be discriminating if he insisted on ladies. Religious and educational institutions are exempt from this provision of the law with respect to their religious and educational activities. Since, at this time, there have not been too many cases processed, decided, collected and published, it is hard to accurately delineate the area where such preferences or limitations due to minority status will be allowed within the exception. Presumably, common sense will prevail and the past pattern and present attitude of the employer will help to indicate if his position is based on rational business reasons or is merely an attempt at subterfuge.

The law specifically states that preferential treatment for veterans and American Indians is permissible. It waives the anti-discrimination rules in the event of national security requirements which could dictate the contrary, and it states that discrimination against Communists is allowed.

It is important to realize what the law does not do as well as what it does do. There is no requirement in the law to correct an already existing imbalance. Thus, if Corporation C in Alabama has 500 workers, all white, the law does not require it to discharge some of these and replace them with Negroes. It would, of course, affect C's hiring of new help and the job conditions of these people. No company is forced to make changes in its existing work force.

Preferential treatment of minority groups is not required. On the contrary, to take such action would on the face of it violate the law. Thus, if an employer in south Texas having only "anglos" working for him announced that he wanted to hire solely Mexican-American people and so advertised, he would be acting contrary to the law. Moreover, the percentage of minority groups in the community is deemed to be irrelevant. An employer in the New York area who has his work force evenly divided among $\frac{1}{3}$ Negroes, $\frac{1}{3}$ Spanish speaking people of Puerto Rican descent or birth, and $\frac{1}{3}$ others, could not take affirmative steps to preserve this ratio. Nor would he automatically be found not guilty of discrimination simply because the racial or ethnic composition in his plant mirrored the percentages in the community as a whole.

The law permits personnel officers to continue to give tests to prospective employees prior to hiring them. However, the tests must not have built-in bias in the sense of being loaded for or against any particular groups. Thus, if such an examination requires a scholastic or cultural background that significantly large segments of a minority group could not be expected to have, it could then be questioned. Based on the assumptions of some educators that many substantially segregated Negro schools in the South do not provide as good an education as public schools open to whites, it may be argued that prejudice is already written into a test based on general educational achievement. It will take time for guidelines to be established.

The provisions of the law require that there be no discrimination by employers against men or women because of their sex. Provided that a person can do the job, he or she is entitled to it. As a result of the law, if you are an employer in a covered industry it means that you cannot refuse to hire a male secretary although you may prefer a woman; nor may you decline to employ a lady executive albeit you would be happier with a man in the job. In addition to

affecting personal tastes, there may be some economic consequences of implementation of this rule. For example, if women start
working in a place that has been exclusively male, or vice-versa, it
may require installation of separate dressing rooms, lounges and
lavatory facilities.

The Equal Pay Act of 1963 requires equal pay for equal work.
This hits at the practice of second class economic citizenship for
women and forbids financial discrimination based on sex. Wage
rates include not only straight wages paid, but also minimums, maximums and overtime differentials. Furthermore, the law provided
that pay rates of men could not be reduced to achieve equality.
There are special provisions defining the coverage of this Act and
there are some qualifications. For example, temporary assignment
on a red circle rate may be allowed if for less than one month.

When a woman is unable to do the heavy work that a man must
do on a job, then there is no compulsion to hire her. But the distinction between job functions must be a real one in order to justify
pay differentials. Example: Mr. A and Miss B both work in a mail
room. Mr. A gets a higher pay rate than Miss B. For nearly half of
the time A and B both do the same work of filling, sealing, stamp-
ing, addressing and stacking envelopes. The rest of the time Miss B
continues to do this, but Mr. A bundles large sets of envelopes,
packs them in cases, and loads the cases on a truck for hauling to
the post office. Since Mr. A must perform this job function and
Miss B does not, it would be legitimate to pay Mr. A a higher
hourly wage for all of his hours worked. His job requirements are
different than hers. However, if A and B had entirely the same type
of work to do all of the time, then they would have to get equal pay.
An argument that the employer needed a man to stand by in case
heavy work came up, if in fact the man did not perform it, might
well be considered an excuse to circumvent the law.

With regard to payment of supplementary obligations, the pattern appears to be that payments may be unequal if the end results
are the same or if the payments for the benefit are the same, the
actual benefit may be different by virtue of sex. Thus, if life insurance policies on men and women of the same age carry different
premium rates, the cost for the man being higher, the employer
has either of two options. First, he may insure all workers—both
male and female—for $1,000.00 of life insurance and not violate
the law by paying a higher premium to obtain this coverage for
the men. Alternatively, he may pay the same premium for all

workers even though the men receive $1,000.00 of life insurance coverage and the women get greater insurance for the same money. Contracting for different retirement ages for men and women for whom pension payments are made is also permissible.

Records concerning the sex of employees must be kept at least three years by the employer. The government has the right to check these. If the employer does not adhere to the equal pay requirements, he can be found guilty of violating the Fair Labor Standards Act. Just as in other cases where this law is disregarded, the underpaid employee may institute a civil suit for restitution. In some cases there may be criminal sanctions imposed for violations of this law.

There has been no major Congressional legislation to prevent job discrimination against persons because of their age. However, there is emerging a pronounced public policy to discourage any reluctance to hire older workers. Statements by Federal officials have been made indicating that government contractors should not discriminate in this regard. Recently there has been under consideration the enactment of a general law to strengthen the rights of older people to equal employment opportunity. Possibly some opposition may arise from those who point out that the employment of older people may inflate the cost of pension plans and welfare programs providing health and life insurance.

In order to implement the equal opportunity law, employers who are covered by its provisions must file certain forms. The E.E.O.-1 was sent to most covered employers for them to complete and return. This requires information on minority group employment. Government contractors are responsible to see that their sub-contractors comply. Employers in the Plans for Progress program also have reporting requirements.

Another major way in which equal job opportunity is being promoted is through court and N.L.R.B. decisions concerning race relations and the labor law. In pre-election campaigning, the Board has taken an increasingly stricter stand against inflammatory propaganda. While a frank and honest discussion of racial issues may be permitted, statements that arouse and incite to hatred are not; and, if they are made, they may result in an overturning of the election results. The theory behind the Board's position is that its function is to try to ascertain through an election the true sentiment of the employees. If emotional appeals are made which overcome reason, or outrageous lies are told which can mislead people, then the ballots do not really reflect the free and deliberate choice of the voters. This Board policy was first enunciated in a 1962 opinion. The Board held that the employer's propaganda against the union which depicted them as integrationist and in favor of "race mixing" precluded a rational vote on the part of the white employees. The Board did say, however, that one party can truthfully disclose the racial position of the other and if it "does not deliberately seek to overstress and exacerbate racial feelings by irrelevant, inflammatory appeals, we shall not set aside an election on this ground."

There have been cases where unions used pleas for racial consciousness for an opposite effect. In these cases the unions trying to organize predominantly Negro workers appealed to racial solidarity or pride. The Board has allowed this on the rationale that it does not stir up hatred. But, in a similar case, a Federal Appeals Court, applying the Board's own standards set down in the 1962 case, held that such appeals were not to reason and that the election should be set aside. This divergence of opinion remains substantially unresolved at this time.

A union is charged with representing all of its members equally. If it can be shown that a union refused to represent some members because of their race, the Board can rescind the union certification. And, a union may be charged with an unfair labor practice if it refuses to handle a grievance raised by a worker because of that individual's race. Moreover, unions cannot lawfully bargain or agree to contracts that discriminate against groups of employees due to their race. Evidently, some unions still have segregated locals of white and Negro members. There is no clear cut Board ruling existing now that bars this if the union represents all members equally. But, a collective bargaining agreement allowing discrimination between whites and Negroes will not be a bar to an election.

The trend of cases, in this writer's opinion, indicates that the Board and courts are increasingly going to hold to account the employer or union which discriminates. By putting such parties to a very real disadvantage vis-à-vis the labor law, efforts will be made to curtail discrimination. Self-interest, if no nobler purpose, should disincline companies and unions from prejudiced positions. The consequence to the biased will be their own loss of rights under the law, which can indeed be harmful.

The entire concept of comprehensive equal opportunity as something enforced by Federal laws and policy has been initiated only recently and is developing swiftly. The employer no longer is limited only by his conscience nor is he guided solely by his views or moral precepts. Now the Congress, the courts and the Board have all promulgated rules or criteria to which employers must adhere. To avoid difficulty, management must learn these standards, be alert to their modification and implementation and adhere to the law.

36

The Employer
and Union Administration

A review of the laws regulating the administration of unions is appropriate for management because these requirements can directly or indirectly affect labor-management relations. After a period of investigation the Senate Select Committee on Improper Activities in the Labor or Management Field—known popularly as the Mc-Clellan Committee—recommended legislation which eventually emerged as the Labor Management Reporting and Disclosure Act. This was signed into law by President Eisenhower on September 14, 1959 and is known also as the Landrum-Griffin Act. Its adherents believed that the law would ensure and preserve democratic rights for rank and file union members and eliminate undesirable practices.

A most important element of the law was the enactment of the "Bill of Rights" for union members. These include equality of rights for all union members; freedom of speech and assembly; the right to vote before dues and fees may be increased; and the right to sue the union. Other rights enumerated are the assurance of access to union records; recovery of misappropriated union assets; information about union activities; and, specifically, the right to inspect contracts entered into by a member's union other than the particular agreement affecting him; the right to sue for trusteeship violation and protection against arbitrary disciplinary action by the union. This last assurance provides that, other than for failure to pay dues, union members cannot be punished or expelled unless they have the opportunity of "due process," with all the procedural safeguards and protections of notice that such a principle involves.

To implement these rights various rules were promulgated as well as requirements for reports making disclosure. The constitution and by-laws of a union, as well as reports on union administration, policies and finances, must be filed with the Secretary of Labor. And the Secretary may investigate in the event of a failure to file or a false filing and institute court action. A wilful failure to file, the making of a false statement or the withholding of a material fact are criminal offenses and can result in penalties of a $10,000 fine and up to a year in prison. Union members have a qualified right, providing they can show good cause, to inspect these reports.

In addition there is certain other information which some union officers may have to file. Paralleling the responsibility of management agents, labor representatives must file, for example, if they receive payments from management to influence their course of conduct as labor officials. Wages paid to employees, who also happen to be union officers for their work for the company are, of course, not improper or illegal and do not require a filing.

The days when a union boss or ruling clique could, by edict, raise dues and force their members to pay more money are gone. Today a union cannot increase dues, obligations or initiation fees or levy assessments unless certain procedures have been followed. In a local union, for instance, such financial changes can only be made after a majority of the local, by secret ballot, so vote at a meeting specifically called for that purpose, or after a secret referendum. Similar safeguards exist at other levels of union organization.

Collective bargaining contracts negotiated by a union must be available to all people covered thereby including both union members and non-union employees. This obviously reduces the opportunity for an unscrupulous union official to conspire with the same kind of employer and allow management to do less for the people than it is contractually obligated for.

Union election methods are regulated and there are specific procedures geared to democratize elections including the nominating process, requirements for notice of elections, the right to campaign, etc. Even the frequency of elections is regulated so as to prevent the perpetuation in office of an unwanted leadership. A national or international union must have elections at least every five years with the members voting by secret ballot or through delegates at a convention provided these persons were themselves selected by secret ballot.

Local unions have a minimum requirement of one election in three years and this must be by secret ballot of all members in good standing. Intermediate bodies, for example joint boards and joint councils, are required to select officers at least once in four years by secret ballot of members or votes of officials who were chosen by secret ballot.

State laws cannot contravene these Federal requirements. Union officials may not use dues or other funds of the membership to meet their campaign expenses nor may employers contribute to the campaign chest of an incumbent labor leader or his opponent. Records concerning union elections for officers including the actual ballots must be kept for at least one year.

This Federal Act also provides for the regulations of trusteeships. This is, in effect, the superimposing of appointed leadership on a trade union organization with the suspension of the right of the rank and file union members to elect their own leaders.

Trusteeships generally are imposed by the international union leadership on a subordinate group when it is deemed necessary to eliminate corruption or gangsterism and to aid in regenerating the democratic process. Or, if a union's leaders are not administering the current collective bargaining agreement or otherwise fail to properly represent their members, a trusteeship may result. In some cases higher union leadership used the device of a trusteeship arrangement to throw out union leaders who were in opposition and to control local treasuries. As such, in a power struggle, locals could be turned into pawns with the membership as the ultimate loser. Consequently, the Congress believed it necessary to put limitations on a union's right to institute and maintain a trusteeship arrangement with its own locals. The act is not designed to eliminate the concept of trusteeship. This is recognized as a legitimate function of the parent organization that may often be necessary to protect its standing in the long run. The law does, however, seek to curb abuses of the use of trusteeships for political purposes and to prevent manipulation of locals against the interests of the membership. For example, delegates of local unions in trusteeship may not vote in conventions unless they are chosen by secret ballot, and transferring of funds is prohibited. Trustees must file reports of their actions which are open to all.

Part of the reason for passage of this regulating law were the revelations before the McClellan Committee of irregular practices committed by some union leaders. As a consequence, the law imposes a fiduciary obligation on union officials. Embezzlement of union funds was made a federal crime, rather than just a state offense. This permits federal enforcement; and allows investigating agencies such as the F.B.I. to have jurisdiction of such cases and places the responsibility for prosecution with U.S. attorneys. The result of this fiduciary obligation is that a union officer must treat union funds with a higher degree of care than he would handle his own money. He must deal with these funds and make financial decisions as a prudent man should. Neither negligence nor ignorance can be counted on as defenses to accusations of mishandling of union funds. It was anticipated that some union leaders might be powerful enough to get exculpatory language placed in union constitutions or by-laws and so it was further legislated that a union cannot by its own action exonerate a union official from such legal liability. Thus, even if a union resolution stated that their treasurer would be free of fault if funds were misappropriated due to his carelessness, such enactment would have absolutely no effect on the government's right to proceed, nor would it serve as a legal defense for the accused.

To further ensure high standards of financial management, the law requires the bonding of certain union officials. Obviously, this puts the bonding company in a position of reviewing the records of union officials who must be bonded. Theoretically, in case of refusal of an insurance company to issue a bond to a union official question would arise as to his legal right to serve in such a position. One of several features of the law which some union officials view with disfavor, the bonding requirement comes in for particular criticism. Opponents point out that the majority of union officials are not corrupt and have never committed any offenses which would raise doubts as to their honesty in financial dealings. They complain that the cost of bond premiums places an added burden on union treasuries. They argue further that a truly dishonest man will not be more effectively curbed if his defalcation hurts a bonding company instead of a union treasury. And, they maintain that officers of corporations who handle shareholders' money and have equal opportunity for embezzlement are not required to be bonded. Without discussing the merits of these arguments, this issue is raised here to illustrate that the "democratizing" requirements of the law were not unanimously welcomed as equitable or fair.

A union officer or employee who embezzles, steals or misappropriates union funds can be fined $10,000 and imprisoned for five years, if convicted. Moreover, if his acts violate state law as well as the federal law, he may be tried for the state violation, since the federal law does not pre-empt the field. The law provides penalties for the union official who infringes on the union members' rights by violent interference. Here again, state courts have concurrent jurisdiction.

Unions are limited in the amount of loans which they can make to officers. Two thousand dollars is the total amount of loan which may be outstanding to any individual at a given time. Unions and employers are both forbidden to pay on behalf of union officers any fine imposed on them for violation of the Landrum-Griffin law.

Federal laws have barred those convicted of certain crimes and Communists from holding union offices for certain periods. However, the U.S. Supreme Court has declared that portion of the law prohibiting Communists from leadership is void.

The governmental fostering of what many consider greater union democracy has ramifications which affect the employer. The strength of a corrupt union's ruling clique and the grip of bossism have undoubtedly been weakened. On the other hand, courageous and responsible union leadership may find itself challenged more often than in the past.

Two phenomena which disturb many observers of the labor-management scene have been attributed by some to the increased measure of union democracy. The first is the unratified settlement the second is the unnecessary arbitration.

During the past several years, there has been a rash of instances where union officials have negotiated a hard-bargained settlement with management, only to have the rank and file members reject the terms. There is no legal requirement that the full membership vote to approve an agreement negotiated between their leadership and management. However, union officials, influenced by the law, consider this a democratic procedure and also believe that to seek direct guidance from their constituencies is a wise and worthwhile policy.

The consequences of an unratified settlement can be serious. The negative vote does not say what the people will accept, only that they are not satisfied with what they got. Thus, union leaders returning to the bargaining table can only ask for more, but usually have no clear gauge of what will be enough. The leadership is, of course, down-graded because of what amounts to a vote of no-confidence and management can, with some justification, be reluctant to bargain again with union officers who cannot "deliver."

The classic advice to management in this situation is usually: "Stand firm on your final offer and do not raise the bid." But, often the exigencies of business and the realities of economics dictate an improved offer so as to end or avoid a strike. When, through a failure to ratify the first settlement, a higher package is ultimately obtained, the lesson is not lost on the rank-and-file, and management negotiators will approach subsequent bargaining sessions very gingerly. In fact, at the next contract negotiation, they may decide not to go to their best figure with the union negotiating team for fear that again the settlement will be overturned and they will have to go higher. This puts a new dimension on bargaining—holding something back in anticipation of renewed bargaining after a supposed settlement. In turn, it is more difficult for the union leaders to accept the so-called final package—now less than the maximum possible—and more likely that the rank and file will again vote down a settlement.

Union leadership may feel more secure to turn down an offer of the company even if it means a strike than to accept a settlement which might be rejected by the membership. It is politically more sound for labor leaders to be at odds with management than with their own members. Moreover, this reaction may spread to management. It is conceivable that after the union accepts an offer, management's team will regretfully announce that its superior or Board of Directors has vetoed its settlement and that it will have to negotiate further and downward.

A rank and file failure to ratify a negotiated settlement can set off a cycle of problems which in turn produce other problems. The result can make good faith bargaining difficult and distort the negotiating process. If union members continue with frequency to kick over settlements negotiated by their leaders, many established concepts of collective bargaining may have to be re-examined. To be successful, as presently practiced, collective bargaining must operate in a framework in which most of the principal negotiators on both sides are responsible people, and where these spokesmen have authority to speak for the elements which they represent. When either negotiating party is irresponsible or loses control of its situation, collective bargaining, as we know it, may fail and the achievement of a rational and equitable solution becomes more difficult.

Obviously, management is directly affected by the caliber and quality of union leadership. A union official can choose either to follow or to lead. If he simply reflects the wishes of the rank and file, he may find his life easier. If he attempts to lead, he may diminish his popularity. This practical problem confronts union officials on a day to day basis. A business manager of a local may be convinced that to push for too high a settlement, even if obtainable, could put a weak company out of business. In some ways, it is easier to insist on and get the big package and have the company go out of business a few months later. However, assuming the jobs are valuable and the company not exploiting, the wiser course in the long run may be to counsel moderation and hold the negotiators back from getting the maximum possible. Job security can be more significant and of greater value to the workers in the long pull than the illusion of a big raise and soon thereafter a defunct company. However, to choose this positive alternative requires courage and can result in disfavor. It forces the union leader to persuade and restrain and educate his membership. It puts him in the position of recommending something that is to management's benefit. There are almost always ambitious insurgents who will call such a leader a "sell out artist" and run against him in an election on a platform calling for more militancy and less concern for management.

The same result can occur if a labor leader tells a member he is wrong and management is right.

Some union officials may insist on arbitration even when they believe they are wrong. They may figure it is better to have an arbitrator say that the union or its members are at fault than to say so themselves and incur the enmity of members. Obviously, this approach can lead to problems for management and can be costly in both time and money for the employer and the union.

A responsible and courageous union leader, on the one hand, or paradoxically enough a corrupt one, on the other, may tell the member that he is wrong and the company right and refuse to arbitrate. The dishonest leader will do so if there is a sweetheart deal, regardless of the merits of the controversy. The honorable labor official will do so for several reasons, but only when he genuinely believes the company is right. Firstly, as a matter of principle he will not want to stand for a proposition that is unfair. Secondly, to hold an arbitration costs the union members money which will be wasted if losing is a foregone conclusion. Thirdly, if a guilty man is defended then others may follow in his footsteps with bad consequences for the company and the job security of all workers. For example, when a worker is repeatedly and inexcusably late and absent for work, a good union leader may not contest the company's disciplinary action. He will realize that excessive absences or latenesses on a plant-wide basis might put the company out of business and thereby the majority of the workers, who are on time, would suffer.

The union leader who does take this principled position is, to a great extent, putting his job on the line. Some commentators on the labor-management scene say that ironically as a result of Landrum-Griffin, this type of responsible labor leader is in a more vulnerable position than before. Supporters of the law reply that this situation exists in all free and democratic organizations. They argue that this is a smaller price to pay than to permit the authoritarian rule of union membership by a few.

Management must be as concerned with union leadership as is the trade union movement and it should seek to understand the problems of union officials. Business increasingly recruits executives from colleges and graduate business schools. The success story of the high school drop-out who starts as a stock clerk and ends up as a corporation president is becoming the exception, not the rule, particularly in larger companies. Organized labor, on the other hand, almost always gets its leadership from the rank and file where the most intelligent, able and aggressive men rise to the top. The union leader's knowledge of labor relations is apt to come from on-the-job training and be based on practical experience, while the management representative increasingly comes to a problem with more formal training in law, business administration, engineering, accountancy or liberal arts. In my opinion, it is inevitable that labor will eventually develop training schools for its leadership and a new type of labor leader may emerge— one who first has practical experience and then formal training in labor relations.

All of the developments discussed in this chapter will ultimately shape the course of labor-management relations, and thoughtful employers and their representatives should be aware of these issues and consider them.

37

The Biggest Employer—
How Government Handles
Labor Relations

In 1966 there were close to thirteen million people who were employed by various government agencies in the U.S. More than two and a half million were civilian employees of the U.S. government, or of wholly owned government corporations. About two-fifths of this number worked for the Defense Department and related agencies, and about one-fifth worked for the U.S. Post Office Department. More than seven million individuals were employed by State governments and their political sub-divisions, including cities, counties, school districts and bi-State agencies. There are ninety thousand of these political units in the United States. These seven million persons include teachers, social workers, policemen, firemen, sanitation workers, court attendants and correction personnel, doctors and health and hospital employees, transit workers, laborers and a host of other skilled, semi-skilled and unskilled people.

Congress, in passing legislation encouraging workers to bargain collectively, did not include government employees. On the contrary, the Wagner Act specifically excluded all those in this category from the coverage of its provisions. Nevertheless, unionization has been growing steadily among all types of government workers and it is apparent that the trend will accelerate over the next few years. Most businessmen will watch these developments with interest.

The single largest employer in the U.S.—having more than three times the number of people on its civilian payroll than the entire Bell Telephone System or the whole General Motors manufacturing complex—is the United States itself. On January 17, 1962, the late President John F. Kennedy promulgated Executive Order 10988. This order established collective bargaining rights and procedures for Federal government employees. As a consequence of this Order civilian employees of practically all executive departments and agencies are permitted to join labor unions and to negotiate collectively.

Unionization of Federal employees is not something new. For more than a century, certain U.S. government employees have been in unions. Unions have been particularly strong in certain executive agencies such as the Post Office Department for many years. Nevertheless, this Executive Order has undoubtedly given impetus to a concerted organizing drive by unions on a scale not seen before. Moreover, the Order will remove the reluctance that may have remained in the minds of some individual government employees who had doubts about joining unions. It is estimated that more than 800,000 Federal employees are already in labor unions. And, observers of labor relations developments predict that this number will grow substantially in the next few years. Executive Order 10988 provides for "recognition" by government agencies of unions which represent government employees. There are three kinds of such recognition. First, there is "informal" recognition. This entitles a union to express its views on issues that concern employees of the government. Second, there is "formal" recognition, which is extended when a union represents ten per cent or more of the employees in the bargaining unit. Formal recognition imposes a duty on the federal agency to consult with the union. Third, the Order provides for the granting of exclusive representation rights to a union that represents a majority of employees in the unit. Such status gives a union the right to negotiate for all covered employees of the agency and no other union in the bargaining unit can be formally recognized.

In order to qualify for any kind of recognition, a union must conform to certain major standards. It must not discriminate, be corrupt, advocate overthrow of the government or espouse the right to strike against the government. In fact, as noted elsewhere in this book, U.S. government employees cannot strike at any time, and should they do so, their action is punishable as a felony.

When a union claims that it represents ten per cent or more of the workers in a unit, the Secretary of Labor then nominates an arbitrator who determines which people should be included in the unit. For example, in a Veterans Administration hospital, a question arises—should all civilian employees be deemed an appropriate unit, or should just the skilled operating engineers be considered eligible to vote on whether or not they want to go into a union? The formulation of the unit from the point of view of the government as an employer and the union parallels similar problems in defining units in private enterprise. The arbitrator, after considering the views of the union or unions and of the government, will then make his recommendations.

The union, in negotiating with the government, does not have as wide a scope of issues which it can discuss with this "employer" as it would with a private employer. Because the people which the union represents are civil servants many matters that ordinarily would be subject to collective bargaining are determined unilaterally by the government. For example, wage scales are set by Civil Service standards. However, there are various subjects on which a union may negotiate. These include job categories and classification, grievances, shift and location assignments, safety and sanitary conditions, transfers, standards, work force reduction and many other significant issues. If the unions and the government do not agree, organized labor does not have the ordinary recourse— the strike—which it would have in the same situation with a private employer. Federal employees may not engage in a concerted withholding of work from their employer. Unions cannot hope to deal with the government and at the same time advocate the right to strike or urge their members to strike. The unions, however, are not without some weapons. Unions may employ political pressure and endeavor to get their arguments over to Congressmen and officials in the executive branch of government. Furthermore, unions are not barred from lobbying or from proclaiming their complaints to the public at large and hoping that this, in turn, will build up a favorable political climate for them.

A most significant recourse which the union has when there is a deadlock with the government is to request arbitration. Unlike most labor-management situations, arbitration is not binding on the parties. It is advisory in nature only. Sensible personnel practices, nevertheless, dictate that whenever possible the government executives who are charged with dealing with their subordinate personnel will abide by the arbitrator's award. And, since more and more such decisions will no doubt be handed down, precedents will probably have increasing significance. Some observers believe that there will be a tendency on the part of government management people to abide by the arbitrations whenever they possibly can.

There are many other problems similar but not identical to corresponding situations in private labor relations which, of course, will ultimately arise. These questions involve the check-off issue, the decertification or deauthorization of unions, the position of personnel specialists and supervisors in a unionized unit and many other matters. It is clear that this field of law will continue to develop.

State and local governments are also finding that there is an increasing trend on the part of their employees to unionize. With this, has emerged a greater militancy by organized labor to achieve its goals. Different states, and indeed, various cities will adopt legislation to deal with this situation. In one city alone, New York, there has been considerable friction between unions representing City employees and the City itself as employer. There was a strike on the municipally owned transit system in January, 1966. After that, public health nurses, registered nurses in City hospitals and doctors on the municipal payroll either struck or "resigned" their jobs. At mid-point of 1966, representatives of nearly one-hundred-thousand City employees, including the Uniformed Firemen's Association, the Patrolmen's Benevolent Association, and a Teamster local comprising the sanitation men started to bargain in earnest with the City since their contracts had run out. Despite the Condon-Wadlin Act, a law passed by the New York Legislature in 1947 that barred strikes by public employees, not all union leaders have unequivocally stated that they would not strike against the City or use other tactics involving a partial work stoppage. On the contrary, there have already been strikes in New York by welfare workers and school teachers too; and in the months before negotiations a rash of protests by municipal employees has recently swept the country. Firemen in Atlanta and Kansas City, nurses in San Francisco, welfare personnel in Los Angeles, garbage truck drivers in Youngstown, teachers in several cities, all struck, picketed or made demands on their city governments. The possibility of city employees engaging in a work stoppage cannot be discounted. It is clear that even among public safety employees the "no strike" concept is not sacrosanct. In an effort to solve this problem and to rationalize its labor relations policy, New York City in 1966 was setting up an office of collective bargaining to represent it in negotiating with its employees.

Since various unions of New York City employees were able to flout the State Condon-Sadlin law with relative impunity, there has developed a growing outcry on the part of the public that either the law be enforced as written or rescinded or modified. Efforts are now being made to amend the law. Political considerations, of course, are paramount in the discussions concerning amendment. Obviously, the problems that the City and State of New York are presently facing do and will continue to confront municipalities, states and other political entities throughout this entire nation as growing numbers of these state, county and municipal employees join labor unions, and make demands on their employers.

For many years, in the opinion of a significant segment of the public, there was a simple answer to the question of who could and who could not engage in a strike. It was felt that in most cases, employees of private concerns had the right to strike, while employees of any government agency did not have the right to strike. It is submitted that the logic behind this is doubtful.

To set a hard and fast rule and hold that workers in private enterprise may strike and those working for the government may not is to overlook certain economic realities. In many cases, strikes by workers in private enterprise can do more damage to the economy, and, in fact, the very political safety of our country than a strike by government employees. For example, it is obvious that if personnel of a telephone company were to stop work for a long enough period to cause the phones to go out of order, or if employees of a utility were to strike and thereby stop the delivery of light and heat to an entire city, there would be many far reaching consequences, and it would be of a much more serious nature to the entire populace than if, for example, Park Department workers or the keepers at the zoo were to go on strike. Within the recent past, private civilian employees directly working on defense production have struck and such activities in war time can have dangerous effects. It is submitted that this old dividing line of who can and who cannot properly strike is not a meaningful one. The impracticality of this criterion can be demonstrated in another way. Up to a certain date, bus drivers and subway workers in New York City had a legal right to strike, because they were employees of a private, albeit franchised, corporation. However, as of a certain minute, hour and day when the City took over the operation of these transit facilities, the same individuals no longer had the right to strike. It is clear that these people could not have done less damage at 11:59 p.m. on Thursday than at 12:01 a.m. on Friday, simply by virtue of the fact that the government had taken over the operation of the company. It is suggested that there has to be additional thought and perhaps eventually constructive proposals with regard to a rational and democratic alternative to the right to strike in certain segments of the economy. It is obvious that no government could tolerate a strike on the part of its military forces and that if such an event occurred, anarchy would prevail and the very foundation of the nation would be shaken. It is questionable if a prolonged strike on the part of police or fire personnel could be allowed if an orderly community is to be maintained. There are some people who go further and say that a sophisticated approach requires a recognition that a strike on the part of school teachers which could close down an entire school system for weeks or even months, would have far reaching and serious effects upon an entire community. By the same token, strikes on the part of certain employees of private enterprise, as noted above, can materially affect the economy and the well-being of large segments of the population.

The classic concept of a strike was that the workers withheld their labor from an employer and thereby made him suffer. The employer, in turn, by allowing the strike, deprived the workers of their sustenance, and there was, in effect, a test of strength to see who could last longer. This was primarily a fight between the parties involved, that is, the company and the union. However, in recent times we have seen that often when there is a fight between labor and management, the damage is done not only to the parties that presumably of their own volition have chosen this alternative to settlement but also to the public at large that vitally needs a service or commodity produced by the striking workers and the company. It is patently obvious that a strike involving the entire transit facilities of the City of New York is not a private matter between the employer and the employees, but indeed, affects the economy and the entire lives of the people in the City. These individuals are innocent bystanders to what is going on and cannot individually, independently or directly solve the problems of the workers or of the employer.

In many ways, the problem of governments' dealings with their employees presents in microcosm the broader problem of industrial relations in the private sector. (The consequences of strikes are discussed further in Chapter 39.) The interplay between the evolution of labor-management relations in the public and in the private portions of our economy is obvious. Therefore, the non-governmental employer should watch with interest as events unfold in the continuing history of labor-management relations involving various governmental agencies in the United States and their ten-million civilian employees.

38

Fringe Benefits and Joint Funds
—A Case Study

Increasingly, management finds it is contributing money to joint funds—so-called Taft-Hartley trusts—made up of equal representatives of management and labor. The performance of employer trustees on these funds is daily growing more important. The entire field of pension, welfare, supplementary vacation or holiday or severance funds, apprentice and training funds and industry promotion funds is swiftly becoming a specialized segment of the labor-management field. Nevertheless businesses of almost all sizes must have a general awareness of procedures and developments in this area since they are or may become involved in it.

Pension and welfare funds, to take the most common of the joint funds, are set up as independent entities—neither company nor union controlled in theory. Their purpose is to collect the dollars due as a result of collective bargaining, invest or hold this money, obtain the best possible benefits, and ultimately see that the workers and their families derive the advantages that have been bargained. These funds should receive tax exemption, must file specific reports and make certain publication of their positions. In all of this, management has a definite responsibility. With reference to this, the author published an article in *Pension and Welfare News* in February, 1966. It is an illustrative case study of some problems facing management particularly in this field. Through arrangement with the magazine publishers, it is reprinted here in its entirety.

THE SILENT ABDICATION

A Discussion of Management's Role in Joint Plans

Public policy, as reflected through legislative action, encourages the joint participation of labor and management, in the operation of negotiated "fringe" benefit funds. Unilateral union control of such funds was curbed by the passage of the Taft-Hartley Act in 1946. Existing plans were exempted from provisions of this law, and it did not operate retroactively. However, as to funds established after January 1, 1947 the law required that if employer contributions were made, organized labor alone could not run the funds. Thus in collectively bargained health, welfare and pension funds created over the past nineteen years direction had to be either in the hands of management only or labor and management jointly. in jointly operated funds failure to adhere to the requirement for equal union-management say-so involves not only an invalidly established and maintained fund; but under some circumstances may involve commission of a criminal act.

As a practical matter many funds created since 1947 have had provisions in the deed of trust, the by-laws and other rules that direction be vested in a Board of Directors or Trustees on which half the representation comes from management and half from labor.

While the letter of the law is generally followed, some say that the spirit is often disregarded. In single company joint funds, participation of both elements—labor and management—is often equally matched. But in multi-employer and industry-area wide funds, management trustees often do not work with the vigor nor sustain the level of interest of their union counterparts. This statement may be impossible to document statistically; and indeed, it is recognized as a controversial one. Nevertheless, discussions in and observations of management circles incline some to the opinion that in many instances this is the case.

Management lethargy manifests itself in several major ways. In some situations management trustees simply do not attend meetings. Chronic absenteeism often is a pattern on joint trusts. Barring specific attendance requirements or pressures from the individual employers represented, such absenteeism goes unchecked. Other trustees who may be physically present at meetings often merely lend their corporeal presence but not their ability. Sheer attendance is no substitution for informed deliberation, participation and interested decision making. Some trustees, apathetic, uninterested, reluctant or resigned to play a secondary role simply vote as "yes-men," do not question decisions and as a practical matter may contribute little to the advancement of the trust. Finally, there are trustees who actually attend and take part in meetings but who do little of the other work required of a conscientious fiduciary. They cannot function efficiently as trustees if they do not keep abreast of specific problems or developments affecting their fund such as actuarial surveys, accountants' statements, investment policy, choice of service institutions, opinions of counsel, expense data, administrators' reports, trustee sub-committee deliberations, etc. Moreover, a good trustee should be aware of current legal, legislative and policy developments in the overall field of pension, health and welfare plans, and one who does not follow the general picture is often unable to perform effectively with respect to a specific trust.

Abdication by management of its prerogatives in the joint trust field can lead to many serious results and ultimately have a costly consequence for employers. A board of trustees functions as the "administrator" of a fund. Even if the professional staff of full-time administrators or secretaries and the service staff of firms of attorneys, accountants, actuaries, consultants, banks and insurance companies are all of the highest caliber, they cannot entirely substitute for a poor board, because there remains a function for the board which cannot be delegated to others. In a word this key responsibility of the board is to set *policy*. To delegate this to others can be considered to contravene the law and the trust indenture. Most policy decisions, in the long run, are equally as important to management as to the union and its members. Consider three examples, the first concerning pension plans, the second in the health and welfare field and the third, applicable to all funds.

In a pension plan when additional employer contributions are negotiated the question of how to allocate the proceeds almost always arises. There are innumerable alternatives. Should the plan provide for greater death benefits? Should it include a severance pay feature? Should the number of years required for vesting be lowered or should early retirement provisions be liberalized? If these decisions are not made by the parties in collective bargaining, it is up to the Trustees to act.

The union representing the beneficiaries should generally express its preference first, and serious weight should be given to this; but the ultimate decisions must be made by the entire board of trustees. When the cents-per-hour, percentage, or dollar-per-month contribution is increased and more money flows into the plan straight retirement benefits can be expanded. One critical decision is if the improved pension should go to all retirees or only those who retire after a certain future date. Broadening of a multi-employer fund to cover additional firms, different segments of an industry or wider geographical areas usually has implications that must be carefully considered.

Decisions of this type are not ministerial in nature and cannot properly be delegated. The decision-making involves weighing different rights, equities and values. The judgment that is made is usually not the "right" one so much as the "best" one. If management trustees do not partake in this type of determination then by default it will pass to the union to make the decision unilaterally.

Problems of a parallel nature arise with regard to welfare funds. The concept of a good welfare fund should be to provide the best, most comprehensive benefits for the covered employees consistent with the amount of money to be spent. When selecting a kind of medical care many approaches may be applied. In New York City, for example, a fund can be self-insured and give benefits on an indemnity basis. It can choose to select a plan and have its coverage placed through a commercial carrier. It can decide to seek insurance through Group Health Insurance or United Medical Service, or it can take a prepaid or service plan like the Health Insurance Plan of Greater New York. Alternatively it can choose to operate and staff its own medical facility. Competent welfare plan management requires not only that an initial choice be made among these avenues, but that the selection be constantly reviewed for performance quality with other choices to see if a change would benefit the employees. It is obvious that such a decision cannot be made strictly on a computer or low-bid basis, but involves many other factors.

If a welfare plan finds that its contributions are running substantially and consistently higher than its claims payout, a surplus quickly accrues. The trustees can take different kinds of action. They can publicize to plan members the benefits available to them and encourage greater participation. (Theoretically, although seldom practically, they can recommend a reduction in employer contributions to the parties for consideration at the next negotiating session. Presumably, these payments would be diverted in other directions.) The board can expand the medical care given in terms of greater depth and higher benefits, or extend coverage to include ambulance, psychiatric, diagnostic, anesthesia or home-call benefits. It can advance in ancillary fields of medical care such as paying for the cost of drugs, or dental services or optical benefits or mental care. Finally, the board can take no affirmative action and build reserves if it chooses. The choice of the best alternative is dictated by the needs of the people, the limitation of funds, the services available in the community and various other matters. It is by no means mechanical and cannot be made except after careful investigation and consideration.

Practically all plans—welfare, pension, apprentice training, industry promotion, supplementary vacation or holiday—will, at any given time, have a net balance of funds on hand. The question of investment policy, therefore, concerns almost all funds, regardless of their purpose. Broadly speaking the investment goals of any fund have been three up to now—growth, safety and yield. But the key decision of determining the right "mix" of these elements for investments and the problem of assigning relative weights to those three desired objectives can only be made and solved by the trustees after hearing the advice of their investment counselors, brokers, banks, and others.

The problems in the investment policy field will, I think, soon prove even more challenging to trustees than heretofore. I predict that there will be two additional goals of investment policy which some may seek to add to the three already accepted. With respect to these additional goals the significant problem will not necessarily be to implement them but to determine if they are worthy objectives as a matter of principle.

Firstly, I believe there will be an increasing desire on the part of many to have trust fund assets invested in the most socially useful ways. Thus there may be suggestions that funds be invested in domestic low-cost housing; or in the development bonds of friendly, underdeveloped foreign nations. If there is no conflict with the need for safety and yield, for example, a "socially beneficial" bond or mortgage investment can be favored over one that is not. But what if there is a greater risk or a smaller income? Here a major and tremendously important choice arises and one where advocates of both viewpoints can be deeply involved. Suppose a fund wants to invest a million dollars in a real estate first mortgage. It may have three alternatives ranging from the most safe and high yielding to the least—a mortgage on a seasoned commercial property; a mortgage at a lower rate on an industrial building to be built which will bring jobs to an under employed community, or a mortgage on a hospital in a location that badly needs a medical facility and where the mortgage collateral is a highly specialized piece of property with a great degree of risk. Obviously, there is a clash of objectives in a situation like this. Recently Negro civil rights groups urged boycotting of the municipal bonds of segregated southern communities. A liberal, integration minded fund board may well consider such a plea and act accordingly. The trusted categorical answer of the old-style fiduciary that his job is to manage money without regard to the social nature of its investment may come in for some very serious scrutiny and attack.

Secondly, the concept of using accumulated assets to accomplish a practical trade-union or industry objective will have to be considered. The entire intriguing question of proxy fight stock voting remains to be thoroughly explored. Why should not the board of a pension fund decide to have the fund vote its shares in a publicly held stock corporation for a management slate more sympathetic to the aims of organized labor than not. In the event of a stockholders' fight, voting of blocks of institutional stock can be decisive and, in the proxy fight of one listed company recently, it was said to have been very significant. The next step, of course, is for a fund, within prudent limits, to purposefully invest some of its assets in the stock of a company where a proxy fight is imminent. A gigantic international or continental-sized company with tremendous stockholder diversification and high total market values may not be susceptible to such a move. But many smaller companies—on major exchanges or over-the-counter—might, be sensitive indeed to such activities. The logical evolution of such voting would be reciprocal understandings between various different trusts in the form of mutual assistance associations; one fund helps another today and looks for reciprocity tomorrow. Joint labor management trusts probably have close to ten billion dollars in assets now. Contributions and return on investments are pouring into such funds at an ever-increasing rate. Moreover, these funds being tax free, accumulate dollars at roughly twice the rate of a taxable or profit making enterprise. The joint trust influence that might bear on corporate policy as described here could well be something with which to reckon.

At first glance the observer may think that there is a natural, built-in check on joint funds that will limit this exercise of such pressure. Management trustees, it is assumed, will unquestionably block such a use of economic power. But closer examination indicates that this will not necessarily be true. A conscientious management trustee representing firms already unionized might be delighted to vote fund shares in such a way as to influence management of a non-union competitor to be more sympathetic to organized labor or to force a unionized competitor to come up to his standards.

Proxy voting positions need not be limited to non-union firms. A unionized company unwilling to give a wage increase or change other conditions in an economic collective bargaining negotiation may find its management subject to pressure and the threat of a dissident group of shareholders at the next meeting. Challenges to management can transcend the specific arena of bread and butter labor-management issues. Questions of new plant site location, personnel policy, etc. are all fair game for scrutiny, advice, opinions and perhaps opposition by stockholders, including trust funds. Certainly no one can criticize a stockholder—be it an individual, trust or other institution—for exercising its right to change or preserve a management team which it feels will be best for the enterprise of which it is a part owner.

On the contrary, failure to exercise such prerogatives could be deemed a neglect of duty; and increased participation by informed stockholders in a company's affairs will be viewed by many as fully within the desirable scope of economic democracy.

These examples serve to sketch out some of the highlights of the areas in which the trustees of joint funds are called upon to exercise discretion and make crucial decisions that cannot be delegated. The importance of informed and effective trustee participation cannot be denied. The problem of apathetic trustees then is a clear one. The results of a continuing abdication in the face of the increasing role of these funds in our economy and society can be projected into the future and the consequences are obvious.

Before prescribing cures for a sickness it is often valuable to pinpoint its causes. An awareness of the reasons for employer apathy might facilitate correction of the problems.

Many employers adopt a "do nothing" attitude out of mistaken sense of futility. The union they figure, is, as the name implies, unified. The interests of various employers in a joint fund are often diversified. Some employer trustees, despairing at reconciling divergent views, simply throw up their hands. As a practical matter while diverse and even conflicting employer needs and wants may prevail in some places, particularly among firms in the same industry, one area where there is a great potential for unity of management viewpoint is in the joint trust field. Thus the challenge to an employer trustee representing many firms on a fund board is an interesting and often surmountable one.

Some employer trustees do not manifest concern because the proportionate share of the contribution of their specific firms to the overall fund is slight. They feel that the effect of any fund action when filtered down to their company would be miniscule. Such people fail to grasp their function as trustees. They function (or do not function) as individuals and do not understand that they must act both as delegates of other employers, not represented on the board, and as fiduciaries who are legally responsible to exercise their judgment and best efforts for the advantage of beneficiaries. Equally unfit to sit on a board of trustees are those persons who simply are not interested in their responsibility as trustees or in the fulfillment of the mission of the particular trust fund.

Occasionally one hears speculation that employer trustees do not take an active role because they fear that the union, and the union trustees, would resent this and be alienated. The response to this lies both on the theoretical and practical level. Theoretically, unions should not do anything to undermine the requirement of the law that the management of the fund be joint. Practically, it may be noted that of the many employer trustees whom I have talked with, most felt that the union people generally welcomed employer participation. I have seen many union trustees who have encouraged the suggestions, comments and advice of employer trustees. Lines of communication on well-run trusts are set up so that pertinent information—both official and informal—is equally available to all trustees. Particularly in the field of investment policy, union trustees frequently look to management trustees to play a major role since these employer representatives have often had more extensive experience in money management. My own opinion is that where, practically speaking, union representatives completely dominate a trust fund, it is not that they are denying management trustees a voice so much as moving in to fill a vacuum caused by lack of management participation.

Other reasons for employer trustee neglect include the selection of trustees who do not have time to serve properly, those who do not understand the nature of their function, and those who feel it is "the worker's money" in the fund and are, consequently, indifferent to how it is spent.

More active participation by all employer trustees in trust funds should be encouraged. As a matter of business policy, effective employer participation in trust fund management can result in greater fund economies and in the long run a saving of money for the employer firms. In the eyes of the law a person charged with a fiduciary obligation who neglects that duty does so at his peril. As a purely personal issue, a trustee should function as such or resign from a board and make room for someone more responsible. Finally, from an idealistic viewpoint active participation in a trust fund, where the goal is improving the lot of one's fellow man, is certainly as rewarding as any other form of community activity or social service and should yield a great sense of self-satisfaction to a responsible person.

There are four major ways in which the deficiencies in trustee participation can be avoided.

Firstly, there are various legalistic devices which can be employed to encourage participation.

For example, a quorum can be set at a fairly high percentage of trustees. Thus, if there is considerable absenteeism no business can be transacted due to lack of a quorum. Active trustees will soon put pressure on chronic absentees to do their job and stop causing the time-wasting of a useless meeting. Another more forthright device is to incorporate in the trust indenture the rule that any trustee who misses two or three meetings without a valid reason is deemed to have automatically resigned from the board and is replaced. The other trustees can be the judge of what is a good cause for inattendance. Management may protect itself by seeing that the trust rules require bloc voting, i.e. that even if one trustee is present he casts all the votes for the absentee trustees representing his side of the bargaining table. However, this plan, like the designation of alternatives, and the use of proxy trustee voting may raise questions from a legal viewpoint, since certain aspects of a fiduciary's responsibility cannot be delegated to another person.

Secondly, there are various practical techniques that encourage full attendance at meetings.

These include scheduling at convenient times and places; adequate advance notice of meetings with a follow-up notice or call a day or two before the meeting, and postponement of meetings where it appears there will be much absenteeism. Experience shows that the smaller the board of trustees the more interested and involved the individual trustees are with the affairs of the fund. Consistent with adequate representation this approach might be considered. When the number of trustees is limited, the people who actually serve are often more conscious of their responsibility and less likely to feel that other trustees will do their jobs for them. Some also believe that the greater the frequency of meetings the larger the chance of absenteeism. Therefore, meetings should be held to an absolute minimum to take care of necessary business. If this is done, and the agendas are well organized and the meetings conducted in business-like fashion the busy trustee will be more likely to attend. Advance mailing of the topics to be under consideration at the board meeting is a good idea as it stimulates interest and allows for consideration of problems and canvassing of views in advance. Most of the practical techniques utilized to bring directors of corporations, clubs or other organizations to meetings, obviously apply with respect to trustees. In mentioning this it should be noted that often corporate directors are paid for attending meetings and some suggest that this tangible reward should be given fund trustees as well. The advocates of trustees' fees suggest that this will stimulate attendance and that it is quite fair and proper to compensate trustees for their efforts and responsibility. Persuasive arguments to the contrary are advanced, however. Paying a man to come to a meeting may get him there, but it does not insure that he will bring much with him in the way of intellect. Moreover, to my knowledge there are no "professional trustees" who make their living sitting on joint-labor management boards representing one side or the other. The men or women who do sit usually have a personal financial stake in the industry or their own jobs that directly or indirectly should motivate them to be concerned about their performance as trustees. The trustees being an autonomous group have the theoretical authority to vote themselves high amounts as salaries for acting as such. This could lead to practices which might be legally allowable but are clearly morally wrong and which could eventually raise the question of misappropriation of funds. For all of these and other reasons many labor leaders are opposed to payment of fees to trustees and their view is shared by a lot of management spokesmen. Not only is the therapeutic effect of such payments dubious but the likelihood of it is remote as a general practice.

The third can be summed up in one word—education.

Trustees must be informed of the importance of their jobs. They should know of the increasing importance of trust funds and understand the ramifications of the exercise of their power. They must clearly understand how significant their action or inaction could be; and they ought to comprehend the role of the board of trustees and know that its responsibility cannot be delegated. They should be clearly aware of the magnitude of their legal liability should they fail to exercise normal prudence and diligence. If incumbent fund officials or the fund counsel emphasized this point some potential trustees seeking glory without worry would decline to accept the job; but those who accepted it might perform it better. Oncoming trustees should be invited to meet with the fund's service personnel —the administrator, accountant, attorney, etc. and familiarize themselves initially with the working of the trust.

Generally board meetings are not held in secret. It might be worth considering the invitation of potential trustees to sit in as observers. Junior union officials, not yet on the board, and associates of managements' representatives, all of whom are logical choices as future trustees, can attend meetings. In this fashion they serve an apprenticeship period, and when and if they do join the board they are well acquainted with the problems facing it, and even the personalities of other trustees. Continuing education of all trustees is desirable and to this end participation in and attendance at educational functions relating to trust fund management and reading of relevant publications in the field is valuable.

Finally, better performance will result from careful selection of people to serve as trustees.

This means that selectivity must be exercised when management chooses a trustee to represent it. Top management and those company or trade association personnel charged with the labor relations function must themselves recognize the importance of joint-labor management trust funds. When they see this they also realize that they cannot afford to pick as a trustee someone who will not properly represent their interests.

Those who are elected as trustees should not be junior men unable to exercise their judgment nor should the trustee's job be considered a green pasture for tired executives. The people designated for the position should have a material interest in performing as trustees. In multi-employer joint trusts top executives or qualified industrial relations men of participating companies fit this category. Representatives of a trade association or employer's group in the industry are particularly good as are attorneys who represent such associations or indeed labor relations consultants or lawyers who represent one or more companies contributing to the fund. Such individuals are likely to have a broad view of the picture and will often fit all the requirements.

The good trustee should have all of the qualifications considered here—interest, ability, knowledge, continuing education, awareness of the responsibility and in fact, sincere concern to do a first rate job. All people connected with joint trusts—union, management and service personnel—should combat the silent abdication. And everyone should realize that better trustees mean better trusts.

39

The Future of

Collective Bargaining

The economy of the United States and the world is undergoing many significant changes. It is a dynamic and constantly developing phenomena. Executives and owners of businesses should be aware of the new directions.

Employment and unemployment patterns vary not only from region to region and locale to locale but also among industries. In 1940, 16,000 people worked in the United States for scheduled passenger and cargo air carriers. In 1964, the number was over 153,000. Employment in the coal mining industry has dropped gradually over many years, but between 1962 and 1964 aircraft companies abolished 50,000 jobs. Manufacturing industries do not call for new manpower in the same proportion as the growing service businesses. Job functions are undergoing changes. There are more and more white collar, professional, clerical and technical positions to fill, while the "blue collar" and manual jobs are not growing apace. General Electric, for example, has less than one-half of its employees on a regular hourly rated scale. Traditionally, it has been harder for unions to organize the white collar staff than the blue collar worker. The labor movement will increasingly be faced with the challenge of organizing these people and jobs, or it will find its share of the work force, that is, the proportion of the organized, falling.

Automation has had profound effects on the economy and on collective bargaining and will continue to have accelerating impact.

Unions cannot organize machines and find it harder to win the skilled technicians who run machines than to represent the many workers who used to make what the machine now produces.

And the effect of a strike has been softened in many industries where technological modernization has occurred. Large utilities and chemical plants and oil refineries, using less personnel than previously, can absorb the effects of work stoppages better than firms dependent on human hands for production. The output of automated plants does not necessarily drastically decline if workers are off duty for a period. Supervisory personnel often can keep things going and the strike—probably labor's strongest weapon—is no longer the threat it was in non-automated plants. Unions in these industries, recognizing this change, must look for other defenses. Inevitably, they will realize that to win their points they must seek either government aid or intervention directly, or in the form of more sympathetic laws and rulings about secondary boycotts and allied matters so that unions retain a way of making their adversaries suffer economically. Additionally, labor will turn more towards the public at large and seek to mobilize opinion to support it in its drive to attain its goals.

Trends in patterns of bargaining are changing also. The number of business units covered in single negotiations will tend to be more and their size larger. Two very significant developments occurred in 1966 that are probably typical of future events. Several of the unions that bargain with General Electric banded together to negotiate jointly. The company fought this. The theory behind the unions' action was that in greater unity there is more strength. They planned to have a broad and unified position. Within the AFL-CIO, and particularly its Industrial Union Department, there is an effort to coordinate the strategy and goals of the different unions that bargain with one company or group of companies. Thus, Corporation X may have previously bargained with many different unions representing drivers, production employees, clerical workers, various construction or maintenance craft unions, and so on. In the future it will most likely meet with a combined committee. The aims of the different unions will have been worked out with some degree of joint participation. Compromises may be made within the appropriate segment of the labor movement in advance of negotiations and a united front will be presented to the company. A particular problem arising because the company will not concede something to one element of its workers may, in this type of bargaining, mean a confrontation with all of its unionized employees.

Second, the Teamsters union, at their July 1966 convention, concentrated more power in the hands of the international leadership to negotiate nationwide collective bargaining agreements. This type of action will increase the power and ability of unions to impose uniform contracts on industry. The results of this will be welcomed by some employers but be damaging to others. Presumably such action will go a long way towards eradicating regional differences in labor rates. It will also centralize power in the hands of top international union leaders. The local chiefs and business agents, if shorn of their power to negotiate contracts, will merely remain to service the membership and see that the contract is enforced. The Teamsters have even placed much of the grievance settlement authority under control of their general president.

Another aspect of more inclusive bargaining units is occurring in the garment industry. Previously different unionized companies would be members of trade associations and sign master contracts covering their factories. A sportswear firm would be part of the industry-wide employer association; a scarf firm the same; and so with a dress manufacturer and a coat and suit manufacturer. But, as larger, integrated companies have emerged in the past several years, as a function of the maturing of the entire industry, this pattern has changed. These companies make broad lines of apparel and the fragmented approach no longer applies. Consequently, the International Ladies Garmets Workers Union enter into contract with the companies covering all portions of their operations. Again, the inevitable result is a concentration of the bargaining function in the highest echelons of union leadership.

The trade union movement must increasingly examine and review its own techniques and theories. As noted, automation, the shift in job patterns and bargaining techniques will all affect the union's future strength and standing. Certain very basic questions will, of necessity, have to be pondered and solved by the leaders of organized labor.

One very significant problem, mentioned in Chapters 19 and 36, is the recruitment and training of new union leadership able to cope with these developments. Another will be the search for a rational alternative to the bitter and damaging economic conse-

quences of major strikes. Every time there is a particularly important industry-wide strike—in steel, among the railroads, with the
airlines, on the docks—there is talk of how to prevent such occurrences. Increasingly, there has been consideration of legislation to
stay such stoppages. Usually most consideration is given only to
the question of how to solve the particular strike. However, it is
submitted that there will be a growing realization that this is not
a problem to be solved in a piecemeal basis, but rather that the
resolution must rest on a long range set of principles and their
implementation. Obviously, such a solution can only be found in
alternatives that are acceptable to all parties—labor, management
and the public. It is unlikely that there will be legislation forbidding strikes or forcing compulsory settlements on labor. If a program is to be found and implemented, political reality dictates
that it must be palatable to labor. Should labor's right to strike
be abridged, something will have to be given to it in return. Whatever methods are substituted, if they are to be satisfactory in any
meaningful way, the end result must be a settlement that is fair and
equitable. In my opinion management must recognize that in the
long run curtailment of labor's right to strike will inevitably lead
to significant and parallel curtailment of some management rights.

New York State has a law that forbids workers in private non-
profit hospitals from striking. It requires compulsory arbitration of
disputes if the parties cannot themselves solve the problem. This
means that the ultimate decision on the settlement is taken out of
the hands not only of labor but also of management. If this type
of legislation were to be applied in other fields, involving other
private employers, the same result would inevitably occur.

Most observers believe that decisive government intervention
(as distinct from mere mediation) if it is to be applied at all,
should only occur after the principal parties themselves have ex-
hausted every attempt to solve their problem. Therefore, whatever
opinions one may have about ultimate methods of solving problems
that management and labor cannot themselves solve, I believe that
all responsible people would agree that any aid towards encouraging the parties to achieve voluntary settlements is important.
This requires more research and consideration of the methods of
collective bargaining and the evolution of techniques that will promote completely free and uncoerced settlements. Finally, it should
be added that there are many who firmly believe that any abridge-
ment of the right to strike—whatever the alternative protections

would be—would be more harmful than the effects of a strike it-self. These people feel that limitations would tamper with our economic system as we know it and result in substantial limitation of freedoms in many areas.

The labor movement must also examine itself in terms of its relationship to its own members. Some believe that there is an increasing gap between the thinking of the rank and file members of the union and the leadership that makes decisions. They believe that rather than following the wishes of the membership, the offi-cials of unions should lead them in certain directions. This, too, raises some very vasic questions. But in theorizing, one must re-member that the mainstream of the American labor movement has not been revolutionary in nature, as were the trade unions of many other countries. Essentially, American unions are not out to change the free enterprise or capitalist system; they simply want it to work for them and their members.

The next decade will see changing demands from labor. Un-doubtedly, some major requests will remain. Labor will press for a shorter work week and higher wages. But there will be other proposals of a very different nature. In the decade after the Second World War many innovations in the field of fringe benefits oc-curred. In the next ten years, from the mid 1950's to the mid 60's, there was an emphasis on wage increases and a continuing development of fringe benefits. The next ten years will, in my opinion, bring an expansion of both concepts. Fringe benefit wel-fare funds will undoubtedly be expanded to cover more of the employees' needs. Originally, most welfare funds covered hospital-ization and some medical treatments. More aid in paying doctors' bills will be included and these plans will also be designed or expanded to cover dental care, optical care, psychiatric treatment, drugs, periodic physical examinations, laboratory and diagnostic services and many other needs. The scope of coverage will be widened to include not only the workers but also their spouses and children.

Pension plans will be expanded to integrate with Social Security more closely. There are very important innovations in the pension field pending now. One is the idea of government insurance of private pension plans to protect beneficiaries if a company goes out of business or a fund's assets are mismanaged or misappro-priated. Another is the attention given to the concept of pension portability. This would allow a worker to take his pension credits with him as he moved from job to job or to a different industry or locale. It would promote the mobility of the labor force. It would also make pensions more costly for management since the actuaries could no longer count on pension contributions for the many workers who never serve enough time to qualify for pensions. The money paid in for these people, and its income accumulations, now go to those who work long enough under the rules of the particular plan to have a vested interest in that plan. But, if reciprocity of credits was promoted, obviously this funding technique would no longer operate. Moreover, the aspects of "time-in-service" required in order to get a company pension that today serve to keep employees working for the same employer or in the same industry could cease to apply. Management might find that its pension payments no longer increase the stability of its work force.

Of particular significance will be, I believe, a growing integration of pension and welfare and other benefit funds under one administration and one program. Many welfare plans provide for life insurance and pension funds also have death benefits. At this point there is not much dovetailing or planning of benefits when the plans are separately administered. Questions will increasingly arise. Should the retired worker's medical insurance be covered by the welfare plan that provides such protection for the active workers or is this more properly the function of the pension plan trustees who are responsible for payments to retirees? These questions can be best solved if all the pension, welfare and allied fringe benefits are viewed as an entity. This will mean the development of a more total and comprehensive kind of private social security financed by management. It will mean increased responsibility for plan administrators, and since labor will strive for equal representation on management funds, eventually more responsibility for joint-board trustees.

In terms of direct payments to the workers, there may be more thought given to the guaranteed annual wage in the next few years. Proposed in only a few industries some years ago and then relatively dormant, this suggestion was revived in July, 1966 by Secretary of Labor Wirtz in his efforts to solve an impasse in the construction trades in New Jersey. Like the idea of supplementary unemployment benefits, the guaranteed annual wage would serve to smooth out the cyclical effect of unemployment. A definite and, in effect, insured yearly salary would certainly have tremendous effects on management and necessitate increased production and sales planning efforts, and in some cases, very radical changes in the entire operation of a business.

Another possible development, long disfavored by many unions, may be the growth of profit sharing plans. Particularly in smaller plants where management is thin or in firms where direct labor is a major element in over-all activities, profit sharing or other incentive arrangements have some very interesting potentials. As labor costs increase in marginal industries, management will turn to any hope for survival and this will be one. Plans to cushion technological unemployment and promote freer management use of automation as well as to encourage retraining, as at Kaiser Steel, will appear with greater frequency.

In summary, this chapter is not an attempt to exhaustively list the problems of collective bargaining or clairvoyantly chart its future. It is included so that management may be aware of some of the developments and thoughts in the field of labor relations, and even more important, so that the employer recognizes clearly that there are many problems affecting not only his company but also all industry. Effective management must be aware of these trends and formulate its own thinking and response with respect to them. Truly progressive executives will look to the future of collective bargaining; their companies will benefit from their consideration today of the problems they will face tomorrow.

40

Successful Labor Relations:
Summary and Sermon

"Labor-management relations is a major force shaping the American future. The dealings between companies and unions affect the productive capacity of the entire country. This, in turn, influences the social, political and economic development of our society. Consequently, labor-management relations are also a vital factor in the interplay between America and the rest of the world. Dependent on the attainment of harmony in labor relations is our ability to achieve and maintain a high standard of living for our citizens, to give aid to our allies and to support our defense effort. These are all essential elements in ensuring world peace, the survival of our nation and the well-being of its people."

These are the opening words of this book—the first paragraph of the Introduction. The reader might well consider the impact of labor relations in light of what he has read. Every reader, as a citizen of this country, concerned with defining and attaining our national goals, will be concerned with labor relations. The employer or representative of management is additionally involved on a personal level because his livelihood and the future of his company will be affected by management's labor policies.

Successful labor relations depend on many things. Some of these are not always or entirely within the company's control. These include the state of the economy in general and the financial health of the employer's industry, community or company in particular, the attitudes of the union or unions involved, the position of competitors, the labor market and the supply and demand for the product or service offered.

Other factors which contribute to solid and sensible labor relations can be controlled by management and fall within its sphere of activity. First, management must understand the prevailing laws and rulings which affect it. In this regard, labor relations advisors or attorneys can play a major role. The mission of these individuals, in brief, is to achieve the most efficient utilization of labor for the lowest cost. In this capacity these specialists are aides to top management with particular responsibility in the areas of production, operation and personnel planning. As this book has stated, a professional approach to labor-management problems is absolutely essential. All management representatives charged with the labor relations function must have both background knowledge of their field and systematized methods of assimilating new developments as they occur.

Second, the employer must be aware of the nature of the labor-management relationship. There is inherently an area of conflict between the aims of organized labor and management. Samuel Gompers, one-time AFL president and national labor-leader, when asked what labor wants, is reputed to have answered "More." Labor strives for greater pay and shorter hours. Industry wants profit and tries to hold the cost of labor down. This divergence of desires is a real one, not a mere semantic difference. Many would-be do-gooders say that if communications were improved between the parties the problems would all be solved. This is not true. In this labor-management conflict each side can understand the other quite well and still disagree on basic issues. It is important to recognize this and, understanding that there are different goals, to endeavor to reconcile them.

There are also sectors of the labor-management relationship where the two parties may have joint aims. The good health, growth and stability of the economy means more and better jobs. The over-all and transcending need for sound economic conditions can be applied in individual firms, where the cooperative efforts of both union and management can do much to strengthen the company and the industry.

There is a basic common denominator between labor and management. Both employers and employees are people. All of the parties are human beings and as such they often react alike and have similar needs and aspirations.

Third, management should think out and adopt a comprehensive and integrated policy of labor relations. The policy must fit the times. For example, consider the company in a "union town," already in contract with a labor organization. Reality dictates that the union is there to stay. Trying to break or oust it may be like tilting at windmills. These efforts can dissipate company energy, time and money which could be turned to productive use. As a practical matter this company is probably well advised to realize that it is inextricably involved with a union. Its labor relations policy should be geared to living with the union on the best possible terms for the company. On the other hand, the company with no union, situated in a non-union town or industry, may be correct in deciding that its best course is to make every lawful endeavor to keep unions from organizing its employees. If this is the decision, then careful administration of wage and benefit scales and certain other steps are clearly indicated.

There are still other possible alternatives. A non-unionized company may welcome the advent of a union. Or an already unionized firm may have some particularly pressing reason which motivates it to try to break its ties with the union.

In any of these situations and in other circumstances, the important thing is that there be no aimless drifting and that a definite and planned approach to labor relations be established. Formulating such a program requires a thoughtful analysis of the situation and constant, informed re-evaluation of prevailing policies in the face of new events.

Some company executives may want to consider supplementing these policies with endeavors in the field of political action. Obviously, the effect of such activity will be less direct than the implementation of particular economic policies on the company level. However, broad management action can eventually have significant results for individual firms. All laws which are enacted to deal with labor-management relations are passed by legislative representatives of the citizens. Our democratic system ensures that voters, through their delegates, may change these laws. Moreover, members of Federal and state agencies dealing with labor matters are generally appointed by elected officials and will, in turn, reflect the electorate's wishes.

Unions engage in political action to gain their goals. The AFL-

CIO has consistently spent large sums in lobbying with the Congress, as the Federal listings show. Organized labor helps those nominees for public office that it favors.

Neither labor unions nor corporations are allowed by law to make financial donations to a political campaign, but people from the ranks of both industry and labor may contribute to candidates' campaign funds. And certain lobbying activity is permitted. Instead of chafing at unfriendly laws and administrators, management should consider trying to change these.

Effective political action must be sophisticated. Any statement saying "What labor is for, management is against," is crude and unworkable. The political action which an employer takes must coincide with his particular situation. Often different companies quite logically want different things. For example, labor laws regulate the extent of labor's right to organize. Of necessity, there can be no single, monolithic management position on this. If a company is not unionized it may want as many roadblocks put in the way of organizing unions as possible. But segments of an industry that are already unionized and are being threatened by non-union competition may have no interest at all in lessening labor's chances of organizing their competitors. Furthermore, on certain issues such as world trade and tariff policies, management and labor may fruitfully cooperate.

When management espouses certain laws or seeks to persuade Government to adopt a particular position, it must do so with an awareness of America's political complexion. Labor has more votes than management. Industry's executives are outnumbered by its workers. Many unions are effective in mobilizing these workers politically. To garner sufficient support for its policies, management must rely on the votes of independent citizens who are committed to neither labor nor management. These people, because of their very lack of direct involvement in labor-management problems, tend to be moderate on such issues. When management champions an extreme or unfair proposition, it may only defeat itself because it cannot convince enough independent voters to go along with it. But when the measures it advocates are equitable, it has a good chance of success.

This issue of political action is of great significance because the government is intimately and continuously involved in labor-management relations. Moreover, the importance of high productivity in this country is tremendous. The uninterrupted national output of goods and services is necessary to ensure domestic prosperity and international security. Consequently, there is every reason to anticipate that Government intervention will not diminish over the long term. The nature and direction of government supervision and its intensity will be determined by the electorate. Some management spokesmen will not want to miss the opportunity of furthering their cause through political effort. Such action may be developed as an adjunct to the company's programmed labor-relations objectives.

Fourth, management's representatives must exercise judgment. Top company officials must themselves, ultimately, make their own decisions. To reach proper conclusions they need knowledge of their own company. This means understanding its strong and weak points, knowing its people and comprehending its relation to other economic factors. Good staff work, experience, perspicacity and intelligence will contribute to the acquisition of this knowledge.

It is equally important that the determinations which are made be realistic. There is no room for hate or fear or other emotionalism when it comes to exercising judgment in this connection. An attitude of progressiveness and forward-looking enlightenment is acceptable. Conversely, an attachment to traditionalism and the status quo has a place. But current problems must be solved by people who live in the present and grasp reality. The thought processes of a nineteenth century mind or a twenty-first century mind are not designed to meet issues of the twentieth century.

Management that follows these basic principles will make great strides towards achieving and maintaining successful labor relations.